FACTORS IN
MODERN HISTORY

FACTORS IN
MODERN HISTORY

BY

A. F. POLLARD

M.A. HON. LITT.D. F.B.A.

Fellow of All Souls and Hon. Fellow of Jesus
College, Oxford ; Corresponding Member of the
Académie des Inscriptions et Belles Lettres
(Institut de France) ; and Hon. Director of the
London Institute of Historical Research.

THIRD EDITION

CONSTABLE & COMPANY LTD
LONDON WC 2

LONDON

PUBLISHED BY
Constable and Company Ltd.
10-12 Orange Street, W.C.2

INDIA
Longmans, Green and Company Ltd.
BOMBAY   CALCUTTA   MADRAS

CANADA
Longmans, Green and Company
TORONTO

First published 1907
Reprinted 1910
,, ... 1919
,, ... 1921
. . . . 1924
Second Edition 1926
Third Edition 1932
Reprinted 1945
,, ... 1948

PRINTED AND MADE BY
FLETCHER & SON LTD NORWICH AND
THE LEIGHTON-STRAKER BOOKBINDING CO. LTD LONDON

PREFACE TO
THE THIRD (1932) EDITION

THE demand for a third edition and a seventh reprint of these lectures, delivered a quarter of a century ago, seems to justify an explanation, which would have seemed presumptuous at any earlier date, of the purpose which they were dimly hoped to be serving. They were a sort of prospectus, elaborated during the first two years (1903-5) of a professional connection with the University of London and shaped by the circumstances of a student of history beginning to teach it under conditions, which were on the surface not prepossessing but concealed beneath it a good deal worth seeking for those not ashamed to dig. That particular occupation has now come to an end and the prospect is changed into retrospect.

It was clear that any building would have to begin from the foundations. An attempt had already been made to start from the top and, by means of the pioneer but slender Creighton endowment,[1] to initiate a post-graduate school of history in London. Still earlier, historians of distinction —Sir Edward Creasy, J. S. Brewer, S. R. Gardiner, E. S. Beesly, Sir John Knox Laughton—had derived scanty rewards from occasional courses delivered to casual students ; but a few odd bricks had to stand for a school of history until after the end of the nineteenth century. The university, as such, had examiners and examinees but neither students nor teachers till 1901 : even then it was hard to see how or where to begin the building. There were no endowed chairs of the subject, no scholarships to attract students, and few students to be attracted. The schools which taught history up to scholarship standard did not

[1] See below, pp. 243, 252n., 258.

send their pupils to London colleges, and the schools which
did taught no history worth mention. It was easier to see
that one had to begin at the bottom than to find the bottom
at which to begin. The Inferno was a circle from
which there seemed no escape. No living wage would be
forthcoming for university teachers of history until there
were students' fees to provide it; no students would be
attracted until there were university teachers to attract
them, and school teachers to prepare them for entrance;
and school teachers themselves would be lacking until the
training colleges, from which they were drawn, were staffed
with competent teachers of history. So far as history was
concerned, the university was only a place for stones which
the builders rejected.

Attempts were, however, made to break out almost
simultaneously from various segments of the circle. Within
the university, students were attracted from other subjects,
and soon began in their turn to spread the light in the
schools they went to teach. Outside, the chief assistance
came from the London County Council, newly endowed
with its educational authority by Lord Balfour's Act of
1902, and directed towards history by the stimulus of Sir
Robert Blair and Professor Graham Wallas. Short evening
courses for history teachers[1] led to a permanent evening
school with a regular staff and a four years' continuous
course; a committee, comprising school teachers, teachers
in training colleges, and professors, laboured for two years
on a report on history-teaching in L.C.C. schools[2]; and
the Historical Association was founded to elevate the
circle from its depression and convert it into a spiral of
intellectual co-operation in the interests of all grades of

[1] The first of these courses comprised most of the lectures in this
volume. Another, entitled 'The Evolution of England' (1912)
contained the substance of my volume on England in the Home
University Library, and a third the germs of my *Evolution of
Parliament,* while the lectures given weekly during 1914-17 formed
the basis of my *Short History of the Great War* (1920).

[2] See below, p. 259.

historical education. 'London,' remarked Mr. Sidney
Webb in January 1909, had 'at last become interested in
history.'

There were other schisms to heal in higher intellectual
atmospheres.   The original attempt to begin in London
with a purely post-graduate school[1] illustrated the danger,
already apparent at Oxford and Cambridge, of an historical
education sharply divided between teaching by university
professors and teaching by college tutors; and this
bifurcation was all the more serious because it coincided
with other and even more fundamental lines of divergence.
They took various forms and divided historians into diverse,
almost hostile, camps.   The divergence was obvious in the
different answers given by historians to the questions
whether history was a science or an art, and whether
historical study should be mainly the means of a liberal
education or of a scientific training.   Cognate was the
argument whether history should be primarily a form of
literature and a source of popular influence and inspiration,
or a matter of abstruse investigation appealing only to
narrow, but numerous, circles of experts.   Was its aim to
produce æsthetic satisfaction or intellectual hunger?[2]
Was philosophic thought or technical skill in research the
essential qualification?   Can the historian's mind be both
broad and deep? and if he cannot extend in both dimensions, which is he to choose?   Is it better to know something about everything, or everything about something?

These antagonisms attained formidable proportions, and
it was obvious that a new school must avoid committing
itself to one or the other extreme.   London was saved from
the dilemma less by foresight, skill, or determination than
by the stress of circumstances.   The purely post-graduate
school was impossible without extensive endowments for
historical research which have never been forthcoming.
Its most zealous votaries could only make tentative

1 See below, p. 243.
2 F. W. Maitland, *Collected Papers*, iii, 294.

advances towards their goal by beginning with the more general forms of historical education, and by attracting students whose numbers and fees might yield a basis for guaranteed stipends to which some slight obligation to pursue research might eventually be attached. For while the sole remuneration for teaching history consisted in a share of the fees from pupils who were few and far between, and the teacher had to earn a living by other means, it was impossible to superimpose a further obligation to engage in unremunerative research. Fortunately there was no need to impose it. One of the paradoxical advantages of university chairs without stipends was that candidates were not attracted by pecuniary considerations. Another was that the establishment of university or college chairs was not dependent upon the slender resources of either. The chair of Constitutional History, for instance, owed its accidental origin to these circumstances. There was in 1903 a vacancy in the chair of Constitutional Law and History, and among the candidates were Dr. (now Sir) William Holdsworth and the present writer. The electors wanted to recommend both : 'why not,' suggested the presiding genius ; 'there is no stipend for either,, and it will cost the college no more to have two chairs than one.' So two were devised, one called 'Constitutional Law' and the other 'Constitutional History' ; the first year's fees of the latter came to £25, and of the other to a trifle more. There was no novelty in that : Jowett had been Regius Professor of Greek at Oxford on a stipend of £40. The novelty is the change from professors who answered a call to those who make a profession.

The historian by vocation naturally needed no financial inducement to research, and any intellectual bias towards over-specialisation was corrected by the need for bodily sustenance : he must cast a wide net of teaching or he would get a small catch of fees. A school of history in London had, therefore, to be built on a bridge between the divergences in the historical world ; and it was found easier to make a teacher out of a natural researcher than a researcher out of a natural teacher. No seduction is worse for a student, who wants to become a historian, than an invitation to teach before he has learnt what is meant by research. He reveals his nature by what he chooses to do when given the choice. Hence the value of making the M.A. degree depend upon research : it provides the means, as examinations do not, of selecting students who are at least worth trying as junior university teachers. Undeserved compliments have, however, sometimes been paid to heads of departments for their skill in selecting students to assist them ; for the most part it is the students who select their teacher, and if they choose wisely, come to their own reward. But nothing is farther from the mark than the current criticism of the newer universities that the history in their minds is nothing but specialised detail. Five-sixths of the teaching that is given has to be devoted to general history in preparation for a first degree ; and it has to be given by teachers who can spend but spare time on research. The comparison is not between historians who do nothing but research and those who do nothing but teach, but between those who do nothing but teach and those who do some research as well.

The research is of necessity specialised, because only so can we add to the sum of human knowledge. There are, indeed, amateurs who regard as research their skimming of others' results ; but that is only adding to their own knowledge, while real research means revealing what has not been hitherto known by anyone. The apparent triviality of the detail misleads superficial minds : gold is commonly found neither on the surface nor in bulk. Moreover, as Sir James Jeans has said, the infinitely little may throw light on the infinitely great ; and, while Darwin's deductions dazzled men's minds, their value depends as much on the infinite skill and labour he spent on the minutiæ of nature's evidence as on the insight and imagination which enabled him to discern the bearing of the details upon one another and their relation to nature as a whole. 'The university, says Dr. Flexner, 'will not exhaust its function when it piles up its heaps of knowledge.'[1] It is not the detail but its isolation that makes it barren; the special investigation must always be viewed in its relation to a more general problem. But the specialist cannot very well lose himself in his research when he is tied to teaching large parts of general history; it is the general practitioner who is more likely to lose himself in his generalities when he is not attached to any specific research. At least one of the participators in the organisation of the history school in London found it no small advantage to have been tied for nine years to the severe and specific details of the 'Dictionary of National Biography,' before he had the chance or the task of teaching all periods of general European history for university degrees and the higher civil service examinations.

Experience in fact proves the hollowness of most of the fancied antagonisms in the teaching and writing of history unless, indeed, the experience has been limited to some particular form. Take, for instance, the recent charge that the new historical schools rely exclusively on documentary evidence, ignoring the other 'source' of history, namely, interpretation. Interpretation of what, if not of documentary evidence or of the nearest approach to it that is available? What in any case is the writing of history but the interpretation of historical sources? It may be that much of the history that is written is a selection of documentary evidence cemented by preconceived ideas derived from other than historical sources; and, indeed, historical societies in search of truth often qualify by some adjective the kind of truth they are seeking. But it is a criterion rather than a criticism of university schools of history that they ignore such 'sources.'

It is hardly more to the point to complain that the products of research do not rival the popular appeal of

1 *Universities: American, English, German* (1930), p. 23.

historical fiction or psycho-analysis. A university is not endowed to compete with daily newspapers or circulating libraries, but rather to remedy their deficiencies and provide for investigations which do not attract the man in the street : we think none the worse of the pioneer who is not accompanied by cheering crowds and looks to stiller and smaller voices for his inspiration. The old definition of a liberal education that it consisted of knowing something about everything and everything about something was valid enough under the old individualist liberal dispensation. But it regarded only the individual, and ignored the community ; a nation of citizens who individually knew something of everything would be ill-equipped to deal with a rival whose citizens collectively knew all about everything. A diversity of gifts requires a diversified social culture ; and the rarest need it most. The strongest of socialist arguments is that others than civil servants need—for other than administrative business—release from economic dependence on popular taste in order that society may benefit to the full from the diversity of intellectual, moral, and spiritual gifts among its individual members.

So great are the diversities in the University of London that a kindly but competent critic[1] has confessed himself unable to understand in what sense it is a university at all ; and, if some of the possibilities of 1903 have become the realities of 1931, the way to unity has not been through uniformity or even unanimity. Some surviving difficulties are indicated in a third section added to the chapter on 'The University of London and the Study of History," which may have some general interest in view of the

1 Abraham Flexner, *op. cit.*, p. 231. Dr. Flexner remarks (*ib.*, p. 6) that 'universities are complex and organic institutions; their arms may be sound, while both legs may be broken.' The difficulty with London is not that either its legs or its arms are broken, but that it is all legs and arms. It has also had great men, but 'great men are individuals: and individuals and organizations are in everlasting conflict. The University is an institution' (*ibid.* p. 25).

approaching centenary of the parent of modern universities. The new chapter on 'History and Citizenship' is based on an address to the Conference of Educational Associations in January, 1930, and discusses a question which concerns all who learn as well as all who teach anything at all : it is naturally a post war epilogue to 'The Value of History' which, appended to the second edition, is now prefixed for the sake of unity to the whole. A few notes, explaining some allusions in the text,, and an index have also been added ; and I have included as an appendix part of a memorandum submitted on 26 November, 1918, not so much because it led to the establishment of the Institute of Historical Research, as because it raised the problem of a national policy for universities which, in spite of the Universities Bureau of the British Empire, has hardly yet been touched.

A. F. POLLARD.

INSTITUTE OF HISTORICAL RESEARCH,
September, 1931.

CONTENTS

I.—THE VALUE OF HISTORY

II.—NATIONALITY

CONTENTS

V.—HENRY VIII AND THE ENGLISH
REFORMATION

VI.—PARLIAMENT

CONTENTS

CONTENTS

IX.—CHURCH AND STATE IN ENGLAND AND SCOTLAND

X.—CROMWELLIAN CONSTITUTIONS

XI.—COLONIAL EXPANSION

XII.—HISTORY AND CITIZENSHIP

CONTENTS

XIII.—THE UNIVERSITY OF LONDON AND THE STUDY OF HISTORY

(i.) In 1904

FACTORS IN MODERN HISTORY

I

THE VALUE OF HISTORY

It requires less intellectual effort to express a settled conviction than to explain the grounds upon which that conviction is based; and it is probable that most teachers of history are more firmly convinced of its educational value than able to state clearly and concisely wherein that value consists. This chapter is a crude and individual attempt to formulate a rational basis of principle for the practice in which teachers of history live and move and have their being, and to supply tentative answers to the questions—Why do we study history? Why do we teach it? Why do we think that every child should acquire some knowledge of historical truth? And what advantage will such knowledge be to him from an educational point of view? We exclude material advantage from consideration for two reasons. In the first place, the study of history cannot be recommended as a ready means to a lucrative livelihood. In the second place, the number of those who will seek a living by teaching or writing history will always be a small minority of the nation, while the object we have in mind is the education of all.

Our answers will clearly depend upon the definition of history which we adopt. If we regard it as merely a series of stories dependent for its value simply upon the way it is told, we must be content to accept for it a humble place in the educational sphere. These stories do indeed arouse interest and stimulate imagination; and such questions as,

Where was Homer born, if he was born at all? Where did Hannibal cross the Alps? Who killed the Princes in the Tower, or Amy Robsart, or Sir Edmund Berry Godfrey? Who was the man in the Iron Mask? or What became of Louis XVII? have excited an amount of attention out of all proportion to their historic importance. Their educational value consists in the fact that they lend wings to the imagination, and carry our minds out of the groove of the present into the limitless space of the past; and being thus transported, we are led to compare the past with the present, to measure the distance between the two, and to form some idea of how that distance was covered. In this comparison we have some of the materials for that historical judgment which is essential to the understanding of our environment and to the sanity of our outlook. The idealist unrestrained by history compares the present with Utopia, the desert with a mirage, which he seeks to realise by short-cuts across ' the meagre, stale, forbidding ways of custom, law, and statute '; and thus he becomes a revolutionary. The student of history compares the present with a real past, and by means of a valid comparison gains some perception of the conditions and chances of orderly progress.

The educational importance of such an understanding of our environment and its causes is not in practice realised. The 'hero' in one of Mr. H. G. Wells' novels expresses the amazement with which in after life he discovered that throughout his school career in London not one word had been said to him about the city in which he lived, nothing to explain how that city grew or maintained its existence, or the part which it played in the world. He went through his education ignorant of the mechanism as well as of the spirit of modern life, and of the historical causes which had produced the world of to-day. In short, school education sacrifices the truth that is to be expressed to the methods of expression, and prefers the study of language to the study of man. Important as are the clearness and accuracy of expression which proceed from linguistic training, they are only a means to an end; and educationally it is better to be taught to write wisdom in one language than folly in a dozen, better to be able to tell the truth with a stammer than falsehood with the tongue of angels. The principle of restricting school education mainly to cultivating methods of expression would be sound enough, if we could rely upon several years of further education in the truth to be expressed; but, since most people's education stops when they leave school, room must be found in school curricula for the teaching of subjects which are material to the understanding of environment.

Herein the affinities of history are with literature rather than with language. The content of both is much the same, and the difference lies in the method of treatment. In history we deal with the development of man's action as well as of his thought, and consider both in close connection with the conditions of the age in which he lived. To the student of history the essential thing is not merely the thought itself, but the relation of the thought to the circumstances of the time; while the student of literature contemplates the thoughts expressed therein apart from their historical setting or development. Nevertheless the study of literature is an indispensable element in the study of history because action is the effect as well as the cause of ideas; and a study of literature is one of the best correctives of the unintelligent conception of history as merely a matter of facts and dates.

These facts and dates are the merest framework of historical study. They have no value in themselves; mere lists of facts convey the impression that history is a fortuitous collocation of inconsequential events, instead of a coherent sequence of causes and effects; and dates by themselves obscure the gradual nature of historical evolution. They are useful and necessary solely as means of determining sequences, and without the careful observance of sequences we cannot arrive at causes. But it is the causes which the historical student has ultimately in view; he seeks in the study of history an explanation of how mankind reached its present state of development as individuals, as societies, as nations, and as empires.

Two qualities are essential beyond all others to this understanding. One is imagination, and the other is sympathy; and the cultivation of both by means of historical study is one of the most valuable elements in historical education. By imagination we mean a capacity to dissociate our minds from the conditions of the present, to realise those of the past, and to put ourselves in the circumstances of other times, just as sympathy enables us to put ourselves in the place of other people. History is the most humane of the humaner studies. It demands and it provokes the humaner qualities; and for this reason it differs from the physical sciences. No human sympathy is required or produced by the study of geology, mineralogy, physics, or chemistry, which deal with the lifeless elements of the material world; nor by botany, which is concerned with the lowest forms of life. Biology and anatomy do rise to the level of man, but only as an animal. History is the highest form of science because its subject matter is the highest work of nature. It deals with man as a being who possesses a knowledge of good and evil, a standard of right and wrong, who reasons and judges, creates beauty in art and literature, commands and controls to an ever-increasing degree the forces of nature, and consciously or unconsciously fashions the destinies of this world. If history is not commonly regarded as a science, it is only because it is too complex and too human to lend itself to those summary methods of treatment by axioms, rules, and formulæ which are commonly taken as tests of scientific truth.

It must, however, be admitted that history is not an exact science; and the educational values that depend upon exact and universal truth, if there be such a thing, must be sought in other quarters. But exact statements are seldom correct, unless they deal with the merest details or with abstractions; and we cannot begin history, as Euclid begins geometry, by assuming the most disputable statements as definitions and basing our science upon the assumptions. It is no doubt convenient to assume that a line is length without breadth, but no such line ever existed except as a mental conception incapable of objective illustration or even of visualisation. It is also convenient to assume that one is always equal to one, but the proposition becomes ridiculous as soon as it is applied to the men and matters with which history has to deal. There can be no formulæ in history, because no formulæ apply to human affairs. In our terminology itself we have no constants, but only variants. One of the commonest blunders of elementary historians is to assume that Germany meant in the Middle Ages what it means to-day; and specialists have sometimes fallen into similar error from the same assumption of historical constancy in more abstract terms. A distinguished archivist once adduced the fact that John licensed someone to found a *nova religio* as proof of that king's uncommon liberality of mind. He had not realised that in John's reign *religio* meant a religious house or order; but his mistake was no worse than that of those who imagine that the same monarch endowed his country with modern liberty when he granted a *magna carta* of medieval liberties.

Hence in the study and teaching of history we have constantly to correct misconceptions arising from false assumptions of the exactitude and universal truth of absolute and pseudo-scientific statements, and to emphasise the fact that all values depend upon environment. Even in the sphere of mathematics the child, when he leaves school and has to deal with the realities of life, has to learn that, although he has been taught the numerical equality between one sovereign and other, the real value of every coin depends upon its possessor and upon the circumstances under which he owns it. A pound may mean next to nothing to a millionaire, it may mean almost everything to a labourer out of work; it may even mean very different things to the same man at different times, and the usurer's livelihood depends upon his skilful appreciation of the difference. It is owing to its isolation of the numerical signification from the real values that the statistical method leads to such strange and contradictory results.

Similar mistakes in the past led to similarly futile conclusions in historical and political discussions. Endless energy has been spent in debating, for instance, whether monarchy, aristocracy, or democracy is the best form of polity, as though any one of these forms had any ascertainable value apart from the conditions under which it was to be adopted. In those days of unhistorical and *a priori* reasoning a democrat was supposed to believe in the value of democracy for all men at all times and in all countries. To a historian there is nothing inconsistent in thinking that royal despotism was the best government for England at the time of William I. or Henry II., an aristocracy the best in the eighteenth century, and a democracy the best to-day; or in thinking that to-day a democracy may be best for England, a military aristocracy for Turkey, and a despotism for India. For the value of every form of constitution depends upon the stage of political and educational development attained by the people who have to live under it.

The historical method has produced a like revolution in economic science. The classical economists of the early nineteenth century evolved a body of dogma which they considered to be as universally applicable as the principles of mathematics; their place has been taken by the historical school of economists who realise that the value of economic systems is relative and depends upon environment. Nor have the historical method and the historical spirit yet reached the limits of their triumphs. At a dinner to celebrate the completion of the eleventh edition of the *Encyclopædia Britannica* in 1911 one of the chief theological contributors dwelt upon the distance that had been covered since the first edition, when the religions of the world were summarily classified in two categories as true or false.

The study of history is, indeed, fatal to the habit of setting up absolute antitheses. Luther once remarked of himself and Zwingli : " Either he or I must be the devil's minister." He may have been expressing theological truth, but he was certainly inspired by that primeval combative instinct which it is one of the functions of the historical method to eradicate from intellectual pursuits. It is that combative instinct which breeds the custom of regarding one party or one side of a question as entirely right and the other as entirely wrong ; and men would not fight, literally or metaphorically, if they perceived that they were divided from their opponents only by shades of opinion and insignificant degrees of error. Yet the tendency of historical study is to show that nearly all questions are quantitative ; that is to say, that the question is not whether this party was right and the other wrong, but to what extent this party was right and the other wrong. Real historians are ceasing to be political or ecclesiastical pamphleteers disguised ; hence they find it easier not only to approach an agreement, but to civilise the methods by which, and the terms in which, they express their disagreement. They do not now consider that difference of opinion necessarily comes from original sin or leads to final perdition.

Historical study may thus be used to humanise methods of controversy, and this humanistic function is one of the greatest social services which it can render. For history cannot be divorced from ecclesiastical and secular politics. The injunction to keep them rigidly apart is a counsel of fear fraught with mischief. To separate one from the other is to sterilise history and stultify politics : without history, says Seeley, political science has no root, without political science history has no fruit. We should not indeed allow our politics to contaminate our history, but we should use our historical sense to purify our politics ; and when properly developed, historical methods and the historical sense cannot fail to have that effect. The historical student does not, for instance, concern himself with denunciations of Socialism or of Individualism; he seeks to understand the historical causes which have produced those phases of opinion, and to discover how far each of them embodies practical solutions applicable to the varying conditions of political societies. The only conclusion which his historical studies will lead him to exclude is the *a priori* theory that either is a panacea for all the ills of all sorts and conditions of men.

Historical study, besides fostering the scientific spirit in which alone political issues can be profitably examined, provides also the background without which they cannot be understood or viewed in their proper perspective. For every political issue is the result of historical development, and if we want to know how to deal with it we must appreciate the causes and methods of its growth. Revolutionary efforts made in the past by other countries to remedy social or political evils without reference to their history have pointed the moral often enough; and the need for the safeguards of historical sense grows daily more urgent. There are three main reasons for this urgency. In the first place, political power has been placed in the hands of the masses who are just beginning to feel that they possess it, but have had little or no historical enlightenment on the ways in which it may be used. Secondly, such instruction as they do receive comes largely from sensational journals which seek to increase their circulation by presenting their news in as startling, and therefore as much out of perspective, a light as possible. Thirdly, it did not so much matter what the government did, or who controlled it, so long as the *laisser faire* idea prevailed that government should do little or nothing; but wisdom in government has become vastly more necessary now that there seem to be few limits to the range of governmental activity.

While history provides a sound basis of politics, which is inadequately appreciated, its common employment as a basis of moral instruction is open to serious criticism. In the throes of the conflict with Napoleon a Spanish patriot declared his conviction that the tribulations of Spain were a divine judgment upon it for having neglected for more than a generation the duty of burning heretics. He was trying to explain contemporary history upon what seemed to him moral principles; and this example will probably bring home to most of us the danger of the proceeding. But Carlyle's differentiation between the political morality of Frederick the Great and that of Napoleon is hardly less vicious; and the fact that Frederick won the battle of Rossbach, while Napoleon lost that of Waterloo, affords no sort of proof that the absorption of Silesia was a more moral proceeding than the seizure of Holland or Spain. Yet it is a common assumption that historical success has depended on moral excellence, that truth and morality have generally, if not always, prevailed, and that there is at least a strong presumption that the victorious cause has been that of justice and right. Few Protestants can resist the temptation to ascribe the triumph of the Reformation to its inherent righteousness; few Catholics can regard it as anything but a temporary prevailing of the gates of hell.

There must be something radically wrong in historical methods and assumptions which lead honest men to diametrically opposite conclusions from the same body of evidence. And the fundamental misconception seems to be the idea that historical events are the expression of moral judgments. If we adopt that view, we shall always be driven to emphasise the success of a principle in which we believe, and to explain away the success of one in which we do not, lest our admissions should weaken our belief in the efficacy of our principles. Hence the constant explanation of the triumph of causes which we dislike by reference to tyranny and corruption exercised by the few over the many; because it is so much more comforting to believe that a few men were wicked than that the majority voluntarily embraced or acquiesced in what we think to be wrong.

This anxiety to find in history support for our moral conceptions betrays us into the still more unhistorical dogmas that persecution never succeeds and that right is always might; and we are further led into the fallacy of attempting to judge historical action by a fixed code of morals. We ignore the facts that moral standards are the painful achievement of ages; that there has been a moral, no less than a political, a social, and an economic development in history; and that to judge men of the past by the moral standards of the present is as unhistorical as it would be to apply the strategical criteria of to-day to the movements of medieval armies, or to condemn the Elizabethan Poor Law because it failed to cope with the results of the Industrial Revolution. It is far less depressing to be able to show that there has been a raising of moral standards and that the sphere and the force of the appeal to conscience have from age to age expanded, than it is to submit to the conclusion that no progress has been made in the realisation of man's moral ambitions. But this admission of moral progress involves a recognition of the fact that men who came up to the moral standards of the past do not come up to those of the present, and therefore that their careers do not afford a satisfactory basis for modern moral instruction. Good men approved of slavery, of the slaughter of prisoners of war, of tyrannicide, of burning religious and beheading political dissidents from the established order, of diplomatic fraud, and of pious forgery; and political success in the past conveys even less moral sanction than it does in the present.

The circumstance that the study of history provides no sound basis for moral instruction is, however, no bar to its value as a means of developing critical judgment even in the ethical sphere. The action of men must be referred to moral standards; but those standards should be those of the age in which they lived, and the historical appreciation of the difference between the moral standards of different ages is indispensable to the scientific understanding of the growth of moral codes and conventions. The change in men's judgment of slavery, tyrannicide, persecution, and fraud is in itself an important subject of historical study.

But the spirit of criticism is as essential in all departments of historical inquiry as are imagination and sympathy. History is a matter of evidence, and our methods of treating the evidence are vital to the truth of our verdicts. In the study of history we can only deal with men and events as seen through various *media,* such as records, chronicles, ballads, letters, pamphlets, and histories, all of which are, in varying degrees, incomplete, partial, and distorting; and unless we have some idea of the degree to which our evidences are incomplete, partial, and distorting, we can have no solid foundation for our historical judgments. Hence the study and teaching of history involve constant reference to the canons of evidential criticism and to the methods of historical investigation; and this training supplies the scientific element in historical study, just as the imagination and sympathy necessary for the construction of historical synthesis provide the artistic factor. History like every other study is both a science and an art, because it requires a scientific analysis of materials and an artistic synthesis of results.

To sum up : we believe the study of history to possess great educational value for the following reasons. Only by its means can we understand the causes of the religious, moral, political, social, and economic atmosphere in which we live; and we consider that understanding to be quite as important and quite as educational as training in methods of expression or the understanding of man's physical environment. History is not, however, an exact science because man's mind cannot be measured, weighed, dissected and tested by the same comparatively crude and simple methods as his body. But the fact that it lends itself to experiment does not make matter more vital than mind; and history, in being more complex, is not therefore less exigent of real scientific treatment than physics or chemistry. Few people, moreover, need be chemists or physicists, but every one has to be a citizen; and he cannot be an intelligent citizen if he is ignorant of the history of the world. Knowledge of public action in the past provides the best means of understanding public action in the present, and the safest guide for the exercise of political power. Through the proper study of history we can join the wisdom of Solomon to the counsel of Socrates by trying to get understanding and learning to know ourselves.

II

Whatever I may hope to say or to do in the ensuing lectures, one thing at least I shall not attempt; and that is, to give you a history of England during the sixteenth and seventeenth centuries. An effort of that kind would simply result in the perpetration of yet another of those miserable text-books of English history, which may be necessary but are certainly evil, which prefer knowledge to understanding, and seem expressly designed to nip the bud of historical interest and to clip the wings of historical imagination. It is almost a miracle that any incipient students of history survive this crushing ordeal: if they do, it must be due to the inspiration of the living voice; and no teacher of history worth the name relies upon the compilations which the examination-system compels him to inflict upon his class.

My object is primarily to stimulate imagination, and I make no apology for placing imagination in the forefront of all the qualifications indispensable for the student and teacher of history. By that curious process of deterioration, which the meaning of words undergoes, the word imagination' is commonly restricted to the imagination of deeds which were never done, and of causes which never existed. Properly it includes fact as well as fiction, and signifies the power of realising things unseen, and of realising the meaning of things seen. A portrait is a truer *image* than a fancy sketch; and, when an English ambassador wrote to Henry VIII that Holbein had made a very faithful *image* of Anne of Cleves, he meant that the portrait was true to life. So history can never be true to life without imagination. Facts and figures are dry bones; it requires imagination to clothe them with life and meaning; and no accumulation of materials, no ransacking of archives, will make a man a historian without the capacity to interpret and construct. Not that I wish to depreciate the archivist or the burrower after facts. Solomon can only build the temple after David has collected the materials. And these materials are the most valuable means by which to train and cultivate the imagination. Reading history ready-made is to making it out oneself from documents what looking on at a football match is to playing the game oneself, or what reading a detective story is to tracking out a criminal; and to teach the intelligent use of documents is the first of the neglected duties of our schools of history.

Facts, therefore—I make the avowal at the risk of the laughter of pedants—are only a secondary consideration from my point of view, and they will only be used as illustrations. That phrase is perhaps unlucky; at least it has lately caused some innocent merriment. And, indeed, one's facts should be correct; but their meaning is greater than the facts themselves, and it is with the meaning of historical facts that I am now concerned. It is only when we penetrate the outer husks of facts that we can reach the kernel of historic truth. A fact of itself is of little value unless it conveys a meaning. There is a meaning behind all facts, if one can only discover it; but to discover the meaning of facts is commonly the last object at which the writers of text-books aim. Facts are stated as though their statement were all that is necessary, and as though to remember them were more important than to understand them, as though the end of education were to make the youthful mind a lumber-room of facts, instead of an efficient instrument, trained to perform the duties of life and to discern the features of truth.

So far as may be, then, I hope to bring out the significance which underlies the ordinary facts of some portions of modern English history, and particularly that of the sixteenth and seventeenth centuries. And in this first lecture I want to take what seems to me the dominant note of modern, as distinct from medieval and ancient history—I mean nationality. For modern history deals primarily with the national State, while ancient history deals largely with the City-state, and medieval history with the World-state, secular or ecclesiastical. That, of course, is a very rough generalisation; the transitory empire of Alexander if it can be considered a state at all, was almost a world-state. City-states, too, existed in Italy and in Germany during the Middle Ages, and Geneva, Venice, Genoa, continued the species beyond the latest of the various dates at which modern history is said to have begun. Nevertheless, the City-state is the predominant type of the ancient civilised world; with it Aristotle's *Politics,* the greatest text-book of political science, is almost exclusively concerned. Now, Aristotle says a great many things about the State, which are not yet out of date: its permanence can only be secured by the toleration of all the elements in it, it must pay great regard to education, must have a care of virtue, rests upon justice, is not made happier by conquest, and so forth. His doctrine that it should be economically self-sufficing is perhaps more familiar than indisputable, but his criteria as to its size sound strange in modern ears. It must not be so large that its citizens, gathered in one public meeting, cannot hear the speaker's voice, and a State the size of Birmingham would have appeared to him unwieldy from its bulk. Such an estimate illustrates the difference, made by the development of modern representative systems and the abolition of slavery, between the ancient and the modern state.

The World-state is not less typical of the Middle Ages, though perhaps more as regards its theory than its practice. You remember the Cheshire cat in *Alice in Wonderland,* whose smile remained long after the cat had disappeared. The same phenomenon is common enough in history and in politics; and the idea of the World-state continued to fascinate men's minds long after it had lost material existence. The Roman Empire had become more than an institution; it was the only form in which men could conceive the political organisation of the world. For centuries it had existed; and the contempt and neglect of pagan history, which Gregory the Great impressed upon men's minds, obliterated the knowledge that there had ever been any different political existence. Hence the revival of the Empire in the times of Charles the Great and Otto—a revivalism which reaches its height with Otto III, and the fancied approach of the millennium in the year 1000. Hence, too, the development of the Papacy, which grew up under the shadow, and moulded itself after the form, of the Roman Empire.

Empire and Papacy, said Zwingli, both came from Rome. The law of one was Roman civil law, the law of the other was Roman canon law, and in both cases it was universal. The world was one and indivisible, though it had two aspects, secular and ecclesiastical, temporal and spiritual. In one aspect the Emperor was its head, in the other the Pope. The two spheres were ill-defined, and the struggle between them fills the greater part of medieval history. Papalists compared the Papacy with the sun, the empire with the moon, which only shone with the reflected light conferred by Pope Leo III upon Charles the Great. The empire was like the body, temporal and transitory, the Papacy was like the soul, spiritual and imperishable.

Popes claimed by right both swords, the temporal and the spiritual, but entrusted the temporal sword to the emperor, because the execution of justice was menial work beneath their spiritual dignity. Imperialists retorted with arguments drawn from Biblical injunctions of obedience to the powers that be and from the Scriptural recognition of the divine ordination of authority. The clergy might be the bearers of the keys, but it was only in the capacity of turnkeys— a more menial office than the execution of justice. And so the contest waged in the closet and on the field of battle, with sword and dagger and spear, with bell, book and candle. It was ever a strife between two powers and two jurisdictions, both claiming to be universal and international. Although the voice of nationality is heard in the councils of Philip IV of France and in the wars of the fourteenth century, the world is still to Dante one monarchy and the emperor Henry VII is its monarch.

This absence of nationality is characteristic of all medieval institutions. The empire is *ex hypothesi* an international organisation. It is associated with the German monarchy as a rule, but that is only an accident. The empire, claiming all the world as its subjects, knows nothing of aliens; they are a modern invention. Alfonso of Castile is a candidate for the empire; he fails, but his Spanish nationality is no bar to his pretension. Later on, Henry VIII and Francis I are candidates for the imperial throne; German sentiment is against them, but there is no law to exclude an Englishman or a Frenchman. Any one can hold an imperial fief; a Pole or a Spaniard is the same as a German in the eyes of the law of the empire; they are no more foreigners than a Saxon or a Suabian. Law, in fact, is in the Middle Ages international. There are, it is true, various kinds of law, civil law, canon law, feudal law and folkright; and the differences are pronounced enough. But they are not national differences. Feudal custom is much the same, wherever you meet it in Western Europe. The tenant-in-chief, the mailed knight, the *curia regis,* the lord's demesne, the castle, rights of jurisdiction, obligations of defence, are everywhere. We are taught, indeed, that feudalism was introduced into England from France; but recently a French scholar has repaid us the compliment by asserting that feudalism was imported from England into Normandy and thence spread throughout France. The honour is apparently not coveted. But no one people invented feudalism; it grew out of disorderly conditions which were common all over Europe, and therefore it assumed a common form.

If feudal law and custom were not national, still less so were Roman civil and Roman canon law. The emperor was the fountain of one; *quod principi placuit legis habet vigorem* wrote Ulpian. The Pope was the fountain of the other; *habet omnia jura in scrinio suo,* said Clement VII. The State might resist the application of canon law as the English barons did in 1236, and the Church might forbid the study of civil law as did Popes Honorius and Innocent III; but in both cases it would be two universal claims contending in a particular locality, rather than a national contending against a universal sentiment.

As with laws, so with letters. The Middle Ages had their *Esperanto* ready made and natural in growth. Every one in Western Europe who could write, wrote the same language, and that was Latin. History was easy to the monkish chronicler because his original documents were all in the same language. Intercourse with foreign scholars was robbed of its impediments and perhaps some of its amusement; and the barriers, which now obstruct the interchange of intellectual currency, had not yet been erected. Alien and foreigner were not yet terms of insult and contempt,. The literature, on which youth was nourished, was not painted red nor adorned with Union Jacks. Vernacular tongues were spoken as dialects are to-day, but they were not written; and national literatures only arise when the Middle Ages decay. The Bible was the same wherever it was read; the same Vulgate text served for English and Italian, for German and for Spaniard. And although there was room for local option in the matter of ritual, its broad outlines were the same in every church and chapel of the West. The universities were international institutions; a national university would have seemed a poor and narrow thing, and academic organisation was based upon the idea that at least four nations would be represented in each university. Even the

wars of the Middle Ages were not national; the greatest
are the Crusades; then there are wars between Empire and
Papacy, and lowest of all comes the feudal strife of vassal
against vassal or vassal against his lord; there is no really
national war before the Hundred Years' War between
England and France.

Religion also was cosmopolitan; the Church universal
was visible as well as invisible. It had divisions of course.
There were laymen and priests, secular priests and regulars,
monks and friars. But the sections were horizontal, not
vertical; they ran all through Western Christendom, and
did not divide it into geographical parts. The monastic
orders were peculiarly international; the whole world was
their parish; their general chapters were cosmopolitan
parliaments; and the rigidity of their international
character brought them into sharp collision with the rising
national spirit of the sixteenth century, and made them
the first spoils of the Reformation.

The change from this partially-realised ideal of unity to
the modern diversity of national tongues and national
churches, national laws and national liberties, is the
greatest factor in the evolution of modern from medieval
history. We may express it by means of a diagram.

	England	France	Germany	Spain
Folkright				
Feudal Custom				
Civil Law				
Canon Law				

Take the feudal, civil, and canonical varieties of medieval law and custom. They are separated from one another by horizontal lines, which spread all over Western Europe, recognising no distinction of nationality. So with ecclesiastical institutions, dogma and ritual, seculars and regulars, monks and friars. But what happens? Imperceptibly vertical lines begin to traverse the horizontal lines. Feudal custom in England is differentiated from feudal custom in France; for instance, by the Salisbury oath of 1086 William the Conqueror makes every man's duty to his king superior to his duty to his lord. Canon law is limited in England where it is not limited abroad; for instance, in 1236 the English barons refuse to assimilate the laws of England to those of the Church universal with respect to the legitimation of bastards by the subsequent marriage of the parents. English common law[1] modifies and moulds all other kinds of laws. As the vertical lines get deeper, the horizontal lines tend to become obliterated, and feudal custom, civil law and canon law, tend to become merged in national systems of English, French, German, and Spanish law. In the sixteenth century, the canon law, so far as it is not embedded in the common law, becomes binding on the laity only *in foro conscientiae*. The struggle between the civil and the common law is more prolonged and calls for treatment later on. But eventually they too are merged in a national system.

In the same way the somewhat obscure vertical line between the Church in England and the Church abroad grows clear and sharp, and the horizontal lines grow dim. There is no room in an aggressively national system for international institutions which refuse to compromise their universal character, and the monks and friars disappear. The Thirty-Nine Articles are not the articles of any but the Anglican Church; the Book of Common Prayer is its

1 Common law is the one law which is not common over Western Europe, but is common over all classes in England. It is the law of the *Curia Regis*, and is the first kind of *national* law.

unique and priceless property. The Church *in* England has
been nationalised; it has become the Church *of* England.
It is the same abroad : *cujus regio, ejus religio* was the
maxim of the Peace of Augsburg (1555) in which the
territorial princes of Germany asserted the fact that they
had conquered in the Church as well as in the State.

Language and literature, too, become nationalised. We
can scarcely say that either a national language or a
national literature existed in England before the fourteenth
century, before the days of Langland, of Wycliffe, and
of Chaucer. For Anglo-Saxon is not English, nor is it
literature. A national German language and literature
arise about the same time. French, Italian, and Spanish
are perhaps earlier, because less original. The Bible is
translated into these vernacular tongues, and is nationalised : it is no longer the same in England, France,
Germany, and Spain : and the more idiomatic the translation, the more popular it becomes. Luther's New
Testament and the Authorised Version of the English Bible
would never have been great national forces had they been
exactly alike. Universities lose their cosmopolitan character,
and for the time suffer severely by the change : indeed
they rarely flourish amid national animosities. So, too,
patriotism began to invade the schoolroom, and in Queen
Elizabeth's reign we find the author of *De Proeliis
Anglorum*—a sort of sixteenth century *Deeds that won the
Empire*—writing to Burghley to point out how much better
it would be for English schoolboys to study his book than
Ovid's *Metamorphoses*. He actually obtained an advertise-
ment from the Privy Council, but nations had not yet
invented national anthems. They began in the eighteenth
century, a fact which possibly led an eminent statesman
to declare that before that age patriotism did not exist.

From these illustrations of the working of the nationalist
and separatist spirit we must turn to a more difficult
question. It is comparatively easy to see the horizontal
lines of medieval unity dissolving behind the vertical lines

of national diversity: and there is not much difficulty in discovering that the emphasis of the latter tended to obliterate the former. But it is not so simple to explain why or how these nationalising forces grew, why the national prevailed over the universal, and the centrifugal over the centripetal. There is one obvious and facile answer—national character. But the obvious is always superficial, and the facile is generally false. National character, as Professor Maitland has satirically pointed out, is a wonder-working spirit at the beck and call of every embarrassed historian, a sort of *deus ex machina*, which is invoked to settle any problem which cannot readily be solved by ordinary methods of rational investigation. The rule of the game seems to be, 'when in doubt, play National Character.' It is assumed to be a fixed and permanent force slowly perhaps, but surely, moulding national institutions, shaping national ends, and working out the national destiny. It existed, presumably, from the beginning, and to it are ascribed all national differences. Is liberty the predominant feature of the English constitution and governmental privilege of the French? It is due to national character. 'When Britain first at Heaven's command arose from out the azure main,' it received a charter and a double dose of original independence. When France began to drag out its miserable existence, its people received a double dose of original servility, and a charter which made each Frenchman equal to about one-third of an Englishman. The idea was older than 'Rule Britannia!' 'We must fight it out' exclaimed the disappointed and dispossessed peasants, who rebelled in 1549, 'or be brought into *like slavery that the Frenchmen are in.*' We do not use the word slavery nowadays when speaking of the French, but we often mean much the same thing; and it is an article of the Englishman's creed that whatever differences exist between England and the continent are due to the inherent and ineradicable superiority of English national character.

But what is this national character? Where does it come
from? From our Celtic, our German, or our Norse
ancestors? Or is it due to none of these pure brands, but
to the extraordinary virtue of a very special blend? The
first and most persistent confusion which meets us in this
discussion is the identification of nationality with race.
Now race is one of the vaguest words in the language.
We use it to distinguish men from other animals, and speak
of the human race.   We use it to differentiate various
branches of the human family, and speak of the Aryan,
Semitic, and other races.   We employ it for further
subdividing Aryans into Teutonic and Celtic races, for
subdividing Teutonic races into English, German, Dutch,
and Norse : and we even talk of English-speaking races,
American, Canadian, Australian, and Afrikander. Race
in fact may mean half a dozen kinds of subdivision, so that
it cannot possibly be the cause of any one of those sub-
divisions, and we do not get much further in our analysis
of nationality by identifying it with race.

There is another bar to the identification. A Jew can
no more change his race than an Ethiopian can his skin,
but he can assume English, French, or American nationality with very little trouble. Nationality is a coat which
can rapidly be turned. A few years ago an alien was a
candidate for the House of Commons : he was of German
nationality two days before his nomination : nine days
later he was a patriotic British M.P. The variety of races
which constitute British nationality is astonishing. ' Saxon,
or Norman, or Dane are we ' sang Tennyson : but the
exigencies of time, space and metre prevented him from
giving an exhaustive list. We are also Scots, Irish, Welsh,
German, French, Spaniards and Italians—not to mention
the lost Ten Tribes. From the days of Simon de Montfort
downwards many of the most distinguished British patriots
have not been British in race. Merely to recall names like
Disraeli, Bentinck, Keppel, Romilly, Goschen, Vanbrugh,
Panizzi, Rossetti, Rothschild indicates the debt we owe in

the sphere of law and letters, politics, art, and finance, to men of alien race; and it is a well-known fact that nearly all great English musicians have been Germans, and most great English painters Dutch. It is well for our national achievement that we have had no prohibitive tariff on the import of alien immigrants.

Nor are we peculiar in this respect. Natives of the British Isles have helped to create the armies and fleets, and to build up the polities of most European states. In the eighteenth century you might have found one Irishman directing as prime minister the fortunes of Spain, and another those of Naples, a third commanding the forces of Austria, and a fourth seeking to rebuild the French dominion in India. Scots as a rule restricted their attentions to Protestant countries, but John Law in the early years of that century did wonderful things with French finance. The right-hand man of Frederick the Great was a Scot, and Scots took more than their share in the making of Russia—an article of almost exclusively foreign manufacture. Peter the Great himself had a mother of Scottish birth, and the fact made all the difference between him and his imbecile half-brothers. Catherine the Great was a German. Napoleon himself was not a Frenchman by race: one of his marshals, an Italian, became King of Sweden, and founded the present Swedish line of monarchs. The Kings of Italy come from Savoy. and the Kings of Spain are Bourbons, and the Kings of Belgium were made in Saxe-Coburg. Even in England we have had no kings of exclusively English race since the Battle of Hastings. The conquering Normans were succeeded by the Plantagenets who came from Anjou. The Tudors descended on England from the mountains of Wales, and the Stuarts from over the Tweed: and our last royal families come from Brunswick and Saxe-Coburg-Gotha.

Nationality then is something more and something less than race. It is mutable: it is complex: and compared

with race it is modern. English national character did not
exist when our Teutonic forebears left the shores of
Germany. The tribes, which migrated, were no more
distinct from those which stayed behind than the Pilgrim
Fathers were from the Puritans of the Long Parliament.
The differences between English and German history are
not due to original differences of national character,
any more than are the differences between English and
American history. In both cases the different national
character is due to the different environment and history.
A scientist made the same point the other day, when he
asserted that environment was stronger than heredity.
Nationality is the effect, rather than the cause, of history,
though in its turn it does affect the course of history. It is
not a thing to be assumed without discussion or proof like
the definitions of Euclid : it is a mass of acquired characteristics, each of which has its definite and more or less
ascertainable causes.

We go back to the earliest records of the peoples of
Western Europe. That does not take us back to their
beginnings; for anthropologists, who burrow in barrows
and caves, tell us that tens of centuries of human development and differentiation had rolled by before the earliest
record appears. But the light in these barrows and caves
is dim, and their evidence doubtful. The historian cannot
go far beyond Cæsar for the beginnings of modern Gaul,
nor beyond Tacitus for those of modern Germany and
England : and the first appearance of modern peoples
upon the stage of history is in the rôle of wanderers, having
the slightest connection with the soil. Such property as
they have is easily moved—and lifted. Their pursuits are
pastoral, not agricultural, because flocks are much more
mobile than crops; and primitive man is always on the
move. The soil is no bond and no tie : it has no associations for them. Sentiment does not differentiate one land
from another, but only its fertility and accessibility. Their
relations are personal, not territorial : they are kinsmen

rather than neighbours, and the word 'neighbour' comes comparatively late into the language, not until the system of 'borh' has replaced the kin, and territorial proximity has supplanted the proximity of blood.

This is the first great revolution in human affairs with which we have to deal. For causes, at which we can only guess, the wanderers weary of wandering and make for themselves that novel thing, a home. They settle on the soil, and the soil grips them. Their abode becomes fixed, and so does their horizon. They build huts and they plough the land : their property is no longer movable, and they are tied to the spot on which they live. Their bonds are with those who live near : these may be kinsmen, and no doubt are at first. But they need not be : the stranger within the gates becomes neighbour, and the bonds with distant kinsmen relax. Territorial proximity replaces that of blood as the basis of human society. Then the *genius loci* casts its spell over the immigrants : it includes the effects of climate and the results of previous occupation. The immigrants into Celtic and Roman Britain will not be the same as if they had remained in Teutonic Germany. The Ostrogoth who conquers Italy becomes an Italian, the Visigoth who conquers Spain becomes a Spaniard : the Frank who settles in France becomes a Frenchman, while he who remains at home continues a German : the Norman who conquers England becomes English, and he who conquers Sicily, Sicilian. Subtler still is the influence of climate and geographical conditions ; and hence the value of historical geography. We have been told—I know not with how much truth—that the Yankee is developing the same features, the high cheek-bones, the prominent nose, the straight lank hair, and even somewhat of the colour of the American Indians whom he displaced. We can see under our eyes the process of intellectual and moral differentiation. There are three Englishmen : one stays at home, one goes to Australia, and one to Canada. Twenty years pass, one has become a Canadian, another an

Australian, and the first alone remains an Englishman. The differentiation, once begun, proceeds at a growing pace; and the task of reconciling the new nationalities with the old Imperial unity is the hardest problem of politics.

It is this association of men with different parts of the earth's surface which begins the process of differentiating modern nations from one another, and drives vertical national lines down through the horizontal cosmopolitan lines. But the common ideas which the immigrants take to the various localities combine at first with the influence of the soil to produce similar institutions. Feudalism is more or less common to the whole of Western Europe : the soil becomes the basis and badge of social position in France as well as in England. Everywhere the territorial supersedes the personal relationship, and the kings become owners of land rather than lords of people. Alfred the Great is not King of Wessex, but of the West Saxons, and William the Conqueror is King of the English, not King of England. To call him King of England is as wrong as to call the Kaiser Emperor of Germany : for the territorial sovereign in Saxony is not Kaiser Wilhelm, but König Friedrich August. It is only with John that the King of the English becomes King of England, and the substitution of the territorial for the personal sovereignty is officially recognised.

The change is expressed in many ways. In England the 'hundred' and the 'tithing,' originally groups of persons, become geographical terms. In France public functions are transformed into local divisions : the *bailliage*, originally the office of *bailli*, is soon a portion of territory. The county, at first the office of count, acquires a geographical meaning. Law itself becomes local : it had been as mobile as property, and each tribe carried with it its personal law wherever it went. The Ostrogoths and Lombards carried Teutonic law into Italy, the Visigoths into Spain, the Franks into Gaul, and the Angles and Saxons into Britain.

But it comes under local influence, splits into hundreds of local customs, and becomes territorial. The law of persons becomes the law of the land. Men no longer carry about their own legal atmosphere : they have to breathe that of the land whither they go.

This ' territorialism,' as it is called, is the great bar to national unity. Indeed, national unity is a conception far beyond the reach of men's minds in early times. How do we know that we are a nation and an Empire? Well, we have the *Daily Mail* to tell us so, and *The Times* and other Atlases with maps all coloured red. But the Anglo-Saxons had no halfpenny or any other papers to tell them how great they were, or how little : they could not read or write, and they would quite have failed to understand a map. They had ceased to wander as tribes, and had not yet begun to travel as individuals. All these means for the expansion of men's consciousness were wanting. Their horizon was limited by what they saw, and not expanded by what they imagined. Their patriotism centred round the parish pump or its equivalent. The ' best ' men of the township and the hundred travelled further afield, and had some conception of tribal unity as represented by the shire-moot : but the Anglo-Saxons never got beyond provincial patriotism, and the old English monarchy was never more than a federation of tribal commonwealths, loosely bound together for purposes of mutual defence. The Norman Conquest first imposed some sort of national unity, and Henry II's *Curia Regis* some sort of national law : but the consciousness of this unity was for ages limited to the king and his entourage, to the *Curia Regis* and the royal officials. Even after Parliament appears, the greatest difficulty is to make it national, and to bring home to the constituencies a sense of their national duties. Representation was regarded as a burden right down to the sixteenth century, both by electors and elected. On one occasion the elected knights for Oxfordshire fled the country to escape the honour. The sheriff raised the hue and cry and pursued them like thieves and murderers. One was caught and bound over to appear at Westminster when Parliament should assemble, but the other escaped; and it was the Tudors who first inoculated Parliament with a really national consciousness.

Local interests are potent in the Middle Ages: they hampered the growth of national feeling, but they were less incompatible than national unity with a wider, if more shadowy, universal unity. There is more room for local option in a universal than in a national church : and the idea of universal empire was only possible before the era of national consolidation. It is the consolidation of national unity, the expansion of a local and provincial into a national patriotism, which proves fatal to both the concrete expressions of unity of the world : to the Empire and to the Papacy. England led the way in this process of nationalisation, because Nature had done most of the work by giving England frontiers which no man could change. It was easy to see the geographical limits of English nationality : it was not so easy to trace those of France or Germany, and even now they are not defined beyond cavil. England was almost a water-tight compartment, and within it the elements fused more speedily than over a wider expanse. The cosmopolitan connections of its Angevin kings introduced, it is true, alien elements, Savoyards, Poitevins, Gascons : but the reaction against their dominion in the thirteenth century developed English national consciousness, just as the English attempt to conquer France in the Hundred Years' War provoked the growth of French nationality.

This movement made the fourteenth century the first epoch of English nationalism. It has been called the 'age of the commons': that is because it is the age of the nation. Its battles are fought with a national weapon, the long bow (since become the national weapon of the Americans): its wars are financed by the national wealth of the wool-trade : its armies are formed, not of feudal knights or foreign mercenaries, but by national and voluntary enlistment : and its navy begins at Sluys the national achievements at sea which roll on in triumph to Trafalgar. Political songs show a popular interest in public affairs, and popular feeling is voiced in the poems of Chaucer and Langland, in the tracts and translations of Wycliffe. The House of Commons emerges, and asserts its control over legislation, taxation, and administration. ' What touches all must be approved of all ' is the maxim : and although its application was partial, although the House of Commons is an aristocracy, Parliament is at least more national than it had been before. The advent of the middle class has begun, and middle classes are more national than feudal barons : national consciousness has reached the heart, and fired the imagination of the burgess and the gentleman, though it may not yet have touched the stolid mind of the peasant.

England has begun to differ from other countries, and different environment and institutions will produce different habits of mind, and eventually a different national character. But the process is slow and gradual : the characteristics are not all acquired at once. The Church in England is still much the same as the Church anywhere else in Western Christendom. But there are signs of the coming break. At the Councils of Constance and Basle in the first half of the fifteenth century, the reform movement fails because the Papacy can play off national jealousies. England and Germany side against France, Spain, and Italy ; and foreshadow the religious divisions of the following century. The Papacy itself becomes impossible as lord of the Church universal, because the local and pagan spirit of Italy has laid unclean and impious hands on the Vicar of Christ, and Wycliffe had taught that dominion depended on Grace. The storm came in the sixteenth century · the national State took hold of the Church and made it national too. This, in its turn, was a fresh cause of the differentiation of national character.

Englishmen, nurtured on Cranmer's Book of Common Prayer, on Foxe's *Book of Martyrs,* and on the Geneva version of the Bible, grew very different from what they would have been, had they continued to assimilate the Vulgate, the Roman breviary, and the *Legenda Aurea.* English Puritanism came into the world, and no factor has been more potent in moulding English destinies and character.

One indirect and undesigned effect was the foundation of Greater Britain over the seas : and this again has expanded national character. Doubtless there was evil as well as good in the influence which the possession of Empire had exerted over the national mind. Nabobs and corruption invaded the British Parliament, at the same time that its sense of responsibility was broadened and deepened by the growth of obligations to other races and inferior civilisations; and South African wealth has not been an unmixed blessing in English politics. But it would never have been possible for us to call ourselves an imperial race, had we not possessed an Empire : and that Empire we did not seek with deliberate intent. Religious enthusiasm founded the American colonies; commercial enterprise brought back India in its train. The ambition to make the British Empire the greatest secular agency for good is perhaps the noblest of national characteristics : but it is the latest-born child of national history, and was not the cause of Empire. And so we come round to our original thesis : nationality and national character are the results as well as, if not rather than, the causes of history. We did not start with a national character; we developed one under the stress of circumstances. Environment bred certain acts and classes of acts; acts developed into habits and customs; and habits and custom made and moulded our national character.

III

THE ADVENT OF THE MIDDLE CLASS

A FEW months ago a head-master, who was also a classical scholar, was giving his views on the teaching of history; and he laid it down that any classical scholar could teach history if he were given a week's notice. That dictum reminds me of another opinion, which was expressed by an undergraduate : he remarked that the great thing about history was that it required no thinking. Now I think we must combine these two answers in order to understand them; and we may assume that, in the opinion of these two experts, it is because history requires no thinking that any classical scholar can teach it after a week's notice. The two answers taken together also explain a fact, which has always puzzled me when examining the Matriculation, School Leaving, and Oxford Local Examinations; and it now appears that the appalling ignorance of history displayed by candidates may be due to the circumstance that they had been taught by classical scholars getting up history at a week's notice.

Now, I have no doubt that what this head-master meant by history can be taught by a classical scholar at a week's notice; because that kind of history does require no thinking. To him history is obviously a matter of dates and facts to be learned by heart; and nothing more. But if we were to ask him why there was a Renaissance or a Reformation, why England is English and Scotland is Scottish, why the Spanish Empire decayed and the British Empire developed; if one were even to put some simpler requests, such as ' contrast the nature of the evidence upon which ancient and modern history depend '; or, ' compare the value of the chronicle and the record as sources of history,' I think we should have to wait somewhat longer than a week before we got a satisfactory answer, even from a classical scholar. I even doubt whether a week's research would enable him to state the nature of the difficulties which faced Oliver Cromwell or explain the reasons of his comparative failure and success. Real history has to deal with the problems which have baffled statesmen and thinkers throughout the ages, and the mental equipment required for the adequate discharge of that function is seldom found, and is only acquired at the cost of infinite patience and toil. To pretend that any classical scholar can acquire it in a week is simply to evince an abysmal ignorance of what history really is or really should be.

Now, there are three or four different kinds of questions which every student of history is called upon to answer, some of them elementary, some profound : there is the question when? and the question where? the question how? and the question why? The question when? is the most elementary and the least informing of all historical interrogations. That may sound strange to those who are in the habit of regarding history as mainly a matter of dates. But dates *per se* are almost useless; by themselves, they are merely mental lumber. It may be said that the knowledge of a single accurate date has a certain educational value deriving from its exactitude; and an extravagant importance is often attached to children's knowing that the battle of Hastings was fought in 1066 and the battle of Waterloo in 1815. It may be some corrective of this view, and some inducement to temper justice with mercy in dealing with infants ignorant of these details, if we remember that, as a matter of sheer chronological fact, the battle of Hastings was not fought in 1066, nor that of Waterloo in 1815. For the Christian era is at least four years out of the true reckoning, and all events dated *anno domini* are to that extent wrong. Numberless accepted dates are still more erroneous. You may remember that elaborate preparations were made in

1901 to celebrate the thousandth anniversary of the death of Alfred the Great; on the eve of the celebration a profound but mischievous scholar, without any consideration for the feelings of the organisers of this millenary demonstration, proved that Alfred really died in 899 or 900 at the latest, and that the demonstrators were two years after the fair.

The same uncertainty exists with regard to nearly all dates before the Norman Conquest, and a good many afterwards; even so late as the eleventh century the Anglo-Saxon chronicle, almost a contemporary authority, is some years out in the date it assigns to Canute's visit to Rome. So that whatever value attaches to the committing to memory of these dates must be independent of their scientific exactitude. Dates in fact are valuable not in themselves but only in so far as they enable us to determine the sequence of events, for the sequences are an indispensable factor in ascertaining the causes of history. The mere repetition of dates without reference to their use and meaning involves a repellent waste of time and temper.

The question where? is really more important than the question when?; and it is a much more searching test of a student's understanding of history to inquire where the battle of Blenheim was fought, than when it was fought. Yet I am afraid that for every ten, who could answer the second question, scarce one could be found to answer the first. And among the reforms to be effected in the methods of teaching history none is more urgent than a proper appreciation of historical geography, and a proper use of historical wall-maps.

The next question is that of how?, and this is the subject of nearly all our histories. Few students have yet set themselves systematically to answer the most difficult and most profound of all historical questions, the question why? We take the things for granted, and are content with the outward manifestation, without troubling ourselves about the soul of things which causes those manifestations. Columbus, we know, discovered America in 1492; we accept that as a sufficient statement and proceed to treat it as the origin of New World history, and as one of the principal factors which differentiate the modern from the medieval world. But why did Columbus discover America? why was America discovered towards the end of the fifteenth, and not at the end of the fourteenth or sixteenth centuries? Why does modern, as distinct from medieval, history begin where it does, and not at any other time? This is the sort of problem we should try to solve; compared with it, questions of when, where, and how are almost trivial. History can, perhaps, be little more than a story for children, but there is a time when sober students should put away childish things, or at least cease to regard them as a final object of intellectual effort.

Now, it is not possible to solve these problems completely. History is not an exact science. Nothing that is real and concrete can be exact. Mathematics are exact, but only because they deal with abstractions. Two may be equal to two in arithmetic, but they are generally unequal in real life; no two men are exactly equal to two other men. The same may be predicted about other live and real things; and there is no necessary correlation between two pence and two politicians, except the abstract numerical identity. There is always a gulf between the thing and the mathematical expression of it. By mathematics you can prove that Achilles, moving ten times faster than a tortoise, never overtakes it, if the tortoise has ten yards start; for while Achilles does ten yards, the tortoise does one; while Achilles does one, the tortoise does a tenth, and so on. And, however minutely you subdivide the distance between the two, you cannot get rid of it by mathematical means. But in real life Achilles disposes of the difficulty without much trouble. A line is said to be length without breath, and Euclid does not say that this is absurd. But it is; for a line without breadth cannot be seen, drawn, or imagined, and certainly never existed. The mathematical plane is unreal; to teach it you must leave the realm of reality. When once you have risen to this exalted level, you may be as abstract, as absolute, and as exact as you please. But the truth that deals with concrete things is always relative; absolute truth is an abstract ideal not attained in practical human affairs, and therefore not attainable in their history. History deals with an infinite number of variant facts, just as grammar does with an infinite number of variant uses; generalisations deduced from these facts, like grammatical rules deduced from these uses, are all incomplete, and partially false; there are exceptions to every rule.

With this reminder of the tentative and halting nature of all answers to the question why? of history, I want to suggest some reasons why modern history, as distinct from medieval, begins towards the end of the fifteenth century. I am obliged to insert the qualifying clause 'as distinct from medieval history,' because our terminology is very loose. Commonly modern is merely distinguished from ancient history, and includes medieval; and there is infinite variety of dates at which the commencement of modern history has been placed. Some say that modern history does not really begin until the French Revolution; some date it from Luther's Ninety-five Theses, some from Charles viii's invasion of Italy in 1494, some from Columbus's discovery of the New World. Others go back to the coronation of Charlemagne in 800, to the death of Romulus Augustulus in 476, to the battle of Actium in B.C. 31, or even to the death of Alexander the Great in B.C. 323. Others, again, insisting on the unity of history, deprecate any division into ancient and modern as artificial. But man cannot recognise in practice the unity of Time; even a lecture must have an artificial beginning, though it may seem to have no natural end. So, in history, one must start somewhere, remembering always that our starting-points are artificial; and the line—blurred and wavering though it be—between medieval and modern history is as good a starting-point as any.

Lord Acton makes a bolder assertion : to him this line is clear. ' The modern age,' he writes, ' did not proceed from the medieval by normal succession, with outward tokens of legitimate descent. Unheralded, it founded a new order of things, under a law of innovation, sapping the ancient reign of continuity."[1] With all due deference to so high an authority, I believe this to be an exaggeration. To my mind, at least, the history of the world presents itself as a series of dissolving views, rather than as a succession of separate lantern slides; new light dawns on the screen before the old fades away. Causes are none the less real because they have no fuglemen; the present is none the less rooted in the past because roots are commonly concealed; and the foundations of modern, were laid in medieval, history.

Like most natural processes, the transition was silent, gradual, and in its origin, imperceptible. Who can say precisely when the new bud begins to sap the old leaf on the tree? Two generations ago geologists, impressed by the vast and sudden inequalities which make and mar the beauty of the surface of the earth, imagined in the early history of the globe a series of terrific upheavals. Only sudden and tremendous catastrophies could account for precipitous phenomena. Their reason was too much dominated by the outward manifestation; and erroneous notions of the earth's age led them to compress within a moment the changes of an æon. A more scientific spirit ascribes these features to silent causes working slowly through a multitude of ages; and recourse has been had to the older, truer view that *natura nihil facit per saltum.*

It is just as true in history. There have been changes, sudden in their outward manifestations. The French Revolution is a more striking example of them than the transition from medieval to modern history. But even

[1]Lord Acton, *Inaugural Lecture,* 1895, p. 8.

the French Revolution was the summation of causes, which has been working for ages; even here it is true to say that *natura nihil facit per saltum*. The French Revolution was a high jump rather than a long jump; and the French people, in spite of their determination to cut themselves off the soil on which they had grown, came down from their leap not very far from where they started. The real progress of man often varies inversely with the noise it makes in the world, and with the attention it receives from historians. The outlines of modern history had been fixed before men were conscious that the medieval world was passing away; events do not move as a rule until the direction which they will take has been roughly determined. Men remain where they are until it has been suggested to them that they would be better somewhere else; and this suggestion is more important than the mere mechanical movement of men in the direction suggested.

Answers to questions why? can only therefore be found in the antecedents of the developments under consideration; and if we want to know why the Reformation took place in the sixteenth century, why America was discovered in 1492, why learning came to its new birth at the end of the fifteenth century, we must search the records of preceding generations. No period has been more undeservedly neglected. Even the *Dictionary of National Biography* contains fewer names from the fifteenth than from the fourteenth century, and thrice as many sixteenth as fifteenth century worthies are buried in its covers. The outward manifestations of the sixteenth century have attracted the popular gaze: it is time that students paid more attention to the predestinating causes of the fourteenth and early fifteenth. It is time that we ceased to regard the Renaissance, the discovery of the New World, the Reformation, and the development of nationality as the merely first links of chains suspended in mid-air, and began to regard them rather as links indissolubly bound to old chains which stretch back far into the past. They

were goals as well as starting-points; they sum up old series
as well as begin new ones; and my immediate object is to
attach some parts of modern to medieval history, and to
illustrate the greatest of all historic truths, namely, that
the present is bound up with the past.

I have already attempted to show how the idea of
nationality, growing up during the Middle Ages, helped
to differentiate modern from medieval history. That is
perhaps the weightiest factor in this revolution. We will
now take one or two others, and first ask why it was that
America was discovered towards the end of the fifteenth
century. A short answer would be the paradoxical assertion
that Columbus discovered America in 1492 or thereabouts
because the Turks are an obstructive people. The connection is not quite obvious; but obvious connections are
always superficial, and this connection is more profound.
The Germans have a proverb *Der Mensch ist was er isst*—
man is what he eats. It might be taken for a motto by
those people who believe in the economic interpretation of
history; and, while that interpretation has been pushed to
extremes, it undoubtedly contains a kernel of much
neglected truth. No age and no nation has been quite
independent of its food; even fasting anchorites required
interludes of eating to keep them going in their fasts, and
death by starvation does not appear to have been regarded
as the logical crown of holy life. In the Middle Ages each
country was more or less self-supporting so far as necessaries
were concerned; but for an ever-increasing number of
luxuries they were dependent upon foreign trade. The
great medieval trade routes passed from East to West and
West to East through the Levant. Now, so long as the
Levant was shared between the Byzantine Empire, the
Italians, and the Saracens—a cultured and tolerant race—
there was no great obstacle in the way of this trade. But
in the fourteenth and early fifteenth centuries the Turks,
a destructive race, came and 'squatted' on these trade
routes. Western Europe soon began to feel the pinch;

the arteries through which its trade flowed were choked; and, consciously or unconsciously, men began to seek new routes to the East—routes by which the interrupted communications might be restored.

This was the motive of all the geographical expansion of the fifteenth century. The discovery of a New World, the foundation of colonies, the development of sea-power were incidental results. Each nation was merely intent upon opening up a new channel through which the wealth from the Indies—that is, of course, the East Indies—might flow into its coffers. Even this commercial motive was perhaps unconscious; the new idea invariably appears in an ancient guise, and the earliest commercial voyages may have been undertaken under the impression that they were crusades. Portugal was the first to start, and from its geographical position it inevitably sought to find a route round the south of Africa. Prince Henry the Navigator— we should now call him rather a company-promoter—was the pioneer of these endeavours; and step by step the exploration of the African coast was pushed further and further south. For sixty years from 1426 this process went on. It was no single event, and during this period the commercial motive cast off the crusading shell. But Africa was bigger than men thought; it extended hundreds of miles further south than Prince Henry imagined; and before Diaz doubled the Cape of Good Hope in 1486, it had probably occurred to others that there might be a shorter route to the Indies. This was the idea of Christopher Columbus; he sailed due west, discovered the West Indies, and to the day of his death was unconscious of the magnitude of his achievement. He thought that, instead of discovering a New World, he had merely turned the flank of the Turk and found a fresh route to the East of the Old World.

Other nations followed in the wake of the Portuguese, and the fruits of Columbus's discoveries fell to the Spaniards, under the auspices of whose monarchs his voyages had been made. But, while Spain developed an empire in the West, Albuquerque founded one for Portugal in the East. England and France were later and less fortunate in their early adventures. Their eyes turned north rather than south, and many English lives were lost in the Arctic Ocean. Englishmen went forth, not to find the North Pole, but first a North-east and then a North-west passage to the Indies; and though this quest was hopeless, yet British dominion in Canada was an indirect result of their enterprise. That was still in the womb of the distant future, but other effects of these discoveries were no less great and more immediate. The world was suddenly expanded and its centre shifted. Hitherto the world had been little more than the countries round the Mediterranean Jewish religion, Greek culure, Roman Empire, had represented the sum of human achievement, and they all came from the borders of an inland sea. Great Britain was the Ultima Thule, hovering on the rim of outer darkness; and its people were still accounted barbarians by the polished people of Italy. Rome was the hub of the universe, Venice and Genoa the emporiums of its trade, and the seats of its naval power, and Florence the home of its art and letters. All men's eyes looked towards Italy; but now there came an aversion of gaze, and men's looks were turned outwards. The Mediterranean was deposed from its proud position. Trade and politics became oceanic and not pelagic; the ports on the shores of the Atlantic were no longer outposts on the bounds of a waste, estranging sea, but outlets towards a vast New World. The centre was shifted to the rim; in time Liverpool and Hamburg will take the place of Venice and Genoa.

'Medieval Empire and Papacy shivered at the blow; the inheritors of the new world, Spain, Portugal, France, England, had no dependence on the Empire, and the New World could not be forced into the strait-waistcoat of the old. They still, it is true, depended on the Papacy; Columbus had not called into existence a New World to redress the religious balance of the Old. The discovery of America was not a Protestant enterprise any more than the Bible is a Nonconformist publication; and for more than a century after Columbus's achievement the New World was a Roman Catholic preserve, with a few Protestant wasps buzzing around it. Great changes take long to sink into men's minds, and few realised the importance of these discoveries until generations after they had been made. But the expansion of the world slowly produced an expansion of men's minds; and the ecclesiastical and theological system, adapted to men who believed that the sun went round the earth, and that stars twinkled solely for the benefit of amusement of the dwellers in Western Europe, began to rend, when stretched to cover the science of the sixteenth century; just as some day perhaps current beliefs will be modified by the realisation that the earth is not the centre of the universe, and that probably there are billions of planets more important than that on which we live.

The geographical discoveries of Columbus, Vasco da Gama, Magellan, the Cabots, and the rest, were only the most startling development of those economic changes, which during the fourteenth and fifteenth centuries transformed the medieval into the modern world. They were external and obvious events; there were others less obvious but no less important. These may almost all be summed up in one phrase—the advent of the middle classes. Nearly every movement of this period is a symptom of this middle-class development. The Renaissance represents its intellectual aspect; art, science, and letters had hitherto been ecclesiastical; the Renaissance is a secular, and sometimes even pagan revolt against this sacerdotal monopoly. The Reformation is its religious counterpart, the rebellion of the middle-class laity against the domination by the Church over the relations between God and man. Socially, we see rich burghers competing with feudal lords for rank and title. Michael de la Pole, Earl of Suffolk, in Richard II's reign, is the first English-

man who owed his peerage to wealth derived from trade;
knighthoods are won in the counting-house as well as on
the field of battle; the feudal bars of iron are broken down,
and golden keys begin to unlock the doors of office and
influence. The great ministers of Tudor times, the Crom-
wells, the Cecils, the Walsinghams, all spring from the new
middle, and not the old feudal, classes; and Queen Elizabeth herself was great-grand-daughter of a London merchant. Politically, this expansion shows itself in the
development of the House of Commons at the expense of
the House of Lords and of the monarchy; and, but for
this middle-class aggression, Charles i would never have
laid his head on the block, nor James ii have fled beyond
the sea. Economically, the whole geographical movement,
the search for new trade routes, the foundation of great
companies, the Merchant Adventurers, the East India
Company, the Levant Company are all expressions of the
growth of a commercial middle class.

This in itself meant a revolution destructive of the
Middle Ages. We sometimes call those the feudal ages,
without perhaps any very definite idea of what feudalism
was. But two things are clear enough about feudalism,
Firstly, it was a rural organisation, a system—if anything
so vague can be called a system—based upon man's relation
to the land, and regulated by the conditions of agricultural
life. There were of course towns and cities in the Middle
Ages, but they were always exceptions to the feudal system.
The mass of the population lived in the country, not in the
towns. Secondly, feudalism contemplated, roughly, only
two classes, the lords and their villeins. Now, the industrial
and commercial system of modern history requires two
factors which feudalism did not provide; it requires a
middle class and it requires an urban population. Without
these two there would have been little to distinguish
modern from medieval history. Without commerce and
industry there can be no middle class; where you had no
middle class, you had no Renaissance and no Reformation.

We find two examples in Poland and Spain. Poland was a country whose feudal existence was, unfortunately for it, prolonged into modern history. There were only two classes, the peasants and the nobles; such commerce as there was, was carried on by aliens, Germans and Jews; they inhabited the cities which were never worked into the Polish national system. Hence it was only in the cities that the Reformation made itself felt; there was no Renaissance, and Poland remained the most Catholic country in Europe with the possible exception of Spain. And in Spain the explanation is much the same; fortune had done much for Spain, and its acquisition of the New World might have made it the greatest commercial nation in history. But its long warfare with the Moors had stereotyped the military, crusading, and exclusive character of its feudal class; the nobles declined to adapt themselves to the commercial conditions of the age; Spanish industry and commerce were discouraged by foolish pride and crushed by insane taxation. The middle classes were denied their proper outlets for political, social, and economic expansion; Spain was pauperised rather than enriched by the wealth of the Indies; Renaissance and Reformation found no soil in which to take permanent root, and Spain in the sixteenth century plunged back into the theology of the Middle Ages.

England, on the other hand, has been for centuries peculiarly the land of the middle classes; they give the tone to everything English, good or bad, and English history has been made by its middle class to a greater extent than the history of any other European country. This peculiar strength of the English middle class is a complex factor in our history, nor can it readily be explained. We can perceive conditions even in the Middle Ages tending to foster a strong middle class; but one always has the uncomfortable suspicion that these conditions are as much the effect, as the cause, of the strength of the middle class. One of these circumstances is the absence of impassable barriers between class and class in England. Here there is not, and never has been, a nobility of blood, whatever that particularly idiotic phrase may mean. The younger son of a peer is a commoner, though grandsons of peers often take their place in the upper middle classes; and thousands of members of the middle class in England number peers among their ancestors. The middle class is always being recruited from the nobility, just as the nobility is always being recruited from the middle class. But in Germany, for instance, there was a great gulf between the two; all the sons of a prince were princes, all the sons of a knight were knights, and so on through all the aristocratic ranks. Younger sons of nobles never took to trade; that would be dishonourable, and they took to robbery instead; for there was no disgrace in plundering traders and seizing by force wealth, which it was dishonourable to acquire by legitimate methods. Hence, while in England during the fourteenth and fifteenth centuries the nobles were adapting themselves to commercial and maritime enterprise, in Germany they wrapt themselves up in their noble exclusiveness and turbulence, grew prouder and poorer than ever, and consoled themselves for their poverty by attaching an inordinate value to their birth, and to the customs of their class. Even in the nineteenth century a German minister of state could not bring his wife to court, unless she were of noble blood, and the persistence of duelling is simply another symptom of the same class-pride and prejudice. I took up a novel the other day by a well-known writer and noticed a comparison between the English and German attitude towards duelling; these things, it was remarked, ' do not depend upon civilisation, since modern Germany is probably more civilised than modern England. They depend upon national character.[1] National character we know, is a convenient *deus ex machina*; but duelling is

1F. Marion Crawford, *Greiffenstein.*

a class, and not a national, characteristic. Its prevalence in Germany is due partly to the rigidity and exclusiveness of the aristocratic sentiment which has not been pervaded and civilised by middle-class opinion, and partly to the fact that no strong central monarchy, based on the middle class, arose in Germany to deal with feudal turbulence, for duelling is simply the last surviving form of the private warfare of the Middle Ages. The middle class in Germany received no reinforcements from the upper; the landed gentry remained isolated from the city magnates, and class divisions deferred for centuries the realisation of German unity, and its start in the national race for Empire.

This absence of social castes likewise fostered the growth of self-government in England. The strength of the English House of Commons and the weakness of the third estate in the medieval constitutions of Europe both arise from a similar contrast. The strength of the House of Commons depended on the union in it of the landed gentry, the knights of the shires, and the borough and city members. Now, the knights of the shires were the *barones minores,* the lesser tenants-in-chief; there was no distinction in class or kind between them and the *barones majores,* who formed the House of Lords; and on the continent the *barones minores* clung to their class and formed the noble estate. In England they threw in their lot with the burghers of the House of Commons, and the middle class was reinforced by the landed gentry. To this combination is due the predominance of the House of Commons, and the victory of Parliament over the Crown. Everywhere else the monarchy played upon the jealousy between the three estates, and made itself absolute through their divisions. The depth of those divisions, and the inability of one class in France to co-operate with another, made the Bourbon despotism possible and excusable, though its failure to remove them involved it ultimately in fearful destruction. In England alone the middle classes were not hemmed in by impassable barriers; in England alone was their development a peaceful transformation, and the comparative facility with which these transformations are made has been the making of England. Her constitution is organic, not cut and dried; it grew and was not manufactured; it is not tied up by knots and definitions; it is not obliged to burst because it wants to expand. Of course it is illogical, vague, flexible; but that very adaptability, which has enabled despotism and democracy to employ the same constitutional forms, has rendered violent revolutions as a rule unnecessary. And, if England is destined to turn into a social democracy, the transformation will be accomplished by the same gradual, legitimate, and peaceful methods as those by which feudal England was converted into a commercial middle-class community.

The flexibility of English social and constitutional arrangements was, then, the great condition facilitating the growth of the middle classes; but it did not cause that growth. Its origin was in the revival of trade which followed upon the settling down of Europe after the barbarian migrations. Old trade routes were restored, new ones discovered, and along them grew up great cities like those along the Rhine. Commercial development was followed by constitutional growth; these urban communities demanded a voice in their own affairs; and then, in the eleventh and twelfth centuries, you have the movement for the establishment of communes, in which the management of municipal affairs prepared the middle classes for participation in the wider business of the nation. England lay on the outskirts of this development, and it was not until the end of the twelfth century that the citizens of London purchased from Richard 1 a municipal constitution closely allied to that of Rouen; and other English cities were fifty years behind the capital. The basis of English commercial prosperity in the Middle Ages was the wool, grown largely by the Cistercians and other monastic orders, but handled by lay merchants. At first these merchants were largely foreigners; but with the nationalist movement of the thirteenth century English merchants began to oust the alien, and the expulsion of the Jews by Edward i threw financial business into English hands. Then trade was developed by Edward iii's conquests abroad; naval victories secured English shipping; and the wine trade with Bordeaux became, next to wool, the most flourishing branch of English commerce.

This expansion helped to break up the rigid manorial system, which was already decaying through other causes. Money payments were substituted for personal services, and the villeins slowly won emancipation. Labour became mobile; instead of being fixed to the soil, it sought markets wherever they could be found, and provided employers with the hands without which the great development of capitalism in the fifteenth century could never have taken place. Financial speculation came into vogue; as early as Edward iii's reign we read of a dealer who spread a false rumour of war in order to send down the price of wool.[1] He was banished; but the trick soon became too familiar to involve such drastic treatment. We hear ceaseless complaints of forestalling, regrating, engrossing; our respectable grocers, by the by, are decended from the ' engrossers,' against whom Parliament from the fourteenth to the sixteenth century was never tired of fulminating. Men began to speculate in land and houses, to buy up whole streets and lease out the houses on profitable terms, to accumulate farms and to substitute cultivation on a large scale for the piecemeal agriculture prevalent before; and all these processes were illustrations of the application of commercial methods to the stagnant economics of the Middle Ages. Manufacturers, too, grew up; cloth factories, tanneries, breweries, iron mills, and a host of others. In Elizabeth's reign, for instance, we come across the very modern lament that England supplied the whole world with ordnance, and would smart for it when this ordnance was turned against herself; just as

[1]D'Ewes, *Journals*, p. 166.

to-day some would prohibit us from building ships for foreign navies. So, in one way or another, before the end of the fifteenth century a new middle class, a new social force, had been created, and this force is one of the greatest factors in the making of modern history.

Now commerce and industry quicken the intellect more than agriculture; purely agricultural counties are to-day proverbially sleepy, and a little intellect went a long way in the rural England of the Middle Ages. Nobles themselves could seldom read or write, and even a king was called ' Beauclerk ' because he possessed these two accomplishments. The man who could write was a clerk, a cleric, that is to say an ecclesiastic. The Church monopolised all culture, and hence all art and science were ecclesiastical. But the new middle-class laity, with their sharpened wits, felt a sort of intellectual hunger, and this hunger produced the Renaissance. The Renaissance, has of course, like every other phenomenon, been attributed to one sudden dramatic event, the capture of Constantinople by the Turks; and equally, of course, this attribution is grossly misleading and incorrect. The revival of letters was in full swing before 1453; one of the greatest triumphs of pure scholarship, the exposure of the forged Donation of Constantine, had been achieved by Lorenzo Valla in 1440; Greek was being taught at Florence as early as 1397. In art the revival had begun even earlier; Brunelleschi's Duomo at Florence dates from 1410, and the greatest school of Flemish painters, headed by the Van Eycks, flourished in the fourteenth century. Nearly a dozen universities were founded in Europe between the middle of the fourteenth and the middle of the fifteenth centuries; and numbers of schools sprang up during the same period. In our own land, Eton was founded in 1440 and Winchester College some fifty years earlier. Scholars no doubt fled from Constantinople, and perhaps brought precious manuscripts with them; but they bulk too large in our text-books : at the most they only gave impetus to a movement which had begun before their flight from the Turk. That is one of the important facts to remember about the Renaissance; another is that it represented a lay and a middle-class demand for culture, and not a revival of the ecclesiastical spirit.

The same two statements are likewise true of the Reformation itself. We date it from the publication of Luther's Ninety-five Theses in 1517. But eras cannot be dated by years with any real accuracy; and to say that the Reformation began in 1517 is as misleading as to say that the Renaissance began in 1453. No one can tell exactly when either began; but we can say that the beginnings of both were long before the dramatic events by which we date them. 'With Boniface VIII,' says Bishop Creighton, 'there fell the Mediæval Papacy.' Now Boniface VIII died in 1304, and in 1311 the Council of Vienne put forward the first demand for a general reformation of the Medieval Church. For a century and a half men were making that demand, and expecting it to be satisfied by the convocation of an ecumenical council. The conciliar movement, as it is called, came to a head in the councils of Constance and Basle; but it failed because Europe had become nationalised; the ecumenical machinery of the world had grown rusty, national machinery was taking its place : and time was to prove that only the nations could really reform the Church. Unscrupulous Popes profited by national divisions to balk these ecumenical councils, and every appeal from the Pope to a Council was prohibited. The Pope thought to make legal reform impossible, just as James II did when he threw the Great Seal into the Thames; and the only result was to make revolution inevitable.

That is only one factor in the genesis of the Reformation, which was more than a change in church government. It was the revolt of a laity, growing in intelligence against ecclesiastical tutelage—a tutelage only tolerable, then and now, when the clergy are superior in intellect and knowledge and in character to those over whom they claim to exercise sway. These things were no longer an ecclesiastical monopoly; and conscience and wealth, intellect and pride combined in a strange jumble of motives to repudiate a control which had become galling because its *raison d'être* had ceased to exist. The symbolism which had satisfied rustic minds, because rustic minds can only grasp a symbol, failed to satisfy the keener quest for truth behind the ritual. Men sought out original sources in religion as well as in scholarship, and grew impatient of medieval glosses. Scholastic theology was attacked by pioneers of reform a century before Luther's day. 'If I had read his books before,' wrote Luther of one of them, 'my enemies might have thought that I had borrowed everything from him, so great is the agreement between our spirits.' Popular preachers denounced the vices of the age; numerous translations of the Scriptures into vernacular tongues were made, in spite of the official disapprobation of the Church; and there was a remarkable development of family worship. The revival of religion was non-ecclesiastical; and it was one of the causes, and not one of the results, of the Reformation.

And so, whatever factor we take in the making of that change from medieval to modern history, whether the growth of the middle class, geographical exploration, economic development, the revival of letters, or of religion, we find that the same thing is true about all. They have their roots stretching far back into the past, and buried far out of sight. The growth and decay are silent, gradual, almost imperceptible. The dramatic events which catch the eye and the ear, and by which we date the progress or backsliding of mankind, are, like the catastrophes which convulse the sphere of nature, but the outward and visible manifestations of causes, working without rest, without haste, without conscious human direction in the making of the history of the world.

IV

THE NEW MONARCHY

In my first lecture I drew your attention to the fact that, whereas ancient history deals mainly with the City-state and medieval history with the World-state, modern history is concerned principally with the national State; and to-day my object is to illustrate the development of the national State, particularly as represented by what we call the New Monarchy. For that is one of the prime factors in the history of the sixteenth century. The abstract idea of the State has been expressed in various forms; it has been cast in one mould after another, and so far it has found its most complete and effective expression in the national State. The feeling which bound the Athenian to the City of the Violet Crown, and the Roman to the City of the Seven Hills, now links men to their country, the national State; and patriotism has expanded from a municipal into a national force. How far that patriotism is capable of further expansion into an imperial sentiment, and how far that sentiment is capable of crystallisation in an imperial state is a problem of which none of us will see the final solution. But, into whatever form the idea has been born anew, it has had to develop over again from the beginning, and we must glance for a few minutes at the growth of the national state until it reaches its adult stage in the sixteenth century.

For the state in its infancy may be likened unto a little child. It has no ideas of its own and its earliest utterances are merely the repetition of what it has heard. Its voice is expressed in legislation, and some of you may have studied these early expressions in a book called Stubbs's

Select Charters. That volume has a reputation for dullness, obscurity, and general incomprehensibility; and I am afraid I shall not be believed when I say that, properly treated, it may be made intelligible, interesting, and even at times amusing. Well, in those pages you will find the first attempts of the national state to express its ideas in writing; and it must be admitted that the construction is somewhat crude, the language bald, and the grammar occasionally at fault—as you would expect from a child. The ideas, too, are not new; the laws are not legislation in our sense of the word; they simply repeat what has hitherto been the custom; they are the committing to writing of those things which men had practised as a matter of unconscious habit. Now the child is generally given a governess; so is the State, and its governess is the Church. And the first thing the governess says is ' you must be good.' Those precise words do not occur in Stubbs's *Charters,* but the meaning is conveyed in somewhat more formal terms when a legatine council at York lays it down[1] that the right and proper thing for a newly crowned and consecrated king is to see that peace is kept in Church and State, to prohibit wrong and violence, and to ordain justice and mercy in all his judgments. This is the function of the Church in the Dark and Middle Ages, to educate these growing states in the proper notions of right and wrong, to uphold a standard higher than that of force and fraud, and to set the moral above and before the material order of things. No higher or more necessary duty has been fulfilled by any institution; although one may sometimes think that the anathemas, interdicts, and excommunications employed by the Church to terrorise medieval sovereigns were somewhat like the bogies used to frighten little children. The Church, too, taught the State to write; clerk and cleric are one and the same word; the

1 Rectitudo regis noviter ordinati et in solium sublimati est haec tria praecepta populo Christiano sibi subdito praecipere, etc.— Stubbs' *Select Charters,* p. 62.

writer was a churchman, and churchmen did all the writing in the early Middle Ages. They introduced written laws into England and written wills. They wrote all the history in those times, and perhaps they coloured it too. And they derived a more material advantage from the writing of wills; for it commonly happened that wills written, proved, and administered by clerical· hands contained munificent bequests to ecclesiastical foundations.

As time went on, however, the State began to develop ideas of its own; legislation begins to be something more than the statement of ancient. custom. It begins to enunciate new principles, and the State to enforce them. The State in fact has developed a will of its own, and then the differences with the governess begin. The first real act of legislation dates in England from the reign of Henry II, and so does the first great quarrel with the Church; you find one in the Assize, and the other in the Constitutions of Clarendon. The result of this battle royal is still disputed: whether the victory really lay with the State or the Church, the child was not yet old enough to do without the governess; and it remained in somewhat sulky tutelage, with occasional rebellions, until the sixteenth century. Its sovereignty was denied, and it spent its time, not so much in governing, as in struggling for existence. But by the sixteenth century the child had grown to lusty youth, if not to manhood. The governess was dismissed with what she thought a very inadequate pension; and we hear much of the great spoliation made by Henry VIII The State now boldly claimed omnipotence; and the claim is most forcibly and logically expressed in the *Leviathan* of Thomas Hobbes—the best philosophical comment extant on the Tudor system, although it was written in Stuart times. Sovereignty, he explained, must be absolute, though the sovereign need not be a monarch; it may be a popular assembly, and to-day it is Parliament. It does not merely state law; it does not merely apply law; but it creates law. Instead of being merely a custom or a revelation of God or of nature, law has become a command of the State. Bentham adopted this view when he spoke about the ' omnicompetence ' of the State; and the position is not now seriously challenged. It may be unwise or unjust for the State to do various things; but if it does those things by proper constitutional methods, their legal authority cannot be denied, though their moral validity may be impugned. Within the limits of human possibility, the State has become omnipotent; its growth is complete; from a creation it has become a creator.

This complex and abstract conception of the State has only been evolved by a slow and painful process. The Teutonic invaders of Great Britain had scarcely any notion of the State; their state was simply their kindred, their blood relations. They knew of no such thing as treason; all crimes were merely offences against the kindred, and might be redeemed by money payments to the family. This family system broke down under the stress of war and migration, which produced a specialised military class; and the chief of this class became the king. The Church baptized what war had begotten; and the king became gradually the anointed of God, the fountain of honour and justice, and lord first of the people, and then of their land. He symbolised the unity of his people, and his authority grew in degree as it expanded in area. At first he is merely a tribal chieftain; next he is King of the Mercians, the Northumbrians, or the West Saxons! and finally King of the English. But the English are still divided; there are many dialects, myriad local customs, and diverse methods of thought. The Saxon is not as the Northumbrian; and the antagonism between North and South, which gave William the conquest of England, is hardly extinct until the sixteenth century; the last forcible expression of it is the rebellion of the Earls in 1569, which is as much the last kick of an expiring feudalism as it is a protest against Protestantism. The king is for long the only national representative, and round him centre such national aspirations as emerge from the conflict of local passions. National unity is only personal; the king is the State; treason is an offence against him; and it required a very arbitrary straining of the law to bring it to bear against Strafford with the idea that treason was really an offence against the State, of which the king was only an ornamental expression.

Feudalism, however, was an uncongenial soil for absolute monarchy. The king was the theoretical apex of civilisation, the head of everything; but practice robbed him of most of his powers, and divided them among his barons. The king was *primus inter pares,* little more; and all the talk about divine right, absolute power, and passive obedience is modern and not medieval. Indeed the growth of these things is one of the factors of modern history, and one of the chief features of the age with which we are dealing. As is always the case, the growth is one of events and ideas; it is both material and moral, and it is impossible to disentangle the action and reaction of these two elements upon one another. One school of historians, or rather philosophers, fondly imagines that history is simply the working out of ideas, that political philosophy has moulded events, that force has never conquered truth, that right is might. According to this school the New Monarchy is the material result of the new ideas about kingship which spread in the fifteenth and sixteenth centuries. Another school holds that political philosophy is simply a series of deductions from past experience, of comments on facts already decided, that events have moulded ideas more than ideas have moulded events, that force is the ultimate sanction, that persecution has succeeded whenever it has been steadily and skilfully applied, that might is right. According to this school, the new ideas about kingship were simply the reflection in men's minds of the material achievements of the New Monarchy. Amid the conflict of these two schools one thing is clear, and that is that generalisations are always to some extent untrue. No one really acquainted with history can maintain that persecution has never succeeded; logically, too, it is obvious that if right is always might, then might is often right. If truth has always prevailed, then what has prevailed is often truth; and we set the fatuous generalisation ' whatever is, is true' beside Alexander Pope's still more childish assertion that ' whatever is, is right.'

The correct sequence seems to be that material necessities predisposed men's minds towards a modification of the existing system; this was perceived by the rulers and statesmen of that time, who applied the practical remedy; and then followed the theoretical justification of the accomplished fact. Machiavelli did not invent his *Prince*, he merely painted him from life. Hobbes did not imagine the *Leviathan*; he merely reduced to a dogma the practice of Tudor sovereigns; and, as so often happens, the conditions, which had produced and justified that practice, had already passed away before the philosopher evolved out of it an abstract theoretical system for universal and permanent application. However that may be, the old order of the fifteenth century was in a state of liquidation, and the problem was how to keep society afloat. Every great medieval institution had gone or was going under. The empire had dissolved into nations, the prestige of the Papacy had been dimmed by its Babylonish captivity at Avignon and then by the great schism. Unity gave way to diversity of tongues, of churches, and of states; and the medieval cosmopolitan became the modern nationalist, patriot, separatist. Feudal chivalry and feudal castles had fallen before gunpowder and artillery, the growth of industry and commerce had undermined a social system based on the tenure of land; and the middle classes had sapped the power of the barons. The manorial system had broken down through the substitution of rent for services and the emancipation of the serfs. The revival of learning, the invention of the printing press, the expansion of the world by geographical discovery had removed the

ancient landmarks and delivered the minds of men. There
was a universal welter, a menace of general anarchy. In
France the strife of Burgundian and Armagnac threatened
political disintegration and the destruction of social order.
The Wars of the Roses brought upon England a similar
tale of disasters. Everywhere there was need of a saviour
of society ; everywhere this saviour was found in the king.
' Le nouveau Messie,' says Michelet, ' est le roi.'

National monarchy alone seemed to profit by the decay
of other established institutions ; it survived the Middle
Ages and gained by their disappearance, because it was
the embodiment of the coming force of nationality. Kings
had already reduced the emperor, their nominal lord, to a
shadow ; they now made havoc with the power of their
nominal subordinates, the feudal magnates ; and the
struggle between the disruptive forces of feudalism and
the central authority ended at last in monarchical triumph.
Internal unity prepared the way for external expansion.
France was first in the field. The misery and humiliation
of the Hundred Years' War produced a nationalist reaction,
an outburst of a new French patriotism of which Jeanne
D'Arc is the inspirer and patron saint. The feud between
Burgundian and Armagnac was healed ; by the ordinances
of Orleans (1439) the foundations were laid of a national
army and a national system of finance. The cunning of
Louis XI consolidated the crusade of Jeanne D'Arc. The
remnants of feudal independence were crushed, and France
began to expand at the cost of weaker states. Parts of
Burgundy, Provence, Anjou, and Brittany were incorporated in the French monarchy ; and the exuberant
strength of the new-formed nation burst the barriers of the
Alps, and overflowed into the plains of Italy. Other States
followed the example of France ; Ferdinand of Aragon
married Isabella of Castile, drove out the Moors from
Andalusia, and founded the modern kingdom of Spain.
Marriage had been his method ; but in the arts of successful
matrimony none could compete with the Hapsburgs. *Bella*

gerant alii: tu, felix Austria, nube. Maximilian married
the heiress of Charles the Bold, and united the Netherlands
with Austria; his son, the Archduke Philip, married the
heiress of Ferdinand of Aragon and of Isabella of Castile;
and their two sons were the Emperors Charles v and
Ferdinand I. The former made the Spanish Empire; the
latter founded the Austro-Hungarian monarchy by wedding
the daughter of the King of Hungary and Bohemia. This
union, however, was purely dynastic, not national; and it
was the doom of Austria to be made by the marriage of
princes and marred by the discord of peoples.

The political system of Europe was thus roughly sketched
out, though the boundaries of the rival kingdoms were still
undetermined, and there remained minor principalities and
powers, chiefly in Italy and Germany, which offered an
easy prey to their ambitious neighbours. For both Germany
and Italy had sacrificed national unity to the shadow of
universal sovereignty, Germany in the temporal and Italy
in the spiritual sphere. The German king was also Holy
Roman Emperor, bound by his office to the hopeless task
of enforcing his authority in Italy, and Italy was the tomb
of German national unity. Its own unity was prohibited
by Papal ambition, for the Pope could not tolerate a
secular rival in the Italian Peninsula; and, from the days
of the Goth and the Lombard in the sixth and eighth
centuries to those of Victor Emmanuel in the nineteenth,
every aspirant for the national sovereignty of Italy has
had to meet the bitter enmity of the Papacy. And so both
Italy and Germany were ruled out of the national race,
and had to wait three hundred years for that national
consolidation which their rivals achieved in the sixteenth
century.

This process of unification was not merely material and
geographical. When one country is united with another
it means not only a union of territory but an attempted
harmony of different aspirations, interests, and politics.
Look at the map of Spain, for instance. 'The geography

of Spain,' says a recent writer on ancient history,[1] 'has always been the key to the history and even to the character of the inhabitants. Its peninsular form, and its singularly definite frontier on the one side on which it is not surrounded by the sea, give the country a superficial appearance of unity. In reality it is broken up into separate sections by a succession of transverse mountain ranges which are cut by no great river running from north to south. The dip of the country is from east to west, and accordingly the chief rivers rise near the Mediterranean and flow into the Atlantic. " Nature," it has been said by one who knew Spain well, " by thus dislocating the country, seems to have suggested localism and isolation to the inhabitants, who each in their valleys and districts are walled off from their neighbours." So is explained that powerlessness for combination on a great scale which Strabo absurdly ascribes to the moroseness of the Iberians, whereas that distrustful temper was itself a mere result of the geographical conditions. " They are bold in little adventures," says Strabo, " but never undertake anything of magnitude, inasmuch as they have never formed any extended power or confederacy. On this account the Romans, having carried war into Iberia, lost much time by reason of the number of different sovereignties, having to conquer first one then another; in fact it occupied nearly two centuries or even longer before they had subdued the whole." So, too, when the Saracens conquered Spain they soon split up into half a dozen little Moslem states, and it took the Spaniards four centuries to subdue them, the Spaniards themselves being divided up into nearly half a dozen kingdoms. Nor has this separation entirely disappeared; Spaniards fought on different sides in the War of the Spanish Succession. "It is always dangerous," says a modern description,[2] "to enter into conversation with a stranger in Spain, for there is practically no subject upon

1 W. T. Arnold, Studies of Roman Imperialism, 1906.
2 H. Seton Merriman, The Velvet Glove.

which the various nationalities are unable to quarrel. A
Frenchman is a Frenchman all the world over, and politics
may be avoided by a graceful reference to the ___ for
which Republican and Legitimist are alike pre___
But a Spaniard may be an Aragonese or a ___
Andalusian or a Guipuzcoan, and patrioti___
purely local growth and colour."

Each of the kingdoms, united in ___
form Spain, had its own indivi___
by its peculiar geographica___
instance, is cut off from th___
mountain systems, and r___
than the sea. It was e___
than to unite Germany v___
Louis xiv boasted that the ___
he placed his grandson on th___
Pyrenees exist, and France and ___
Aragon looks towards the sea, t___
aspirations lie in that direction; and___
commerce made its maritime province, C___
progressive and the most prosperous part o___
alone did a middle class and a trading popu___
and even to-day Barcelona is the headquarters ___
tionary sentiment in Spain. Instead of expanding
the mountains, it had first expanded across the sea,
had successfully laid claim to Sicily and Naples. Thes
Mediterranean claims and ambitions, involving conflicts
with France, with the Turks, and in Italy, were the
contribution of Aragon to the future projects and per-
plexities of Spain. The dower of Castile comprised claims
on Portugal and hopes of Andalusia, an oceanic sea-board
with its loopholes to the New World in Vigo, La Coruña
and Ferrol, and a northern outlook through Bilbao and
Santander, whence Spanish trade and Spanish ships sailed
the Bay of Biscay and the English Channel. Castile
contributed to the United Kingdom its medieval pride and
priesthood, its crusading zeal against the Moors and

Indians, and the spoils of Mexico and Peru. The acquisition of Andalusia brought into the joint-stock Cadiz and Gibraltar, the command of the entrance to the Mediterranean, and African ambitions which led Charles v to waste his strength in efforts to conquer Tunis and Algiers. Union was not altogether strength; for with strength it brought distraction between conflicting ambitions and heterogeneous policies. Spain could never make up its mind on which horse to place its money, the Mediterranean, Africa, Europe, or the New World. Charles v rang the changes; now here, now there, hesitating which enterprise to take first, he could never completely succeed because he could never entirely concentrate.

France was more successful because its unity was more real. Unity in fact has been its passion under all its forms of government, and mountain chains have not secluded its people in close compartments. But its origin was as composite and its elements as varied as those of Spain. Aquitaine, which had not been peopled by the Franks, did not become really French until the seventeenth century; and the root, which Huguenotism struck in it, may have owed some of its tenacity to racial bias and the traditions of provincial independence. At any rate, before the rise of Calvinism, the south-west of France was resenting the *Gabelle* and regretting its lost connection with the English Crown. But for the most part union brought real strength to France; and the conflict between the policies, which her various acquisitions brought, was not really ruinous until the eighteenth century, when, during the Seven Years' War, she sacrificed her colonial future in pursuit of European glory. These colonial prospects were the fruit of her union with Normandy and Brittany in the fifteenth century. The Normans, wrote an English ambassador from Paris in the reign of Elizabeth, will be rovers and pirates as long as they live. They were rovers after the style of Frobisher, Hawkins, and Drake; and they brought back to France her dominion in Canada and the West Indies.

The Newfoundland fisheries, developed by Norman and Breton seamen, were the nursery of the French marine, and they were one of the points for which Louis xiv fought hardest in the negotiations for the Treaty of Utrecht. The acquisition of Normandy, Brittany and Aquitaine gave France nearly the whole of her sea-board on the Channel and the Atlantic, and made her the naval and colonial rival of England. But for these unconscious builders of empire in the fifteenth century, there would have been no French in Canada or in India; and the history of English expansion in the Eastern and Western hemispheres would have been widely different.

As Normandy, Brittany, and Aquitaine gave France her Atlantic position, so the acquisition of Provence brought her into the Mediterranean. But for that she would not be in Corsica, Algiers, and Tunis to-day; there would have been no battle of the Nile, no Crimean War, no dual control in Egypt, no Fashado incident. The Corsican ogre would not have been a Frenchman, and no one can fathom the difference which that fact alone would have made in nineteenth century history. The partition of Burgundy by Louis xi. was also a seed-plot of future strife between Valois and Hapsburg, though all the defeats of Francis i did not compel restitution. Lastly, it was the union of Anjou and Orleans with the French Crown which occasioned the French invasion of Italy, and perennial strife therein between French, Spaniards and Austrians. For, just as Aragon brought to the Spanish monarchy its claims on Naples and Sicily, so Anjou brought the competing Angevin claim to France; and the medieval rivalry between the houses of Anjou and Aragon was merged in a more comprehensive rivalry between France and Spain. So, too, when Louis of Orleans became Louis xii. of France, he endowed the French Crown with the Visconti claim to Milan, and no apple of discord produced more strife than that fertile but ill-fated duchy.

All this expansion pointed to closer contact, friendly or

hostile; isolated squatters on a limitless plain or veldt have little communication; but, as soon as they have pegged out claims right up to their neighbours', they see one another more often and watch one another more closely. It was so with these national States. Hitherto diplomatic relations had been rare and spasmodic; ambassadors were only despatched on special occasions; now they became regular and resident. The necessity of watching one another's designs begat the modern diplomatic system; mutual adjustment of each other's disputes produced international law—an incomprehensible idea when all States were theoretically subject to one imperial suzerain;[1] and mutual jealousy of each other's growth gave rise to the theory of the balance of power.

The external development of the area, over which the national monarch ruled, reacted upon the degree of authority which he exercised within his dominions. Every extension of his sway intensified his dignity and power, and lifted him higher above his subjects. Local liberties and feudal rights, which checked a Duke of Brittany or King of Aragon, were powerless against a King of France or a King of Spain. Meetings of the Estates-General in France grew rarer until they ceased altogether in 1614. In Spain the Cortes lost control over taxation and administration, and even in England it seems that the early Tudors, had they been so minded, might have dispensed with Parliament. The sphere of royal authority encroached upon all others; all functions and all powers tended to concentrate in royal hands. The king was the emblem of national unity, the centre of national aspirations, and the object of national reverence. In France and Spain men had many provincial parliaments, but they had only one king.

This monarch gained as much from the growth of the

---

[1] *e.g.* In 1899 Great Britain declined arbitration with the Transvaal on the ground that the Transvaal being subject to British suzerainty there could be no international relations between them.

new ideas as he did from the decay of the old. The Renaissance, the revived study of Roman Civil Law, and the Reformation itself all contributed to the growth of royal absolutism. There seems no direct connection between the study of Greek and political despotism; but indirectly the passion for scholarship took the zest out of politics. Moreover, scholars who worked with their pens had to live on their pensions; and pensions are more easily got from princes than from parliaments. Parliaments will vote huge sums to successful generals, but never a penny to a great scholar or sculptor, poet or painter; for purely intellectual achievements are not as yet regarded as services to the State. And so the host of Renaissance scholars looked to the king and were not disappointed; every New Monarch was in his way a new Mæcenas, and had his reward in the praise of the world of letters, which found as little to say for parliaments as parliaments found to give.

The Renaissance did a more direct service to the New Monarchy. Men turned not only to the theology, literature and art of the early Christian era; they also began to study anew its political organisation and its system of law and jurisprudence. The code of Justinian was as much a revelation as the original Greek of the New Testament. Roman Imperial Law seemed as superior to the barbarities of common law and feudal custom as classical did to medieval Latin. England escaped with a comparatively mild attack of Roman law, because she had early been inoculated with it under Henry II. But the attack proved fatal to maturer constitutions; and Roman Civil Law supplanted indigenous systems in France and Germany, in the Netherlands, Spain and Scotland. Nothing could have suited the kings of the New Monarchy better; common law, canon law, and feudal custom were all of them checks upon despotism. The Roman Civil Law could be used against all; *quod principi placuit legis habet vigorem* ran the maxim of Ulpian, a maxim which could be quoted against Popes as well as against parliaments. Nor was this all; Roman emperors were habitually deified, and men in the sixteenth century were almost inclined to pay similar honours to their kings.

The Reformation itself encouraged this tendency of the Renaissance; and there is no greater error than to think that that movement had anything to do with political liberty. Protestantism, it is true, was originally an appeal to private judgment against authority, but only in spiritual matters. Luther explained to the rebellious peasants of Germany that the Gospel message of freedom for all mankind was not an attack on serfdom; and even in the spiritual sphere the Reformers soon fell into the error of the French Revolutionists when they announced their intention of compelling men to be free. All believed in fire as the proper purge of heresy; they only differed about the heresy and about the rival rights of Church and State to prescribe the fire. They claimed national independence of Rome, but repudiated individual right to dissent from the national Church or the national State. For the State they asserted, if not infallibility, at any rate divine institution and unlimited authority to enforce its will. They proclaimed a right of resistance to the Church and a duty of passive obedience to the State. They reverted in fact to the political theory of the primitive Church; it was part of the Renaissance, the revival of the ancient, and repudiation of the medieval. Now the primitive Church had a simple political theory, which was not by any means original. The writers of the New Testament and the Fathers of the Church were born into the conditions of a despotic system. They accepted it just as they accepted slavery, not as good things in themselves but as a divinely ordained remedy or punishment for the original sin of man. The powers that be are ordained of God, said St. Paul; and working on this basis, some of the Fathers developed the theory that the person and authority of the ruler were so sacred that resistance to him was equivalent to resistance to God Himself. This was the idea borrowed by the Reformers. Cranmer told the rebels of 1549 that, if the whole world prayed for them until doomsday, it would avail them nothing, unless they repented of their disobedience to their king. The Reformers, like some early Fathers, transferred the divine authority of the State, whole and entire, to the particular ruler. Circumstances required a saviour of society and the Reformation consecrated him. ' The new Messiah is the king.'

Nowhere was the king more emphatically the saviour of society than in England. The sixty years of Lancastrian rule were in the seventeeth century represented as the golden age of parliamentary government, a sort of time before the fall to which popular orators appealed against the Stuart despotism. The Lancastrian kings were at the mercy of their parliaments, and parliament in the seventeenth century wished to do the same by the Stuarts; that was their idea of government. But to keen observers of the time the chief characteristic of Lancastrian rule was its ' lack of governance,' or administrative anarchy. The limitations of parliament were never more striking than when its power stood highest. Even in the sphere of legislation, the Statute Book has seldom been so barren. Its principal acts were to narrow the county electorate to an oligarchy by restricting the franchise to forty-shilling freeholders, excluding leaseholders and copyholders altogether; and to confine the choice of electors to local men. It was not content with legislative authority; it interfered with the executive, which it could hamper but could not control. It was possessed with the inveterate fallacy that freedom and strong government are things incompatible, that the executive is the natural enemy of the legislature, that if one is strong the other must be weak. It preferred a weak executive, and strove to compel the king to 'live of his own,' when 'his own' was absolutely inadequate to meet the barest necessities of administration. It failed to realise that liberty without order is licence; that order must be established before liberty can be enjoyed; and that a strong government is the only means of enforcing order. Parliament had acquired power, but repudiated responsibility; and the connecting link between it and the Crown had yet to be found in the Cabinet. Hence the Lancastrian experiment ended in a generation of civil war, and the memory of that anarchy explains much of the Tudor despotism.

The problems of sixteenth-century history can only be solved by realising the misrule of the previous age, the failure of parliamentary government, and the strength of the popular demand for a firm and masterful hand at the wheel. There is a modern myth that Englishmen have always been fired with enthusiasm for constitutional government and consumed with a thirst for the vote. That is the result of ages of parliamentary rule; our thoughts are cast in the mould of the age in which we live; and the interpretation of history, like that of the Scriptures, varies from one generation to another. The political development of the nineteenth century created a parliamentary legend; and civil and religious liberty became the inseparable stage properties of the Englishman. Whenever he came on the boards, he was made to declaim about the right of the subject and the privileges of parliament. National character was supposed to have been always the same, and it was assumed that the desire for a voice in the management of the nation's affairs has ever been the mainspring of an Englishman's action. In reality love of freedom has not always been, and may not always remain, the predominant note in the English mind. At times the English people have pursued that ideal through battle and murder with grim determination; but on other occasions the popular demand has been for a strong government irrespective of its methods, and good government has been preferred to self-government. Wars of expansion and wars of defence have often cooled the love of liberty and impaired the faith in parliaments.

So it was in sixteenth-century England. Parliament had been tried and found wanting. 'A plague on both your Houses' was the cry; and both Houses passed out of the range of popular imagination and almost out of the sphere of independent political action. Men were tired of politics; they wanted peace, peace to pursue new avenues of wealth, to study new problems of literature, art, and religion.

They cared little for parliamentary principles, and vastly preferred that the king should levy benevolences from the rich, than that Parliament should impose taxes on the poor. They did not feel the prick of Morton's Fork nor the weight of Dudley's Mills, and Magna Carta was buried in oblivion; it is not even mentioned in Shakespeare's *King John*. A well-known actor-manager thought that Shakespeare had made a mistake; and, when he produced the play a few years ago, he interpolated a *tableau vivant* representing the signature of that famous document, thus destroying the unity and real meaning of the play. Shakespeare, of course, was faithfully representing the spirit of his age; he appeals to the gallery in the flamboyant patriotism of Philip the Bastard :—

> This England never did, nor never shall,
> Lie at the proud foot of a conqueror,
> But when she first did help to wound herself.
> Come the three corners of the world in arms,
> And we will shock them. Nought shall make us rue,
> If England to herself do rest but true.

So he appeals to national prejudice against Rome in John's denunciation of the Pope :—

> Thou canst not, Cardinal, devise a name
> So slight, unworthy, and ridiculous,
> To charge me to an answer as the Pope,
> Tell him this tale; and from the mouth of England
> Add thus much more; no Italian priest
> Shall tithe or toll in our dominions.

But an appeal to Magna Carta would have left a Tudor audience untouched. The men of that day needed no charm against a monarch who embodied national aspirations and voiced the national will. References to the Charter are as rare in the debates of Parliament as they are in the pages of Shakespeare. Not till the Stuarts came was Magna Carta discovered; and the best-hated instruments of Stuart tyranny were popular institutions under the Tudors. The Star-Chamber itself was hampered by the number of suitors, who flocked to a court when the king was judge, where both the law's delays and counsel's fees were moderate, and where justice was rarely denied merely because it might happen to be illegal. England in the sixteenth century put its trust in its princes far more than it did in its Parliaments. It invested them with attributes almost divine; no one but a Tudor poet would ever have thought of the 'Divinity that doth hedge a king'; or have written :—

> Not all the water in the rough, rude sea,
> Can wash the balm off from an anointed king.
> The breath of worldly men cannot depose
> The deputy elected by the Lord.

'Love for the King,' wrote a Venetian of Henry VIII in his early years, ' is universal with all who see him; for his Highness does not seem a person of this world, but one descended from Heaven.' The new Messiah is the king.

Such were the tendencies which the kings of the New Monarchy crystallised into practical weapons of absolute government. Royalty had become a caste apart; the upper slopes of the feudal pyramid had been swept away in the Wars of the Roses, leaving the king alone in his glory at the top of an unsurmountable precipice. Marriages between peers and princesses had not been rare in the Middle Ages, but they now become almost unknown. Only four instances have occurred since 1485, two of them in our own day. One only took place in the sixteenth century, and the Duke of Suffolk was thought worthy of death by some for his presumption in marrying the sister of Henry VIII. By 1509 there were only one duke and one marquis left in all England. The few peers who remained of the old stock were excluded from government, and the New Monarchs chose their ministers from lawyers, churchmen, and middle-class families. They could be rewarded with bishoprics and judgeships, and required no grants from the Royal estates; while their occupancy of office kept out territorial magnates who abused it for their own private ends. Of the sixteen regents nominated by Henry VIII in his will, not one could boast a peerage of twelve years' standing. The lawyers, too, were civilians, not canonists or common lawyers; that is to say, they were bred in the absolutist maxims of imperial Rome, and looked to their prince for their all. *Ira Principis mors est.* So thought Wolsey and Norfolk and Warham. 'Had I but served my God,' cried Wolsey, 'as I have served my King.' That cry echoes throughout the Tudor age; men paid to the new Messiah the worship they owed to the old; they reaped their reward in riches and pomp and power; but they won no peace of mind. To them there was nothing strange in the union of Church and State, and in the supremacy of the king over both : for, while they professed Christianity in various forms, the State was their real religion, and the king was their Great High Priest. They were consumed with the idea that the State was the end and crown of human endeavour; it was their idol and their ideal. It inspired them, and they became its slaves. This is the real tyranny of Tudor times; individual life, liberty, and conscience were as nothing compared with national interests. Nationalism was young, presumptuous, and exigent; its passion had no patience with the foes to its desires, and its cruelty was only equalled by its vigour. The New Monarchy was the emblem and the focus of these forces; it had a great and an indispensable part to play in the making of modern England; it was strong, un-

principled, and efficient. But its greatest achievement was
that its success made the reception of such an experiment
superfluous for the future. Order is Heaven's first law;
on earth it must always go before liberty. England could
not have done without the Tudors and all their works;
for they gave us law and order. They prepared the way
of liberty; and, now to us who enjoy that liberty, their
works and the methods are hateful. We dream of
revolutions made with rose-water, and think that peace
might have been won by persuasion. It might, had it not
been for human nature. Walking would be much easier,
if, as the Irishman said, you could only wear your boots
six months before you put them on. And the Tudors
might have shut up the Tower, and turned its axes and
spears into pruning-forks, had they only enjoyed the fruits
of the storm and strife of the last three centuries. Moral
and political principles are the slow and painful achievement of ages: and you can no more judge the New
Monarchy by the standards of to-day, than you can apply
to the child the canons by which you approve or condemn
the adult. To use the same test for the sixteenth and
twentieth centuries is to imply that man stands to-day where
he did then, and to ignore the progress of four hundred
years.

HENRY VIII AND THE ENGLISH REFORMATION

IN our last lecture we endeavoured to examine some of the causes which produced the phenomenon called the New Monarchy, and to show how circumstances predisposed men's minds to accept a despotism and called that despotism into existence. It is essential to bear these things in recollection when we come to deal with Henry VIII and the Reformation in England; for both the man and the movement would have been impossible in the forms they took without the New Monarchy. Each in its way is a thorny subject, for both are matters of heated controversy to this day, and it is well-nigh impossible for one who feels deeply on theological questions to speak in a reasonably judicial spirit of Henry VIII. On the other hand, invective is as easy in his case as hero-worship. His wives cling to him more closely after death than they did during life, and Bluebeard is his most familiar nickname. Froude, as you know, was inclined to reverse the picture, and to regard Henry as the victim of the other sex; and even Bishop Stubbs thought that the personal appearance of Henry's queens, as represented in their portraits, while it does not excuse, at least helps to explain the readiness with which he discarded them. Perhaps their children, or rather lack of children, had more to do with it than their looks. At any rate I do not propose to deal in this place with the wives of Henry VIII; their importance has been vastly over-rated; they may have been figureheads of various parties and policies, but a figurehead is not a very essential part of a vessel. We are more concerned with the pilot and the way he weathered the storm.

That may be too flattering a term to apply to Henry VIII. He has often been painted a bold, bad man; but recently we have been told he was a 'flabby coward.' Now it is well to have all points of view represented; any one is at liberty to portray Henry as a flabby coward or as a blood-thirsty villain. But I think one condition should be observed: our picture must be intelligible. Our account of Henry VIII must be an answer to the problem presented by his reign, and we must explain how it came about that he was allowed to do the things he did. From a worldly point of view he was perhaps the most successful of English kings. He achieved nearly everything he tried to achieve, and his work was no mere transient triumph. It has lasted to this day and become part and parcel of England as we know it. He broke the bonds of Rome; he subjected the Church to the State; he destroyed the Monasteries; he completed the union between England and Wales; he defeated the French and the Scots; he developed the parliamentary system; he extended and reformed English dominion in Ireland; he built up the English navy; he flouted both Empire and Papacy, and crushed with comparative ease the only revolt which Englishmen ventured to raise up against him. That does not exhaust the astonishing catalogue of his deeds: he had bills of attainder passed against half the English dukes and half the English cardinals who lived in his reign. Wolsey escaped the Tower by death on the way thither, but More, Fisher and Cromwell were sent to the block. He divorced two queens, he beheaded two others. Parliament gave the force of law to his proclamations, released him from his debts, and empowered him to regulate the succession by will.

Most of these things, it is true, are less extraordinary than they look at first sight. Only four English cardinals and four English dukes lived in his reign; so that only two were attainted and only one of each was actually brought to the block; and of these two Buckingham fell a

victim to his own folly and to Wolsey's enmity rather than
to that of Henry VIII. It was only within limits prescribed
by Parliament that Henry's proclamations had the force
of law; and he was not empowered to leave the Crown
away from any one whose title was undisputed; he could
not have left it from Edward VI. The cancelling of his
debts was probably popular, because it meant that a
burden, which would otherwise have fallen on the
shoulders of the mass, was left on those of a few rich
creditors, who had themselves profited largely by Henry's
spoliation of the Church. Even in the matter of wives
Henry only beheaded two out of six; and of those two, one
was certainly, and the other probably, guilty. And the wife
who survived him had already survived two other husbands
without leaving a stain on her character.

These qualifications must be made, but after they have
been made there remains a remarkable sum; and the
problem is to account for Henry's success, especially if we
regard him as a flabby coward or a bloodthirsty tyrant
whose deeds were hateful to his generation. There is no
objection to calling him all these things, provided that you
make them harmonise with a rational explanation of this
coward's or this tyrant's astonishing success. But the
more cowardly or the more tyrannical you make him out
to be, the more difficult you make your own and your real
task of solving the problem of his reign, or explaining how
it was that Henry accomplished so much, and how it was
that his work lasted so long. Flabby cowards are not as a
rule successful revolutionists, and measures which depend
solely upon the tyranny of one man do not become part of
a nation's policy and of a people's conscience. And it is
not open to any self-respecting student of history to fling
these charges and to leave unexplained the problems they
create. Of course, if your object is to dress up history to
look and sell like a shilling shocker, you may do it with
some impunity and some success; but then you only
appeal to an audience which has never realised that history

is a problem, or in fact that it ever happened at all. The events described in a shilling shocker never happened, and therefore there is no necessity to explain them. The events recorded in history did take place, and therefore we have to make them intelligible.

Personally, I do not think that much can be said for Henry's moral character. I do not believe in the portrait of him as a much-maligned hero labouring for the good of his people; the altruistic motive was, it seems to me, entirely absent from his composition. If he laboured, and he did, at the work of statesmanship and to make the nation strong, it was in order that he might be great. If he was not maliciously cruel to the mass of his subjects, it was because he knew that they would not stand it. If he consulted their prejudices and interests, as he did, it was because he knew that his own position depended on popular support; he made too many enemies to be indifferent to the goodwill of his people. To individuals he was relentless, partly because pity was foreign to his nature, and partly because he knew that he could afford to put down the mighty, provided he spared the humble and weak. *Parcere subjectis et debellare superbos* is the mission attributed by Vergil to the Roman Empire : it was the practice of Henry VIII : in both cases it was a profitable and not an unsound policy. Egotism was the mainspring of his action, the basis of his character, and the root of his vices ; and egotism is a fault which princes can hardly and Tudors could nowise avoid. When you worship a man like a god, you are doing your best to make him a devil ; and some of the responsibility for Henry's egotism must be laid at the door of his people, for they acquiesced in his strong and unscrupulous rule in return for the attention he paid to their material interests. They thought him the only alternative to anarchy and a renewal of civil war : and with all his vices, they preferred Henry VIII. His personal morality was not worse than that of most princes, and the number of his wives is no great argument against him ;

indeed the fact that he married them might almost be taken as a sign of grace in a king. Charles II only married one wife, and he divorced none; but that hardly places his morals above those of Henry VIII.

Henry, of course, made no sort of appeal to the ethical nature of men. He appealed to their patriotism; but, as Dr. Johnson said, patriotism is the last refuge of scoundrels, and its ethical value is sometimes abused. This, however, was no bar to his popularity. Charles II was more popular than Cromwell, in spite of his lack of patriotism. The truth is that nations and parties are strongly tempted to condone the private vices of their champions. Protestants hush up the backslidings of Henry of Navarre and William III, and Catholics those of Mary Stuart and James II; and the peccadilloes of Henry VIII were viewed with a lenient eye by people who welcomed the breach with Rome, the suppression of clerical privilege, and the conversion of monastic wealth to national or at least to secular purposes. The fact is that Henry was as much a demagogue as a despot; he led his people in the way they wanted to go; he tempted them with the baits they coveted most; and he appealed to the most cherished of national prejudices. He did not tread on their toes; he used Parliament, but he did not seek to destroy it. He upheld Catholic doctrine as a whole, because he saw that the mass of the people were not prepared for theological change. But when, towards the end of his reign, he saw that, in spite of the Six Articles and other methods of coercion, reformed opinions were making way, he prepared himself to make further alterations; and the Protector Somerset only carried out the changes which were being secretly elaborated during the last few months of Henry's life.

All this may be described as utterly unscrupulous; and rightly so, because religion should be kept clean from the compromise which dominates politics. High and dry Tories have in recent years accepted the fact of democracy though they opposed its advent; and there is nothing disgraceful in their doing so. But to accept a change of religion from the same motives is unprincipled, and so was Henry's readiness to accept a doctrinal reformation. It was what is called Machiavellian, and indeed Henry VIII is Machiavelli's *Prince* in action. Expediency was the test of everything and not principle; religion was to be subservient to the interests of the State. Fair means and foul might alike be employed if the end was the national welfare. The common law, the Ten Commandments, were all very well as a general rule, but the highest law of all was the safety of the State—or the Church. For the same maxims were employed in the service of the Church; it was almost a commonplace that faith need not be kept with heretics, and that killing was no murder when it served a political or an ecclesiastical end. Nor was this only a maxim of the schools. The fate of William the Silent, of Henry of Navarre, illustrates the practice; and the bulls of excommunication against Henry VIII and Elizabeth were, among other things, licences and exhortations to kill in the open or in secret. Every one, except the victim, agreed that it was better that one man should die than that the nation should suffer.

Acts of Attainder are simply solemn and national assertions of this doctrine. They illustrate another Machiavellian maxim practised by the Tudors, namely, that while the prince should reserve to himself the privilege of mercy, he should devolve on others the odium of rigour. An act of pardon or restitution, even when passed by Parliament, was read only once in either House, and then without amendment and as a matter of course; because it was regarded as especially a royal act. But an Act of Attainder was to be regarded as an Act of the Nation represented by Parliament: it went through all the usual forms. That was the function of Acts of Attainder. There is a ridiculous notion prevalent that they were substituted for trial by jury because it was easier to get an Act through Parliament than to obtain a verdict from a jury. Nothing could be more untrue; it was simplicity itself to pack a jury; it was no easy matter to pack both Houses of Parliament. Moreover, many Acts of Attainder were passed against men who had been already condemned by juries. There are only two or three instances like that of Thomas Cromwell, in which men were executed without legal trial; and the House of Lords, which unanimously passed the Attainder against Cromwell, would have quite as readily condemned him when sitting as a court of his Peers. The motive of Acts of Attainder was to make the whole nation as far as possible the accomplice of the king in these acts of severity. Elizabeth's anxiety to do this in the case of Mary Stuart is notorious; she insisted on shifting the responsibility, and Parliament was ferociously eager to assume it.

The treason laws themselves are merely expressions of this idea, that the security of the State is the first of all political objects, and that expediency may override justice. Traitors are not condemned because they are immoral, but because they are dangerous. Lady Jane Grey was almost a saint, but her execution for treason was strictly legal; the same may be said of Sir Thomas More, and of other victims of Henry VIII. 'Truth for ever on the scaffold, wrong for ever on the throne,' is not a hopelessly false caricature of that time; but the sovereign should not be made the scape-goat for all the nation's sins. In a democratic age history tends to become a series of popular apologies. Grote began it in England with his defence of the Athenian people for the execution of Socrates. But the idea that the people can do no wrong is as absurd as the notion that the king can do no wrong. A people in a passion is just as irrational as a prince in a passion, and is capable of even greater crimes. Popular passions were strong in the sixteenth century, and the violent deeds of the Tudors were the practical expressions of popular feeling. There is no evidence of popular disgust at any of the executions of that time, except perhaps that of Protector

Somerset. Mary's holocaust did indeed produce an impression; but that was because she abandoned Tudor maxims, and sought victims among the people.

This popular acquiescence in Tudor methods is not a pleasant retrospect; but it must not be denied on that account. The Tudors had no means of resisting a determined nation. Henry VIII's standing army consisted of a few yeomen of the guard and gentlemen-pensioners; he had no secret police or organised bureaucracy; his only fortress of commanding strength was the Tower of London, and Charles V's ambassador thought that in 1534 it would be easier to drive him from the throne than it had been Richard III. He mistook the temper of the people; the Pilgrims of Grace had little difficulty in overrunning England north of the Trent in 1536. Had England south of the Trent been of the same mind, Henry VIII's government would have succumbed without a blow. He was saved by the voluntary efforts of the mass of his subjects; the Pilgrimage was not suppressed by professional soldiers or foreign mercenaries, but by English yeomen. There was only one occasion on which England rose as one man against the government; that was when Northumberland tried to set aside the Tudor dynasty, and then the national will prevailed without one drop of blood being spilt. We are therefore forced to the conclusion that Henry VIII on the whole represented the wishes of the majority of the English people, or at least of the politically effective portion of the people. That does not mean that individual acts were popular; the divorce of Catherine of Aragon never was, nor was the execution of Sir Thomas More. But these acts did not disgust the people so far as to make them seek a change of government. There was in fact no opposition prepared to take office in Henry's place; no rival had even a plausible claim to the throne. Charles V had thought at one time that the Princess Mary might be substituted for her father; but Englishmen were not likely to prefer a half-Spanish queen, who would be merely an

agent for Charles, to the English king; and Charles himself soon abandoned the idea as hopeless. The Papal
system of jurisdiction had few adherents in England,
and Henry was very careful about touching Catholic
doctrine.

And so it came about that Henry survived papal threats,
imperial preparations, and domestic faction; and went on
step by step adding to the royal autocracy. The history
of his reign is one of gradual development, both of
character and of policy. In his early years he was a slave
of Vanity Fair; athletics were his passion, and in the
hunting field, the tennis court, the tourney, and the ball-
room, he was more than a match for the best of his subjects.
Serious matters of statecraft were left to Wolsey, who was
king in everything but name, although from the first Henry
took a profound interest in the Navy, in learning, and in
theology. His book against Luther, which was the work
of his own brain, is a remarkable performance for a king;
and Erasmus speaks, not only of the zeal, but of the
courtesy and good-temper, with which Henry conducted
the theological discussions which were then the fashion at
court. No previous king had been so well educated; he
knew Latin, French, Spanish, and some Greek; he was a
first-rate performer on musical instruments; and one at
least of his anthems is still occasionally sung in English
Cathedrals. As time wore on, the athletic mania wore
off; and Henry began to take an active interest in
administration; this alone would in the end have been
fatal to Wolsey's position, for Henry had to be master in
whatever sphere he chose to shine.

Wolsey's policy had, moreover, been anything but a
success. One of the greatest of English diplomatists,
Wolsey was nevertheless bound to fail because he fought
against the strongest forces of his age. In this respect he
was like Metternich, another great diplomatist, who sought
by diplomatic means to put back the hands of Time. By
peace and parsimony Henry VII had secured for England

real wealth and a still greater reputation for it. Wolsey, turbulent and ambitious, used this wealth to foster England's and his own influence on the continent. He was favoured by the intense rivalry between Charles V and Francis I; and at the Conference of Calais in 1521 he figured as the arbiter of Europe. This proud position was not supported by adequate military strength; it depended on Wolsey's skill and on England's wealth, which enabled her to act as the paymaster of Europe. But by 1523 the balance at Henry's bank had disappeared; fresh taxation became necessary and recourse to Parliament. The Commons proved refractory, and granted inadequate supplies. Wolsey next tried loans and benevolences; many counties resisted, and ominous words were used. It was obvious that the nation would not find the means for Wolsey's spirited foreign policy; and the Treaty of Cambrai in 1529, which settled the affairs of Europe for the time, was arranged without consulting Wolsey. His influence, which had gone up like a rocket, came down like the stick. His diplomatic judgment also had been at fault. England was not really the arbiter, but only the makeweight, in the European balance; her influence depended on the maintenance of that balance. But in 1521 Wolsey put the weight in the wrong scale. The result was that at Pavia in 1525 France was utterly defeated, and Charles V became almost dictator of Europe. The feeble efforts of Wolsey to restore the balance between 1526 and 1528 only confirmed the verdict of Pavia. Wolsey's policy had failed at home and abroad : it was time for a change of system.

Nor was this all: in the Parliament of 1515 ominous complaints were brought against the exactions and privileges of the Church. Most dangerous quarrels, records the Clerk of Parliament, broke out between the laity and the clergy; and Wolsey in alarm urged upon Henry the speedy dissolution of Parliament. Hitherto, since Henry's accession, there had been a meeting of Parliament on an average once a year : now eight years passed before another was called. Financial difficulties compelled the summons of that of 1523, but from that year not another was called till Wolsey's fall. Why this sudden abandonment of Parliamentary sessions in 1515? In an address to an early Parliament of the reign, Warham, who was Lord Chancellor as well as Archbishop of Canterbury, had insisted upon the necessity of frequently consulting Parliament. What had caused that necessity to disappear? The anti-clerical proceedings of the Parliament of 1515 supply the answer. Wolsey dreaded an attack on the Church : keen-sighted observers were already muttering about its coming subversion. The clergy, it was said in 1515, were so unpopular that a London jury would convict a clerk, were he as innocent as Abel. The Pope had been openly denounced; heresy was spreading, and in 1511 Henry's Latin Secretary complained to Erasmus that the holocaust of heretics had caused the price of wood to rise. Now Wolsey's position and prospects were bound up with the maintenance of the ecclesiastical and Papal system. His immense authority as Cardinal and Legate was merely a Papal agency; it would disappear with the abolition of the Papal jurisdiction. Parliament must therefore be kept at arm's length lest it should attack the Church. And so he sought for fourteen years to rule without Parliament and by means of clerical influence. Under his régime the chief ministers were ecclesiastics, much to the disgust of the secular nobility, who soon began to cast about for means to ruin Wolsey and destroy the political predominance of the Church. The failure of Wolsey's policy delivered him into their hands in 1529.

Now all this was independent of the question of divorce, to which the whole Reformation in England has been most inaccurately ascribed. The divorce was merely the occasion of a Reformation, which would certainly have come without it. It is not possible to believe that England would have remained permanently within the Roman Catholic

Communion when every other country, in which Teutonic strains were dominant, broke away. The importance of the divorce lies in the fact that it alienated from the Papal cause the monarchy, which might for a time have postponed the rupture. Henry VIII was not omnipotent; no ruler can accomplish anything except with the help of collaborating forces; and he would never have been able to repudiate the Roman jurisdiction, had it not been for the popular dislike of clerical privilege and Papal control. Henry was able to turn the balance; and it was the Pope's refusal to grant him a divorce from Catherine of Aragon, which first inclined Henry against the jurisdiction, which he had defended with so much zeal against Luther.

The divorce, as we must call it (though the Pope said there was no divorce, and Henry said there had been no marriage), was itself the outcome of various circumstances. Anne Boleyn was certainly not the only or the principal one of them; for as early as 1514, when Anne was only seven years old, there were rumours at Rome that Henry intended seeking a divorce from Catherine because she failed to produce the requisite heir to the throne. That was the real question. Henry VIII had no surviving brothers and no legitimate sons. The succession of females to the English throne was not recognised. The Lancastrian title had been based upon the denial of this right; Henry VII's own mother had been excluded although all his hereditary claim was derived through her. Matilda was the only woman who had tried to seize the English throne; and no one desired a repetition of that experiment. Apart from domestic disputes the succession of women seemed to threaten national independence. The succession of Isabella of Castile had been followed by its union with Aragon: that of Anne of Brittany by its incorporation with France: that of Mary of Burgundy by its absorption in the Hapsburg dominions. England did not wish to be absorbed by any other State. She did not mind absorbing Scotland, but that was a different matter. She wanted an English king and Henry VIII a legitimate heir. By 1525 it was certain that neither wish would be fulfilled so long as he remained married to Catherine. He thought at first of recognising his illegitimate son, the Duke of Richmond, as his successor. Possibly it was the appearance of Anne Boleyn which decided him to prefer a divorce. There were precedents enough in his immediate family circle : both the husbands of his sister Mary had been divorced by Papal sanction, and the same favour was accorded to his other sister Margaret. Not so very long before, a king of Castile had been licensed by the Pope to take a second wife, on condition that if within a certain period he had no issue he should return to the first; and Clement VII himself was inclined to favour a similar solution of Henry's problem. But he could not, and he would not, grant the divorce. He was perfectly frank about his reasons : the Church, *i.e.* himself and Rome, were, as his secretary wrote to Campeggio completely in the power of Charles V, Catherine's nephew. The defeat of Francis I at Pavia had led to the establishment of Spanish dominion in Italy : the sack of Rome in 1527 had emphasised that fact, and in 1529 the Pope made his humble peace with Charles. That bargain was almost a family compact; the Pope's nephew was to marry the Emperor's illegitimate daughter, and the divorce proceedings in England were to be quashed.

Thus was the breach provoked, and the Reformation begun. Henry appealed from the Pope to Parliament; and a working alliance was formed between King and Parliament against Pope and Church. Parliament wanted the restriction of clerical privilege, powers, and jurisdiction; Henry wanted the abolition of Papal control and of the legislative independence of the Church. The first thing was to fill the government with laymen instead of ecclesiastics. Wolsey fell as a matter of course : the offices of Lord Chancellor, Lord Privy Seal, and Secretary were transferred to laymen, who since 1529 have, with the exception of Mary's reign, always governed England.

Then, one after another of the outworks of the Papal system fell, First-fruits and Tenths, Appellate jurisdiction, power of appointing bishops, and so forth. Now it might have been supposed that this destruction of the Papal domination would have liberated the English Church. But nothing was further from the mind of ' the majestic lord who broke the bonds of Rome '; and every step in the annihilation of Papal control was accompanied by another towards the establishment of royal control. First-fruits and Tenths were not abolished : they were transferred from Pope to King, and so was the power of appointing bishops, for the pretence of election cannot be regarded as anything more than a solemn farce; episcopal chapters were granted licence to elect, but they were liable to *praemunire* if they did not elect the king's nominee : and no chapter yet has braved that penalty. The Church did not become autonomous; supremacy was simply taken from the Pope and given to the King.

This truth is wormwood and gall to many of us to-day with our belief in religious freedom : and criticism of the Reformation is directed not so much at what was done, as the way in which it was done. The Church in England, it is said, should have been liberated from Rome and then left to work out her own salvation. That was not a solution which occurred to any one then, and it was not practical politics. The strife was not between the Church of England and the Church of Rome, but between the universal Church and national State, as it had been throughout the Middle Ages. These were the only two recognised authorities, the only powers capable of carrying out the Reformation. All ecclesiastical powers were in theory derived from the Papacy : the archbishop exercised jurisdiction, but only as *legatus natus* of the Pope : Wolsey tried to reform some monasteries, but only as Papal legate : they were agents of the Pope, and an agent is bound by his master's will. When they act against it, they are acting *ultra vires*. Now the Papacy had refused to reform :

General Councils had tried in the fifteenth century and had failed. The work was left to the national State, which could act on its own authority. Hence Parliament, and not Convocation, is the instrument of reform: the measures of the Reformation are not canon laws, but Parliamentary statutes: the Book of Common Prayer itself is legally a schedule of an Act of Parliament. It cannot be altered by Convocation, it can by the Houses of Parliament. The Reformation in its external and constitutional aspect is simply the last and greatest conquest of the State, the assertion of its authority over the Church, and of its absolute, undisputed supremacy within the national frontiers.

The result was to nationalise the Church, to transform it from the Church *in* England into the Church *of* England, to make its services, ritual, and articles of faith national rather than catholic. The breach once accomplished with Rome, differentiation set in by a law of nature. The Bible was made English; an English Litany was compiled, then an English Order of Communion, and then an English Book of Common Prayer, enforced by an English Act of Uniformity. Finally an English definition of the faith in the shape of the Thirty-Nine Articles was evolved. All these things were intensely national, for the spirit which produced them was that of national revolt. The same spirit had something to do with the dissolution of the monasteries: they were the least national of all ecclesiastical institutions: everything about them was cosmopolitan, and they were regarded as the most obstinate papal strongholds. It was difficult to harmonise them with a national system, and so they disappeared. There were of course other and more material reasons. Their wealth was an irresistible temptation to Henry VIII, and it provided him with an irresistible lever. Monastic spoils were held out as a bait to Henry's nobles, landed gentry, and commercial magnates to confirm their zeal and faith in Reformation principles. It was understood during the

Reformation Parliament that monastic lands should be the reward for their support against Rome. But even greed was not the ultimate cause of the dissolution. It is probable that kings and nobles were greedy for land in the thirteenth and fourteenth centuries, but they did not dare to attack the monasteries. The real cause was that monastic life had lost its savour. Testimony to this fact is not confined to the famous ' Black Book ' compiled by Cromwell's visitors, which disappeared in Mary's reign. A commission of cardinals appointed by Paul III acknowledged the existence of widespread abuses, and every country in Europe found it necessary to adopt sweeping measures of monastic confiscation. France, Austria, and even Spain followed the example of Henry VIII in the eighteenth century, when England had already outstripped them in the race for national greatness. And over and above these comparatively sordid motives a few had come to believe that it was nobler to stay in the world to save the world, than to go out of the world to save one's own soul.

All this turned to the profit of national monarchy, and Henry VIII boasted that as far as England was concerned, he was King, Emperor, and Pope all rolled into one. ' Imperial ' was one of his favourite adjectives : he named a ship the *Henry Imperial*; his crown, he said, was an imperial crown, and England an imperial realm. Parliament and Convocation took up the strain : they meant that England had not emancipated itself from the Pope to throw itself into the arms of that other medieval monarchy, the Empire; and they zealously propagated a legend that Constantine the Great had really granted England imperial independence, while his alleged donation to the Papacy was forged. The legislative and jurisdictional authority of the Pope had been transferred to the King : but it was not true to say that Henry VIII was Pope of England. His power was a *potestas jurisdictionis,* not a *potestas ordinis* : he did not claim the spiritual functions of the Pope, or even those of a bishop or a priest. The administration of the Sacraments, baptizing, confirming, marrying, and burying were all left to the clergy : and ' Supreme Head of the Church' was an offensive phrase, which conveyed to many more than Henry thought of claiming. The title ' Supreme Governor,' which Elizabeth preferred, included everything that Henry wanted. He claimed control of the machine, but he did not pretend to supply the motive power. He insisted upon selecting the channels through which spiritual blessings flowed, but he did not imagine that he was the channel, nor the source from which they flowed. He was willing, to use his own words, to leave to the clergy control of men's souls, provided the State had control of their bodies.

But within the sphere of ecclesiastical jurisdiction and legislation he was supreme. The papal power had in these matters been absolute; every sort of check had been repudiated; the papal will was law; *habet omnia jura in scrinio suo*, as Clement VII said of himself. This had all been transferred to Henry VIII, with the somewhat *bizarre* result that he was at one and the same time an absolute monarch in the Church and a constitutional monarch in the State. He could reform the Church by injunctions, when he could not reform the State by proclamations. He could in person condemn for heresy, when he could not for murder or treason. This ambiguous position led to some confusion in the Stuart times. Those monarchs arrogated the same absolutism in the State that they legally possessed in the Church; and the dispensing and suspending powers, which they constitutionally exercised in the ecclesiastical sphere, they extended to the temporal sphere. On the other hand, Parliament sought to apply the constitutional limits which bounded the royal authority in the State to the royal authority in the Church; and there you have one of the underlying sources of antagonism between King and Parliament in the seventeenth century —an antagonism which is more ecclesiastical than political, and arose inevitably from the fact that the Tudor settlement of religion was a compromise tenable only so long as the Tudor dictatorship remained in force.

The supremacy over the Church was in fact a royal and not a Parliamentary supremacy. Elizabeth quarrelled with every one of her Parliaments on this question. The sovereign was, in her opinion, supreme over both spheres, ecclesiastical and temporal; but Parliament had only to do with the temporal sphere : Convocation was co-ordinate with, and not subordinate to it. In this she was more ecclesiastically minded than Henry VIII : or perhaps it would be truer to say that she dreaded Parliament more. She had little to fear from Convocation ; and she supported it, not because she loved it more, but because she loved Parliament less. This was the germ of the Stuart policy : Parliament was the aggressor, it threatened both King and Church, and both formed a defensive alliance against it. The victory of the State over the Church in Henry's reign had been a personal victory for the King; but Parliament soon claimed to be a better representative of the State than the King. It wanted to control all the royal prerogative ; it succeeded so far as temporal matters were concerned, but was not so successful in the ecclesiastical sphere. The royal supremacy fell into abeyance between Parliament and the Church : and the result has been ecclesiastical anarchy from which an escape has not yet been found.

There is one other remark to be made about the method by which the Reformation was established in England. It was the work of a government and not of a prophet. There was no Luther or Calvin in England, because the strong monarchy did not favour individual enterprise as did the political anarchy of Germany and Switzerland. The result was perhaps less truth, but greater order. To Luther or Calvin truth could be the first and almost the only consideration. A government has to consider not merely what is truth, but whether truth can be translated into action and imposed on a people. This restrained the exuberance of theological debate, and England came through the Reformation without a religious civil war. It also came without a clear-cut system of theology; the formularies of the English Church are composite in origin and represent the working of various minds : they are like the policy of a cabinet, full of compromise, not entirely satisfactory to any one, but tolerable to many. A government always tries to strike an average; the Tudors did so in the Church of England, but an average is anathema to all extremes.

From this it follows that the Church of England has never been really Lutheran, Zwinglian, or Calvinistic. After the first breach with Rome there was a natural tendency towards Lutheranism; Cranmer passed through a Lutheran phase, and between 1536 and 1538 an attempt at accommodation between the Lutheran and Anglican churches was made. But Henry himself categorically refused to concede the three demands made by Lutheran envoys to England, and the Six Articles reaffirmed England's allegiance to Catholicism. Political changes in 1540 made an alliance with the Lutheran princes unnecessary : Cromwell fell, and Anne of Cleves was divorced. The Catholic reaction was only temporary, but the next wave of Protestantism was Zwinglian rather than Lutheran; and Henry Bullinger, Zwingli's successor at Zürich, was the oracle of the advanced reformers in the reign of Edward VI. The Calvanistic phase, although it is often antedated, came later, not till Elizabeth's reign when the Marian exiles had returned from Geneva. Its success in Scotland made it more formidable than Lutheranism or Zwinglianism had ever been, and in the seventeenth century it seemed that the Church might become Calvinistic. But by that time the Anglican system had taken root and fortified itself in the national affection. The Book of Common Prayer, the Anglican theology of Hooker and the Caroline divines, were antidotes against Puritanism; and later on the development of the secular and latitudinarian spirit produced an atmosphere uncongenial to the severity of Calvinism. Wycliffe, indeed, is more representative of English theology than any foreign divine; he anticipated practically all the Protestantism that the English Church adopted in the sixteenth century. Possibly he anticipated more; he was not a bishop, and he did not breathe a spirit of compromise. He was perhaps more of a Puritan than an Anglican; and he pointed to heights or depths to which the Established Church never rose or fell. But the path which he illumined was the path which England took, however much she may have stumbled on the way and however far she may have stopped short of his ideal; and the Morning Star of the Reformation in England was also its guiding light.

VI

PARLIAMENT

THE circumstances of which we have been speaking in connection with the New Monarchy were anything but favourable to the development of Parliamentary independence and prestige. Indeed, everywhere but in England Parliamentary institutions almost disappeared. The States-General met for the last time in France before the revolution in 1614; the Cortes of the Spanish Peninsula grew insignificant. In Germany the Imperial Diet and the provincial assemblies lost much of their influence, and ceased to control the territorial princes. The same tendencies threatened the future of the Houses of Lords and Commons. Parliament in the sixteenth century seemed to meet only to register the monarch's decrees and to clothe with a legal cloak the naked despotism of his acts. It is commonly asserted that they were packed with royal nominees and dragooned by royal commands. How far this picture is true we must now inquire.

Of the weakness of Parliament at the end of the fifteenth century there can be no manner of doubt. That was the natural result of the failure of Parliament under the Lancastrians to secure respect for law and order; and this general effect was supplemented by particular causes. The House of Lords was enfeebled through the slaughter of nobles on the battlefields of the Wars of the Roses, and through their proscription by the victor in times of peace. The process of attainder not merely disposed of the individual peer, but debarred his descendants from office and honour. So the old lines died out: new creations were rare, and the creatures were subservient. It was not till the reign of Charles I that the peers began to show any signs of independence; and then they were goaded into opposition, not by public wrongs, but by personal jealousy of the upstart Duke of Buckingham. The spiritual lords were somnolent, and the lassitude of the Church was the prelude to its fall. The reason was that it had linked its fortunes with those of the nobility: bishops and abbots were generally younger sons of peers upon whom they depended for political support; and when the secular peerage committed political suicide in the Wars of the Roses, the spiritual peers were left powerless before the throne.

The House of Commons was never quite so destitute of spirit, though it reached low-water mark in the later years of Henry VII. Various acts of its own contributed to its decline. By an Act of 1430 the county franchise had been limited to the forty-shilling freeholders, and forty shillings in those days was equivalent to at least forty pounds to-day; as the leaseholders and copyholders were excluded from the vote, it is clear that the county electors were reduced to a narrow oligarchy, and their representatives could speak for a small fraction only of the nation. In the boroughs there was every variety of qualification for the franchise; but the general tendency in the fifteenth century was to restrict it to the governing body of the borough, and to make that governing body less and less dependent on the populace. Another Act of the Lancastrian period had made residence a condition for election, so that only local men could be chosen. These local men, like their constituencies, had only a local consciousness; they were not really interested in national affairs, and they resented being called away from their homes and their businesses to attend at Westminster to matters with which they honestly felt incompetent to deal. They tried to comfort themselves with their wages, and to make something out of their necessities by executing commissions in London for their local friends. Neither

proved very satisfactory; a member of the Reformation
Parliament complained that his residence in London cost
him far more than his wages, and the King was pestered
with petitions from members for licence to go home before
the session ended. As late as Elizabeth's reign the Lord
Chancellor apologised to Parliament for its summons as
being a necessary evil. Violent methods had sometimes
to be employed to bring members up to Westminster; and
I have already mentioned the instance in which the two
elected members for Oxfordshire fled the country to escape
the burden. There were instances in which the Recorder
of a borough was bound, as part of his duties, to represent
the borough in Parliament.

The constituencies, too, felt Parliamentary representation
to be a burden rather than a privilege, and many suffered
it to lapse. They objected to finding wages for their
members, and in 1539 a friend of Cromwell's induced one
or more constituencies to return his nominees by guarantee-
ing that they should get their representation done for
nothing. This frame of mind rendered it easy for county
magnates to secure seats for their friends. An aspiring
politician in Elizabeth's reign writes to the Earl of Rutland
saying that he desires for his learning's sake to be a member
of Parliament, and asking if the Earl has a seat to spare.
The Duke of Norfolk could return ten members in Sussex
alone. The Bishop of Winchester was in the habit of
nominating various burgesses in his bishopric.

These were abuses consequent on the lack of patriotism
and national consciousness on the part of the constituencies.
When Henry viii sent a peremptory order to a certain
knight to represent Cumberland in Parliament, it was not
because he wanted to pack Parliament, but because nothing
short of a royal command addressed to an individual could
produce a representative at all from so distant a constituency; the gentlemen of that district found Border
raids far more exciting than Parliamentary oratory.
Parliamentary representation was an irksome duty; men

could no more resign a seat in Parliament than they can to-day resign their obligation to serve on juries or pay rates and taxes. That prohibition remains in form to-day, though the spirit has departed. You have all heard of the Chiltern Hundreds, for which M.P.'s apply when they want to resign their seats; the point is that that stewardship is an office of profit under the Crown, the acceptance of which by an Act of William III vacates a member's seat; and it is only by this cumbersome, roundabout method that a member can divest himself of his Parliamentary duties. He cannot resign in a straightforward way. The same incapacity to resign then applied to ministers of state, and the fact must be borne in mind when criticising those Tudor officials who held office successively amid all the changes of Henry VIII, Edward VI, Mary, and Elizabeth. Resignation was regarded as an almost cowardly dereliction of duty to the State; a member could not in fact resign, unless the King gave him leave; and again the form has remained to this day. The King must accept a resignation before it can become effectual; if he refused, the minister would have to remain in office. Practically he never does refuse now, but he often did so in the sixteenth century.

Such were the Parliamentary conditions when the Tudors ascended the throne: a great deal of Parliamentary lassitude, and indifference to Parliamentary questions on the part of the nation at large, a marked tendency on the part of many constituencies to let slide their Parliamentary representation, both on account of the expense and because they thought that the monarchy would look after their interests as carefully and as effectively as their members; and an extreme reluctance on the part of possible candidates to undertake the irksome burden of Parliamentary duties. A realisation of these conditions will, I think, tend to modify our view of the action of the Tudors with regard to Parliament. We hear so much of the despotism of the Tudors and the tyranny of Henry VIII, and we apply the same phrases so constantly to the government of the

Stuarts, that almost insensibly we are led to conceive of the two kinds of rule as being the same in character, and to attribute to the Tudors the same antipathy to Parliament, the same desire to dispense with it, that we find in all the Stuarts. That Parliament survived in the sixteenth century we think must have been in spite of, and not because of, the Tudors; and, considering the circumstances of the time, we are somewhat at a loss to explain how it was that Parliament survived at all. In fact Parliament was in abeyance for considerable periods, for instance during the latter years of Henry vii's reign and during Wolsey's domination; and had the Tudors as a whole been as averse to Parliament as those two statesmen, it almost seems as though the Parliamentary system might have suffered serious, and perhaps irreparable, damage. But we shall find that Henry viii especially was anything but hostile to his Parliaments; that under him the Parliamentary system is extended and developed; that Parliamentary privileges are asserted and maintained; and that Parliament is educated up to a national sense of duty. Parliament in fact owes much more to the Tudor monarchy than a democratic age is willing to admit; it was not so exclusively its own creation as parliamentarians would believe. Now we must not believe that this development of Parliament was due to any desire on Henry's part to limit the royal prerogative or to any royal belief in popular self-government. It was due to his desire to be great himself, and to his perception of the facts that a king at issue with his people can never be really great or strong, and that a house divided against itself cannot stand; he sought to make Parliament not the rival, still less the master, but the foundation, of the royal authority.

In the clearness with which he perceived this Henry viii stands alone among the Tudors. Part of the credit may be due to Thomas Cromwell, but not all; for Thomas Cromwell would have gone farther in the direction of destroying Parliament than ever Henry dreamt of doing.

The adoption of this policy may also have been due in part to Henry's realisation of the extent to which his wishes and those of Parliament coincided. He might have been as little sympathetic to Parliament as Elizabeth was, had he discovered the same antagonism in it and the same desire to dictate to the Crown. However that may be, there was considerable variation in the Tudor attitude towards Parliament; and it is necessary to be a little careful in our dates, or we shall fall into one of those generalisations which Bishop Stubbs says are *ipso facto* false. A royal *parvenu* like Henry VII felt at first the need of Parliamentary countenance and support; he represented, moreover, the Lancastrian cause; his ministers and especially Cardinal Morton, were imbued with the Lancastrian tradition, and the Lancastrians had always depended upon Parliament. Consequently, during the first few years of Henry VII's reign Parliaments are frequent; no fewer than five were summoned between 1485 and 1497. But before the end of the century Henry had established himself firmly on the throne; he had been recognised by Europe; all the serious pretenders had been removed; there remained, it was said, not a drop of doubtful royal blood in England. Then Cardinal Morton died; and between 1497 and the end of Henry's reign only a single Parliament (1504) was called. It was the longest interval (1497-1504) between one Parliament and another since Parliament had existed, and was perhaps the most critical period in its history.

The death of Henry VII seems, however, to have revived the Lancastrian tradition. Henry VIII, who was not eighteen at his accession, left the government to ministers like Archbishop Warham and Bishop Foxe, who had been trained in Morton's school. Warham in his opening address as Lord Chancellor to the Parliament of 1511 dilated on the necessity of frequent Parliamentary sessions, and between 1509 and 1515 there were six different sessions— an average of one a year. But in the last two of these sessions the House of Commons began to voice popular opinion against the Church; an act was passed limiting the benefit of clergy, and petitions were presented complaining of clerical exactions. Convocation replied by attacking the House of Commons; ecclesiastics cried out that the Church was in danger. A Cardinal now controlled the government of Henry VIII; in alarm he urged upon the King the speedy dissolution of Parliament, and for fourteen years he tried to govern without one. His ecclesiastical despotism may be compared with the eleven years' tyranny of Charles I; in both cases the absence of Parliamentary grants led the government to adopt arbitrary expedients—loans and benevolences by Wolsey, ship-money by Charles I; and in both cases, in Pym's words, he who went about to break Parliament was himself broken by Parliament.

The summons of the Reformation Parliament of 1529 was the natural accompaniment of the fall of Wolsey, Before it met, every intelligent observer knew what its programme was going to be : churchmen like Wolsey and Campeggio called it the utter ruin and subversion of the Papacy and Church in England. Ecclesiastics were to be eliminated from the government; clerical privileges were to be restrained and clerical property to be reduced; papal jurisdiction was to be repudiated and papal taxation to be removed. On this platform King and Parliament were agreed; and from 1529 to Henry's death in 1547 rarely a year passed without a Parliamentary session. The Reformation Parliament sat from 1529 to 1536; within a few weeks of its dissolution another was summoned in June 1536. A fresh general election took place in 1539, and the only year between then and Henry's death in which Parliament did not meet was in 1541. During the eighteen years which elapsed, from the time when Henry took the government into his own hands until his death, there were only three in which Parliament did not sit. This example was followed by Henry's immediate successors; there were five sessions of Parliament in the six years of Edward's reign, and five in the five years of Mary. Elizabeth was not so regular with her Parliaments; her marriage and religion were sources of perennial dispute between her and her subjects. The alliance between the King and Parliament against the Church had been transformed into one of Queen and Church against Parliament; and there were only thirteen sessions during Elizabeth's reign of forty-five years. She discourages rather than encourages Parliamentary liberties, and she was far more arbitrary than her father had been in her treatment of members. There is no precedent in Henry VIII's reign for Elizabeth's denial of freedom of speech and imprisonment of Wentworth; her *régime* is a half-way house between Henry VIII and Charles I; and it was Henry VIII who accustomed the nation to that idea of Parliamentary participation in government which proved a fatal stumbling-block to Charles.

It may seem paradoxical to represent Henry VIII as less tyrannical than Elizabeth; but he certainly humoured his Parliaments more; and, indeed, in other respects it is not easy to justify the discrimination usually made between the two monarchs in favour of the Queen. She was certainly not more truthful than her father; she was by nature quite as callous; and in policy as devoid of scruple. Her suppression of the Rebellion of the Earls in 1569 was as sanguinary as Henry's suppression of the Pilgrimage of Grace. There was as much justification for the execution of Fisher and Sir Thomas More as for that of Father Campion. Elizabeth treated Lady Catherine Grey as harshly as Henry treated Catherine of Aragon; and the fate of Secretary Davison was scarcely more fortunate than that of Thomas Cromwell, though Davison had given far less cause for offence. There were fewer executions, but there was also less necessity; for Henry VIII had shown once for all that no miracles would happen to protect the heads of disaffected churchmen; Cardinal Allen escaped

the fate of Cardinal Fisher by keeping at a prudent
distance; and the only rival claimant to the throne was
put to death. The title 'good' when applied to Queen
Bess has no more moral meaning than the phrase a 'good'
actor. It means that she was good for the purpose then
required; she was an adept in political sharp practice, and
the incarnation of national prejudice. But she did not
understand Parliament as Henry VIII did. She took to
scolding it, and on one occasion through the mouth of her
chancellor she denounced members as 'audacious, arrogant
and presumptuous,' and upbraided them for 'meddling
with matters neither pertaining to them, nor within the
capacity of their understanding.' In the latter years of her
reign there is little to choose between her relations with
Parliament and James I's, except that she could yield on
occasion with grace, while James could not; and on its
side Parliament, as it told James I, forbore much in consideration of the Queen's age and sex: it did not feel quite
equal to the taming of the shrew.

There is not, however, much difference of opinion about
the relations between Elizabeth and her Parliament. The
crux of the question occurs in the latter half of the reign
of Henry VIII; and the common view seems to place
insuperable obstacles in the way of a rational explanation
of the history of that epoch. The usual assumption is that
not only the Church but the nation as a whole was opposed
to Henry's policy, and that the people only assented to it
through Parliament because Parliamentary elections were
controlled by the Crown; because members were royal
nominees; because freedom of speech was suppressed
inside as well as outside the two Houses; and because
Parliament itself had no option but to register in servile
submission the royal decrees. Now if this were all true, it
would leave unsolved the riddle how Henry VIII was able
to impose his will on the nation in the face of opposition
from every quarter. Some people seem to imagine that
when you have said he was an absolute despot, you have

explained everything: you have, as a matter of fact, explained nothing: absolutism is not a mathematical quantity which you can call into existence by assuming it. The question is how he came to be absolute, if he was absolute, which he was not; and the only answer given is some loose and ill-informed talk about the servility of the people and the servility of Parliament. Now the English people are not by nature servile; nor were they in the sixteenth century. If you reckon up the kings of England between the Norman Conquest and the sixteenth century you will find that half of them were temporarily or permanently deprived of power by popular or baronial insurrections. Foreigners in the sixteenth century used scornfully to contrast the turbulence and waywardness of the English people with the loyalty and obedience of other nations. Indeed, I once heard an exponent of the ordinary view urge almost in the same breath that the insurrections of the sixteenth century proved the unpopularity of the Tudors, and that popular acquiescence proved the servility of the people. I do not think that argument will hold water, nor do I think that the evidence bears out the alleged subservience of Parliament.

It is true that the House of Lords showed little initiative or independence; and that can easily be explained. The lay peers were dependent on the Crown; they had ceased to represent the military forces or the wealth of the realm; even its landed property was no longer so exclusively in their hands. They stood on no independent basis, and the spiritual peers who formed a majority of the House were first rendered powerless by their unpopularity and then reduced almost to insignificance by the disappearance of the abbots from the House of Lords at the dissolution of the monasteries. No similar conditions explain the supposed insignificance of the House of Commons. It is obvious enough that there was general harmony between the House of Commons and the King, and this is sufficient proof for those who imagine that Parliament must always

have been subservient unless it was in chronic opposition
to the government. But there is no proof that this accord
was secured by the despotism of the King or the servility of
Parliament; that contention really rests on the utterly
unproved assumption that Parliament and people were
opposed to Henry's policy. If you want to establish the
charge of servility you must prove not merely that Parliament did what Henry wanted, but that it did so in spite of
its own desires and principles.

Now the means by which Henry viii is supposed to
have secured this subservience are these: interference
with elections; creation of new boroughs especially subject
to royal influence; bribery and corruption; and intimidation of the two Houses of Parliament. With regard to the
first it is only possible to say that neither of the extreme
views can be true. It is clear that there was occasionally
royal interference in elections, but it is equally manifest
that members of Parliament were not all royal nominees.
Where the truth lies exactly between these two extremes
cannot be determined; because such a solution would only
be possible if we had complete and impartial accounts of
every borough and shire election which took place in
England during the Tudor period. Such materials do not
exist; even today it is difficult to say exactly how much
bribery takes place at a general election, and even judges
have been criticised for the point at which they have drawn
the line in various constituencies between legitimate and
illegitimate expenditure. The most flagrant instance of
royal dictation occurred at Canterbury in 1536, when after
80 citizens had met and elected two members, a command
came down from Cromwell to quash the election; where-
upon 97 citizens met and chose the candidates recommended
by the Court. But this is the most extreme case known;
and, after all, the exception should not be taken as the rule.
We are told that this ounce of fact is worth a pound of
theory. It is perfectly true that an ounce of fact is worth
a pound of theory, but unfortunately the pounds of theory

are not all on one side, and ounces of fact will stray from one scale of the balance into the other. There would be no difficulty in deciding between ounces of fact and pounds of theory, but we have to decide between so many ounces of fact and pounds of theory in the one scale, and so many ounces of fact and pounds of theory in the other. In 1529, for instance, we have a pretty full contemporary account of the election for the city of London: as was the custom, one member was chosen by the Lord Mayor and aldermen, and one by the common Council; there is no hint whatever of royal interference. We have also an account of a disputed election in Shropshire where the rival parties canvass and cabal in the most approved and modern fashion; but again there is no hint of royal dictation. A few months after Henry's death there was an election in Kent; the Council recommended Sir John Baker, who had been Speaker of the previous Parliament, and was Chancellor of the Exchequer. The electors resented this attempt at dictation; the Council thereupon apologised and said that nothing was further from their thoughts than to rob the constituency of its accustomed freedom of election; but they would take it kindly if Sir John Baker found favour in the electors' eyes. But the electors refused to be mollified, and Sir John, despite the Council's influence, had to find a seat elsewhere. Testimony to the same effect is given by a contemporary pamphlet called *The Complaynt of Roderick Mors*, which upbraids the electors for the kind of representatives they chose; they preferred, laments this Radical, 'such as be rich or bear some office in the country, often boasters and braggers; be he never so very a fool, drunkard, extortioner, never so covetous and crafty a person, yet if he be rich, bear any office, if he be a jolly cracker and bragger in the country, he must needs be a burgess of Parliament. Alas! how can any such study or give any godly counsel for the Commonwealth?' Here the whole responsibility for the character of members of Parliament is thrown on the constituencies, and not upon the alleged practice of royal nomination. The influence is not that of the King or the Court, but the corrupt influence of wealth. And we find precisely the same complaint made in Cecil's papers in 1559. 'Merchants,' it is said, 'have grown so cunning in the task of corrupting, and found it so sweet that since the first year of Henry VIII there never could be won any good law or order which touched their liberty or estate; but they stayed it, either in the Commons or higher house of Parliament, or else by the Prince himself, with either *le roy non veut* or *le roy s'avisera;* and if they get the Prince to be advised they give him leave to forget it altogether.' It is not easy to harmonise this picture drawn by a contemporary hand with the fancy modern sketches of a Parliament simply registering royal edicts.

On the other hand, there were some exceptional constituencies in which royal nomination was the rule; at Calais, for instance, the King nominated one member, the other was elected, and the same custom appears to have been observed in royal boroughs. These were probably few in number; and the great mass of nominees returned to Parliament were the nominees of great magnates like the Duke of Norfolk or the Bishop of Winchester. Smaller lords sometimes enjoyed this privilege : the Copley family, who were lords of the manor of Gatton, returned the members for that borough, because, we are told, 'there are no burgesses there.'

But of any general or systematic attempt to pack the Parliament of 1529 there is no evidence; and, considering the thousands of letters and state papers surviving from that period, the argument from silence is particularly strong. There is one document which has been taken to prove the packing of this Parliament, and that is a well-known letter to Cromwell concerning his election to Parliament, and his undertaking to conform to the King's wishes therein. If he would give this undertaking, he was to be nominated for Oxford or one of the boroughs in Hampshire. The letter has been misunderstood, because Cromwell was seeking to enter the King's service, and his engagement was to be taken not as a member of Parliament, but as minister to the King. The presence of such in Parliament undoubtedly enabled the government to influence Parliament, but so does the presence of ministers to-day, and it would be a poor sort of government which had no such means of exercising influence. Perhaps, too, it is worth noting that Cromwell was not, as a matter of fact, elected for any of the constituencies suggested in this letter; he actually sat for Taunton. More interference is traceable in the general election of 1539, when Cromwell endeavoured to secure the election of personal adherents in some constituencies; but the futility of his efforts is apparent from the fact that this very Parliament passed the bill of attainder against him without a dissentient voice. Equally futile was the one real attempt made in the sixteenth century to secure a packed Parliament. This was in March 1553, when Northumberland's unpopularity had driven him to his wits' end to find means for carrying on the government. That the method was unusual is obvious from a letter from Renard, the Spanish ambassador, to Charles v when he asks in August 1553 whether Charles would advise Mary to summon a general Parliament or an assembly of notables after the fashion introduced by the Duke of Northumberland. Even this assembly proved refractory, and Northumberland's attempt and those of James i and Charles i all go to prove the inadequacy of the packing of Parliament as a method of government. The mere fact of the attempt being made is evidence of a conscious antagonism between King and people which only existed in Tudor times under Northumberland and Mary; in each case it was proof, on the part of the government, of failure, and an omen for the speedy reversal of its policy.

The case with regard to the creation of boroughs breaks down even more completely, at any rate as far as Henry viii is concerned; for recently published Parliamentary records show that only some half a dozen new boroughs

were created before Northumberland's *régime;* and there
is no evidence to show that a single one of these creations
was due to sinister motives rather than to Henry's policy
of extending the Parliamentary system by granting
representation to new centres of population, and by
bringing within it Wales, Cheshire, and Calais. The creation
by Northumberland of eleven new boroughs in Cornwall,
where Crown influence is said to have been predominant,
does look suspicious; and Mary's and Elizabeth's large
additions to the number may perhaps be ascribed to sinister
motives; but I doubt it. The Journals of Parliament,
which was usually vocal enough on its privileges, contain
no hint of resentment at these alleged attempts to pack it;
and it is questionable whether the movement originated
with the government at all. At any rate, we find in
Elizabeth's reign that a committee was appointed by the
House of Commons to consider the claims of various
boroughs which had allowed their representation to lapse
and now wanted to recover it; that among these boroughs
were Tregony, St. Germains, and St. Mawes in Cornwall,
which are usually supposed to have been created by royal
command to suit the royal convenience; that the member
for Tregony, instead of being a minion of the government,
was Peter Wentworth, one of the most courageous and
assertive champions of Parliamentary liberty who ever
opposed the Crown or suffered in the Tower; and that
his brother Paul, who was scarcely less distinguished as a
Parliamentary critic of the Crown, sat for Liskeard, another
Cornish borough. If these Cornish boroughs were really
created in order to make the House of Commons subservient,
the Crown was indeed hoist with its own petard; it rather
looks as though these Cornish boroughs, with their zest for
Protestantism and the sea, were nurseries of political
independence rather than of political subservience.

Of bribery employed by the Crown to corrupt Parliament
there is scarcely a trace in Tudor times, except in so far as
the dissolution of the monasteries was a gigantic bribe.

Henry VIII was too lordly, Elizabeth too parsimonious, to lavish bribes on individual members of Parliament. There was of course that subtle form of influence by which hope of promotion induces members to prophesy smooth things to those who can promote. "Preferment,' runs a verse from Scripture, 'cometh neither from the East, nor from the West, nor from the South,' and an ambitious divine in the reign of George III selected this as his text when preaching before Lord North, then Prime Minister. So long as ambition remains a human motive, men will always flatter the powers that be; and one is rather surprised at the amount of independence shown even by the Privy Councillors in the Parliaments of Elizabeth. They did not by any means merge their character as members in their character as ministers; and were habitually associated with their fellow-members in urging upon the Queen advice which they knew would be distasteful to her. The Tudors, even Elizabeth, always knew, while the Stuarts did not, how to distinguish between courtiers and councillors; flattery was not a road to the Council, however much it might pave the way to the Court.

Lastly, we come to the idea that Parliament approved of the measures of Henry VIII solely because it had no option in the matter, because, whatever its own views may have been, it could not venture to express disagreement with the King by voice or by vote. Against that contention I can only say that no one has yet produced a single instance in which Henry VIII punished or attempted to punish a member of Parliament for any vote or speech within the walls of Parliament. Bishop Gardiner, writing to Protector Somerset in 1547, categorically states that there was complete freedom of speech in Parliament in Henry's reign, and apologises for the length of his letter by comparing himself with members of the Lower House who thought that, once on their legs, they had a right to go on as long as they liked. The principle was formally admitted in 1512 in Strode's case; and about the same time we find

Convocation enviously petitioning for the same freedom
of speech as was enjoyed by Parliament. Nor was this
freedom accorded because members always spoke smooth
things. In the Reformation Parliament two members
urged Henry to take back Catherine of Aragon as his wife
and thus avoid the necessity for the military and naval
expenditure for which he was seeking a Parliamentary
vote. Others hotly asserted that if Henry taxed his people
more he would meet with the fate of Richard III; plain
speaking could not further go, but impunity accompanied
it. So, too, the House absolutely refused to pass the bill
for the pardon of the clergy unless the laity were also
included. Henry grumbled a bit, and said he could if he
liked pardon the clergy wtihout Parliamentary sanction,
which was true; but he thought it wiser in the end to
yield. This was not a solitary instance; many bills in
Henry's reign were rejected or amended by the House of
Commons, and the idea that Parliament did nothing but
register royal edicts cannot stand for a moment after an
examination of the Parliamentary proceedings of the reign.
Similar instances might be quoted from the reigns of
Edward VI, Mary, and Elizabeth. Under Somerset the
Commons rejected measures favoured by the Protector for
the amelioration of social distress; under Northumberland
they rejected a treason bill; under Mary they rejected her
first bill for the restoration of Roman Catholicism; under
Elizabeth dozens of bills were rejected by small or large
majorities. Of course no one denies that pressure was
brought to bear; the point is that that pressure was
neither violent nor unconstitutional, that it often failed,
and that Parliament was a free force to be reckoned with
and not a negligible quantity of dependants on the royal
will.

Another privilege, upon which Parliament prided itself,
was freedom from arrest, not merely for its members but
for its members' servants. It was claimed by the House
in 1543 and acknowledged by Henry VIII in a remarkable

speech, in which he asserted that the royal dignity never stood so high as in the time of Parliament, when he as head and they as members were conjoined and knit together in one body politic, so that an offence to the meanest member of the House was an offence against the King and whole Court of Parliament. Herein he was adumbrating the sound constitutional theory that the King in Parliament is the real sovereign, and expressing that unity between King and Parliament which gave him his extraordinary strength. He arrested no member; and even Elizabeth, who violated this principle by the imprisonment of Peter Wentworth, paid homage to it by pretending that the punishment was not for any words spoken in the House of Commons. Henry's system was in fact the reverse of the Stuart system; he tried to have as much, they as little, as possible to do with Parliament. He sought Parliamentary authorisation for all his acts; they sought to show that their acts needed no Parliamentary sanction. He consulted Parliament on all sorts of questions in which there was no constitutional obligation for him to do so; they refused to consult Parliament on questions in which it was constitutionally obligatory. He could use Parliament, and did not wish to dispense with so valuable a weapon; they could not use Parliament, and wished to do without it. To them it was a stumbling-block, to him it was a stepping-stone.

And so it was that Henry VIII encouraged, fostered, and developed Parliament; he respected its privileges, he recognised its authority, he extended its sphere; and he helped to forge the weapon which was to overthrow the monarchy. This was no part of his design, but he was not responsible for the Stuarts; he even sought to exclude them from the throne. Nor would he have developed Parliament if he had been conscious of Parliamentary opposition to his policy. He was an opportunist, and his system was based on the circumstances of his time. Those circumstances changed; they ceased to exist in Elizabeth's reign. Both parties began to get independent and a little arrogant. Parliament began to think it could do with a little less monarchical help and supervision: and the monarchy thought it would be happier without its Parliamentary mate. Their mutual affection cooled, but no divorce was possible. Parliament and the Crown were bound together by law and necessity, and the result was an acrimonious domestic struggle as to which should be the predominant partner. The decline of the monarchy begins in the reign of a Queen, which, perhaps, was proper and was certainly natural in an age which did not believe in the equality of the sexes. But it was mainly due to the growth of Parliament and of the forces which it represented. Parliament, encouraged and educated by Henry VIII, grew conscious of its strength. Internal peace produced prosperity; Puritanism begat a stubborn and stiff-necked generation impervious to the wiles of Tudor Queens. From the palmy days of Athens dominion of the sea has been associated with democratic impulse; and English and Dutch sea-dogs could not brook a despotism. Elizabethan literature signifies an awakening of national consciousness. Even religious controversy had forced men to take one of two sides, and thus to think and form opinions for themselves. The Spanish dominion of Queen Mary's reign provoked a national reaction; and Elizabeth had not been long on the throne before Parliament began to assert its voice against the Crown. Its advice was not always wise, and its ground against the government was often badly chosen. It could not force the Queen to marry, but it went further in the attempt than any modern Parliament would do; and its arguments against the Queen of Scots were both futile and ferocious, betraying more theological passion than political wisdom. It needed training and experience before it could be trusted to manage national affairs, but it was feeling its feet. It had got the idea that it was to be something more than the sleeping partner in the government. Men began to keep journals of Parliament as records of importance. It afforded a sphere for ambition; and ambitious men began to seek a seat in Parliament. For the first time heirs to peerages are proud to sit in the House of Commons; and it is in keeping with the part played by the family of Russell in English Parliamentary history that the first two instances of this practice, now so common, are those in which the eldest sons of the first and second Earls of Bedford secured election to the House of Commons. Membership became a privilege rather than a burden. Men were ready to pay for it; not merely to serve without wages, but to pay constituencies for electing them, and the first instance of the bribery of a constituency occurs in Elizabeth's reign.

This meant a new spirit of Parliamentary pugnacity; and the assertiveness of the House of Commons provoked many a quarrel with the House of Lords and much resistance from the Crown. Parliament passed many measures distasteful to the government, and no sovereign vetoed more bills than Queen Elizabeth. She began to impugn the privileges of Parliament; she tried to deny the right of the Commons to decide whether a Parliamentary election had been valid or not, and she failed. Possibly it was at her instigation that Speaker Onslow, who was the Queen's serjeant-at-law, omitted to claim the privilege of free speech in 1566. The omission was reprobated by the House, and this experiment was not repeated.

The divergence increased after the Spanish Armada, when men felt that the external danger had passed away, and that there was no longer need of a royal dictatorship hedged about with special sanctions and endowed with special powers. And the last years of Elizabeth's reign shade off imperceptibly into the first years of the Stuarts, For almost every claim put forward by James 1 and Charles 1 you can find a precedent under Elizabeth. In 1601 Mr. Serjeant Hele averred in the House of Commons that the Queen had as much right to all the lands and goods of her subjects as to any revenue of her crown:

'at which,' says the Parliamentary diarist, 'the House hummed, and laughed, and talked.' 'Well,' quoth the Serjeant, 'all your humming shall not put me out of countenance.' The Speaker intervened and the Serjeant proceeded, and 'when he had spoken a little while, the House hummed again, and he sat down.' The Stuarts went no further than this Elizabethan Serjeant; but there came a time when the House did more than hum, and laugh, and talk.[1]

[1] For a fuller treatment of this subject, see my volume (vi in the *Political History of England*, and my *Evolution of Parliament* (2nd ed., 1926).

VII

HITHERTO we have been dealing mainly with the monarchy and with the upper and middle classes of English society in the fifteenth and sixteenth centuries; for Parliament, it must be remembered, only represented a small fraction of the population; and it is not until very recent times, indeed, that the bulk of the English nation has found adequate means of expression in the House of Commons. Now, human nature being what it is, the class which has enjoyed power has always exercised it, consciously or unconsciously, in varying degrees in its own interests. Aristotle pointed that out long enough ago, and Hobbes on that supposition based his plea for a monarchy: the interests of a monarch, he said, would be those of the whole nation. That contention is hardly borne out by the records of history. Henry 1 had barely elaborated an efficient governmental machine before Richard 1 and John began to use that machine to extract money from their people for their own particular ends. The possession of a sharp sword is always a strong temptation to use it; and overgrown armaments are always a threat to the peace of the world. So the possession of absolute power inevitably tends to make its possessor arbitrary and to impair his character. We can trace that process in Henry VIII in Elizabeth, and in almost every monarch who has wielded despotic sway. But aristocracies have not been much better. As soon as the English nobles had weakened the throne, they proceeded to usurp its powers and use them to strengthen their own position and privileges. Their land had been granted to William the Conqueror's barons to be held as a trust, and on condition of its bearing the whole burden of national defence. Gradually the obligation was repudiated, and the trust was turned into absolute property to be enjoyed as the owner pleased, instead of being administered in the national interest. The House of Lords was, in the days of Edward I, an assembly of royal nominees selected by the King for particular purposes; there was no idea that the son was necessarily fit for this function because his father had been, and eldest sons were not summoned, as a matter of course, to the Upper House. The Crown could exercise its discretion; but in the seventeenth century, by a decision of the peers themselves, and not by any Act of Parliament, it was established that the Crown had no rights in the matter, and the House of Lords became hereditary. By the same influence the land-tax, which had been an easy substitute for the feudal obligation of military service, was shifted on to the brewers; and special laws were passed to protect the game of the landowners; whole districts in the Highlands have been depopulated to provide sport for dukes and marquises, just as William the Conqueror created the New Forest. Elsewhere forestry and agriculture have been sacrificed in the same class interest. Then in their turn the upper middle classes became predominant; they controlled the House of Commons, not the House of Lords; but, when in the eighteenth century the House of Commons had seized political power, it was no more inclined than the Stuarts had been to share it with others. The reporting of speeches, the publication of division-lists, and the presence of strangers in the House were all prohibited, lest, as it was said, there should arise some idea that members were responsible to some authority outside the walls of the House. It was this repudiation of responsibility to the nation which laid the House open to the intrigues, the corruption, and intimidation of George III; the King could never have defied the nation; he could defy a corrupt and irresponsible House of Commons.

So, too, the dominant interest of the middle classes was mercantile, and thus we get the mercantile system. The influence of money competed with that of land; Ireland was ruined and colonies lost in order to protect the English commercial classes; and sordid interests had much to do with wars of the eighteenth century. Even the great Revolutionary war began as much because the French opened the Scheldt and threatened to make Antwerp the rival of London as because they had cut off the head of their King. In the wars of the Spanish and Austrian succession England fought largely in order to secure a share in the Spanish-American trade; and the price for which England and Holland sold their alliance to Austria was the prevention of the Austrian Netherlands from competing with their commerce or forming an East India Company. The war against Napoleon would not have been waged so persistently had it not incidentally delivered into England's hands the carrying trade of the world. Now this middle-class predominance is passing away, and there are not wanting signs that the masses, to which power has come by reason of numbers, are demanding a long-deferred share in the good things of life and of politics. Whether democracy will be more national in its outlook and less dominated by class interests than monarchy, aristocracy, and *bourgeoisie*, remains yet to be seen.

It will therefore be readily understood that in the sixteenth century there was little sympathy between Parliament and the mass of the people, and that there was a good deal of social discontent, which could find no outlet except by way of revolution. Indeed, this lack of sympathy was one of the causes for the weakness of Parliament against the Crown in the sixteenth, as well as in the eighteenth, century. The peasants were much more concerned with the thousand and one petty tyrants of the village than with the one great tyrant on the throne; and they were rather inclined to look to the tyrant on the throne to protect them against the tyrants of the village, from whose ranks the county members of Parliament were invariably chosen. This trust in the monarchy was only repaid in a very partial manner, for the peasant was not politically effective; he had no vote, and the Tudors always wanted a *quid pro quo,* and expected political support in return for any favours which they might bestow. They chose the strongest forces on which to rely : and Protector Somerset found to his cost that the good wishes of the peasants and of town proletariat were little protection against the solid ranks of the landed gentry and middle classes.

The social unrest of the sixteenth century was the result of the break-up of the feudalism of the Middle Ages. Feudalism was essentially a conservative organisation of the social system; and it is commonly spoken of as though it combined all the evils which it is possible to inflict upon mankind. But this is by no means a fair statement of the case; feudalism had its advantages even from the point of view of the peasant. It is true that he had little liberty, but he also had less worry than he has at the present time. The struggle for existence was not so keen, and he was more secure of food and lodging than he is under the economic conditions of to-day. He was not treated with much respect, but he was treated with a certain amount of care. He was looked upon as being something like a beast of burden, and his rights were extremely few. But men pay a certain amount of attention to their horses and their cattle, because their usefulness depends upon their health and strength. So the value of the villein to his lord depended upon his being clothed and fed in such a way that hunger and want did not impair his capacity to perform the services expected from him by his lord. The feudal lords had a direct personal interest in the well-being of their dependants, which is wanting in the present economic system. The whole of society was bound together in a close mutual relationship,and was regulated by an infinite series of minute and careful rules. Its rigidity prevented development, but progress was not desired. The ideal of the Middle Ages was, like the old Greek ideal, conservative, not progressive : it was σῳ'ζειν τὸ ἦθος, to preserve the existing type of social and political organisation. Although the caste system was never developed in England to anything like the same extent that it was abroad, it was practically impossible for the peasant to rise out of his class, except through the portals of the Church. Even in the city-states of Northern Italy, which are usually considered democratic, liberty was collectivist and not individual. As societies they were free, as individuals they were not. The individual member of the proletariat was tied throughout life to one fixed class, one trade, one corporation, one parish, one quarter of the city. His status was fixed as rigidly as that of the villein, and everything was regulated for him from the cradle to the grave. The only vent for individual exuberance consisted in those faction-fights, which were the most permanent and apparently the most popular of all these medieval municipal institutions. In the rural districts the organisation was not so close, but the fixity of social arrangements was as rigid. The number of holdings was almost stationary, and the number of families fixed. Population accordingly did not increase, and it is supposed to have remained much the same from the Norman Conquest down to the close of the Middle Ages. Now, the growth of population is one of the great factors in producing competition; and thus one of the greatest stimulants of modern times was lacking in the Middle Ages. Everything was, in fact, regulated by custom, not by competition; and custom is perhaps the most characteristic word of the Middle Ages. When Henry II draws up the Constitutions of Clarendon, he professes merely to be enacting the good old customs; the dues which merchants pay on their wares are customs; the usual way in which land is held is customary tenure.

This excessive regulation produced stagnation, but even stagnation has its advantages; it does not encourage strife, and class-rivalries are not so bitter as they afterwards became. The Peasant Revolts of the fourteenth century are a sign that the Middle Ages are passing away. They proclaim that the stagnation has come to an end, that the peasant has caught a glimpse of better things, and that he wants to reach those things by speedier paths than what Wordsworth calls the 'meagre, stale, forbidding ways of custom, law, or statute.' The ultimate causes of this discontent were perhaps due to an improvement in the position of the peasants themselves; for it is not when things are at their worst that men rebel. They rise in hope, and not in despair. It has often been remarked that the economic position of the peasant in France at the end of the eighteenth century was better than it had been earlier, and better than that of the peasant in Germany or Russia at the same time. Yet it was in France that the Revolution broke out. So, towards the close of the Middle Ages, a certain amelioration in the lot of the agricultural labourer had preceded the rising of 1381. Services had been largely commuted for rents, and the serfs had achieved their emancipation, though some remained in bondage as late as the sixteenth century. Then came the Black Death, which swept off so large a proportion of the population, and depleted the labour market. The scarcity of labour enabled the labourers to raise the price of their labour, and to demand higher wages. The landlords tried to meet this move by compelling them to return to a state of serfdom; and this attempt caused the discontent which culminated in the Peasants' Revolt.

The suppression of that rising did not, however, mean a return to the old conditions; the peasants were not reduced to their former serfdom, their wages did not materially suffer, and it has been maintained that the fifteenth century was the golden age of the agricultural labourer. Evil times were, however, in store. The rapid development of wealth always depresses those who do not participate in it. You can feel the same thing when a millionaire, or a group of millionaires, arrives at an hotel at which you have been staying. Prices at once begin to rise, and attendance on your wants to droop. After a time you find that your resources do not permit you to stay; they may have been all right before the advent of ostentatious wealth, but this advent has depressed your position, and also, perhaps, your spirits. So, in the fifteenth century, the advent of a capitalist class depressed the condition of the peasants in England and over the greater part of Western Europe. It was not merely that the peasant became relatively poorer than he was before; he also suffered directly through the application of commercial ideas to the system of land-tenure. The merchant, who had made a fortune in trade, used it to purchase landed estates, and thus to make himself a gentleman; but he could not avoid importing into his new position the principles, or lack of principles, which he had practiced in the old; he could not help trying to make money out of the land, because he had been making money all his life out of trade or manufactures. Now, the old feudal lords had not regarded the land as something out of which money was to be made; they had looked upon the land as a source of men rather than as a source of money. Their first requisite had been services not rents; they wanted men to fight for them. 'The law is ended,' ran a proverb of the time, 'as a man is friended'; and a numerous body of retainers was the best guarantee for the peaceable possession of one's own property, and the most promising means of securing other people's. Even when not required for private warfare, the tenant was wanted to plough his lord's land, or reap his lord's crops. The feudal lord could do without money, but he could not do without men. He might work his estates so as to produce as many men as possible; he would not work them so as to yield the utmost farthing in cash.

All this was changed when the peaceful business-like trader took the place of the warlike feudal lord. Private war was not to his taste; and retainers were looked at askance by Henry VII and his successors. Land as a source of men began to lose its attraction; but, as a source of wealth, it was more sought after than ever. It was regarded as an investment, and was exploited on purely business principles. Competition supplanted custom, and the excessive regulation of the Middle Ages gave way to *laisser faire.* The cash-nexus, as Carlyle called it, became the principal tie between the landlord and his tenants. Instead of mutual obligation of service and defence, there was mutual suspicion, each party competing with the other in its efforts to get the best of the bargain. The capitalist, as usual, had the advantage; and free contract commonly means the exploitation of the weak by the strong. There can be no really free contract except when the two parties meet on something like equal terms; and when a man's living depends upon his getting a job, he is hardly at liberty to decline an offer.

The position of the capitalists was, moreover, enormously strengthened by a momentous change which took place in the methods of cultivation, and made agricultural labour almost a drug on the market. The somewhat primitive methods of medieval production, the lack of capital, and the economic arrangements of the village community had made cultivation on a large scale impossible. But these conditions had now been altered; capital was forthcoming, and business capacity; and men began to see that the old system of *petite culture* was economically wasteful. They began what was called engrossing lands, that is to say, they accumulated a large number of holdings, allowed all the tenements but one to decay, turned out the independent yeomen, and put in their places a number of hired labourers. That is one of the three processes to which the name of enclosure is loosely applied. Another of these processes was the conversion of arable land to pasture; and this was still more prejudicial to the peasants than the change from cultivation on a small scale to cultivation on a large scale; for even cultivation on a large scale requires a certain amount of labour, but pasture requires scarcely any labour at all. When a sheep-run was formed out of a number of holdings, one man and a dog could do the work which formerly required dozens of yeomen; and many thousands of peasants were thus thrown out of employment.

The third of these processes was the enclosure of common lands; and the legal rights and wrongs of this question have been much debated. If we believe with Freeman, J. R. Green, Bishop Stubbs, and others, that the original Anglo-Saxon village community was an association of freemen owning its land in full proprietorship, then all these enclosures were wanton usurpations on the part of the lords at the expense of the commoners. If, on the other hand, we believe that the original Anglo-Saxon community was not free, but dependent on a lord who really owned the commons, then there was nothing illegal in these enclosures, and the lords were only recovering a right which they were in danger of losing through the prescription enjoyed by their tenants. The Statute of Merton in 1236 had permitted the lords to enclose as much of the commons as they desired, provided they left 'sufficient' for their tenants. This may be interpreted as either the assertion of an ancient right or the creation of a new one. In any case, the fact that it was passed during the reign of Henry III, when the power of the Crown was almost in abeyance, illustrates the way in which the nobles used their opportunities in their own interests. Nor was it of much practical importance to the peasants whether they were suffering from the assertion of a long-lapsed right or the creation of a new disability. In either case the material hardship was the same. These enclosures would be made for one of two purposes—either to convert the open lands into enclosed pasture land, or to convert them into enclosed arable land; but the former was fifty per cent. more profitable than the latter, and consequently was by far the more usual process with the landlords.

All these changes went on with enormous strides after

the middle of the fifteenth century; and they involved a social dislocation almost unparalleled in English history. To them must be ascribed many of the evils which theological prejudice has attributed to the religious Reformation. Nearly a century ago William Cobbett, who had no particular theological axe to grind, wrote a history of the Reformation, in which he represented that movement as a revolution of the rich against the poor; and that line of argument has been taken up by writers whose main object has been to undo the work of the Reformation by casting discredit upon its character. But the social revolution was not the product of the religious revolution, though the two movements doubtless had something common in their origin; neither would have taken place but for the development of commerce, capital, and a middle class. But the only way in which the Reformation directly affected the social revolution was that the Dissolution of the Monasteries brought into the general stream of tendency lands which might otherwise have remained outside. On the other hand, the only scholar,[1] who has gone at all thoroughly into the materials for the history of this agricultural crisis, declares that there is little evidence for the conventional assertion that the monks were kindlier landlords than the laymen.

The social revolution was due to causes entirely independent of the religious and doctrinal movement. It was not the Reformation which made sheep-farming more profitable than corn-growing, and cultivation on a large scale more economical than cultivation on a small scale. Nor was it the Reformation which necessitated the employment of foreign mercenaries by the English government, and impaired the learning of the English universities— both of which developments have by a somewhat curious logical process been ascribed to the theological shortcomings of the English government. The first argument is that

[1] I. S. Leadam, *Domesday of Inclosures*, 1517-18 (Royal Hist. Soc., 2 vols. 1897).

the religious changes were so unpopular that the government could not rely on the fidelity of English troops, and so were driven to hire Germans, Spaniards, and Italians. The second is that the Reformers were ignorant Iconoclasts, who delighted in spoiling the universities. Both results may be traced with much more reason to the effects of the social revolution. The employment of mercenaries was due to the decay of the material on which the English military forces had been based throughout the Middle Ages, namely the yeomen. Military service had been a local rather than a national obligation; and, although the forces were paid by the Crown, they were equipped and provided by the various localities, and it was the common calculation that each parish in England could furnish one man to serve abroad in case of need. But, when the yeomen were evicted in thousands, and their tenements destroyed, this system broke down, not only through lack of yeomen, but because, in the words of a contemporary, 'shepherds be but ill archers,' and neglected those martial exercises for which the yeomen, whose place they took, were famous. A national standing army would not then have been tolerated by the nation, nor could it have been maintained by the feeble financial resources of the government. It was necessary to have recourse to the readiest expedient, and foreign mercenaries were the only trained force ready to hand. So with the decrease of the universities, it was due to the financial straits of the class which had furnished the mass of university students—the yeomanry. For university education and, still more, university endowments were originally intended for the poor and not for the rich. But yeomen ejected from their lands were in no position to send their sons to Oxford or to Cambridge, and the University of London did not then exist; just as to-day there are schools whose prosperity varies inversely with the degree of agricultural depression. So the numbers declined, and the barbarous idea grew up, whish still survives among the backward classes in England, that a university education is a privilege to which only a rich man's son has a title, and that university endowments, bestowed for the sons of the poor, can only be rightly enjoyed by the sons of the rich.

These were some of the indirect results of the economic transformation. It was the immediate results which impressed contemporary observers, and they were startling enough. We have the unemployed always with us; but the 'unemployed' question of to-day is a bagatelle compared with the problem created by the enclosures of the sixteenth century. According to one calculation made in 1548, three hundred thousand men had been thrown out of work by the decay of agriculture—or about ten per cent. of the whole population. Here was the raw material out of which the revolts of Tudor times were made. These persons, complained one of the Supplications presented to Edward vi's government, 'had need to have a living. Whither shall they go? from shire to shire . . . by compulsion driven, some of them to beg and some to steal.' A great number of them, wrote a Bishop to the King, 'are so pined and famished by the reason of the great scarcity and dearth of all kinds of victuals which the great sheep-masters have brought into this noble realm, that they are become more like the slavery and peasantry of France than the ancient and godly yeomanry of England.' The severity of the statutes against vagabondage betrays the alarm of the governing classes, and the frequency of their repetition testifies to their failure to produce any effect. 'They be cast into prison as vagabonds,' wrote Sir Thomas More, 'because they go about and work not whom no man will set at work, though they never so willingly proffer themselves thereto.' Added to the misery of unemployment was an enormous inflation of prices caused by the influx of precious metals from the gold and silver mines of Mexico and Peru, the scarcity of victuals, and the debasement of the coinage. Without going into details, it may be said that the price of the ordinary necessaries of life trebled during the first half of the sixteenth century, at a time when the overflow of labour kept wages almost at their former level.

The government was neither blind nor indifferent to this condition of affairs, but no English government had hitherto been called upon to deal with so complex and serious an economic problem; and statesmen, who had little knowledge of economic science, were not likely to have much success in solving economic problems. The only alternatives which presented themselves to Parliament and to the Privy Council were forcible repression either of the peasants or of the landlords, or of both. Really remedial measures were quite beyond the intellectual horizon of that age; and perhaps the crisis was one which no legislation could meet. It is certain that the old medieval system could neither be retained nor restored; and the only question is, whether the transition from medieval to modern economic organisation could have been effected with less disorder, less permanent injury to the poor, and less unfair advantage to the rich. England has been described as a Paradise for the rich, a Purgatory for the intellectual, and a Hell for the poor. There is more truth in that somewhat truculent antithesis than is pleasant, and it is grievous to reflect that modern poverty is the creation of modern wealth. There was, of course, poverty in the Middle Ages, but there was no such immeasurable distance between the very rich and the very poor; no poor law was found necessary until after the social revolution of the sixteenth century; and starvation in the Middle Ages was the occasional result of pestilence or war, and not the regular concomitant of normal economic conditions.

The earliest official recognition of the evils of these changes appears to have been the Lord Chancellor's speech at the opening of Parliament in 1484, when he lamented that the body politic was daily falling into decay through enclosures, through the driving away of tenants, and through the 'letting down of tenantries.' The Yorkist policy of siding with the lower orders against the squire-archy was to some extent adopted by the Tudors, and in 1489 and 1515 Acts were passed against the accumulation of farms by wealthy individuals. But the only serious attempt to check enclosures in Henry VIII's reign was made by Cardinal Wolsey in 1517. He may very probably have been inspired by Sir Thomas More, who at this time was high in Wolsey's favour, and had just published his *Utopia,* in which enclosures were severely censured. However that may be, Wolsey appointed a commission of inquiry in 1517; and as a result of its labours, he issued a decree for the laying open of all enclosures made since the accession of Henry VII. Even this was only a flash in the pan; proclamations to the same effect as the decree were issued in 1526, but neither decree nor proclamation had any appreciable result. The old enclosures were not destroyed, and new ones were made as rapidly as before. Wolsey was immersed in his spirited foreign policy and in his designs on the Papacy; then Henry VIII followed with his domestic and ecclesiastical embarrassments; and the advocacy of remedial measures for the social discontent was left to a few individual thinkers and writers. Some of them were Catholics, like More, Thomas Starkey, and Thomas Lupset; others, like Henry Brynkelow and Robert Crowley, were Protestants; and they held advanced ideas on other subjects than the question of enclosures. Brynke-low, for instance, urged that all the proceeds from the dissolution of the monasteries should be devoted to the purposes of educational endowment—a suggestion which, had it been adopted, would have made England education-ally the best endowed country in the world. He also thought that both Houses of Parliament should sit and vote together, for, he said, 'it is not riches or authority that bringeth wisdom.'

But it was not until the reign of Edward VI that this party of reform obtained any real importance. The most energetic exponent of its ideas was a certain John Hales,

who has falllen into undeserved oblivion; he was supported
by the reformers, Latimer and Lever, and Cranmer was in
sympathy with their aims.   But the movement came
rapidly to the front mainly because it found a champion
in the Protector Somerset himself.   Their cardinal principle
was that man was born primarily for the service of God
and of the commonwealth.   'It is not lawful,' declared
John Hales, 'for man to do what he lists with his own;
but every man must use what he hath to the utmost benefit
of his country.'   'Let us have,' he said in his charge when
acting as enclosure-commissioner, 'this godly opinion with us,
that nothing can be profitable that is not godly and honest,
nor nothing godly and honest whereby our neighbours and
Christian brethren, or the commonwealth of our country,
is hurt and harmed.'

From their insistence upon the paramount claims of the
community, this party was called the Commonwealth's
Men; and in the first Parliament of Edward's reign they
introduced various bills to give effect to their ideas.   One
was entitled 'For the bringing up poor men's children,'
and it may have embodied a socialistic suggestion, made
by Brynkelow in the reign of Henry VIII, that a certain
number of the poorest children in each town should be
brought up at the expense of the community.   Other bills
were introduced to secure leaseholders from eviction, and
to prevent the decay of husbandry and tillage.   But these
were all rejected either in the House of Lords or in the
House of Commons, and the only social reform which
found favour in the eyes of Parliament was the famous Act
providing that collections should be made in church for the
benefit of the poor, and that confirmed vagabonds might
be sold into slavery.   This was hardly calculated to soothe
or satisfy the dispossessed peasantry, and early in 1548, if
not before, they began to revolt in various counties, while
others of them preferred the more peaceful method of
petitioning the Protector.   In response to these armed
protests, petitions, and perhaps also to Latimer's famous

sermon 'Of the Plough,' the Protector issued in June 1548 his proclamation against enclosures, and appointed a commission of inquiry into the whole question. The proclamation spoke of the 'insatiable greediness' of those by whose means 'houses were decayed, parishes diminished, the force of the realm weakened, and Christian people eaten up and devoured of brute beasts and driven from their houses by sheep and cattle.' The commissioners were to inquire into the extent of enclosures made since 1485, and into the failure of previous legislation to check them,, and to make returns of those who broke the law.

Some one has said that the way to an Englishman's heart lies through his pocket : certainly, when you touch his pocket, his spleen at once becomes active. And this attempt to inquire into the illicit gains of the landlords during the previous sixty years provoked the fiercest resistance. The official classes had always looked askance at the Commonwealth party; Somerset's own colleagues went into secret opposition, and in the counties an organised plan was formed to burke the inquiry. Only the commission over which Hales himself presided ever got to work at all; and no stone was left unturned to balk its efforts. 'I remember,' said Latimer, 'a certain giant, a great man who sat in commission about these matters ; and when the townsmen would bring in what had been enclosed, he frowned and chafed, and so near looked and threatened the poor men that they durst not ask their right.' The landlords, complained Hales, had the juries packed with their own servants, and such was the multitude of retainers and hangers-on that it was impossible to make juries without them. Tenants were threatened with eviction if they gave information against their lords ; and the juries were sometimes indicted because they presented the truth. 'As it pleaseth my landlord, so shall it be.' Other frauds were employed : one furrow would be ploughed across a sheep-run, and then the sheep-run would be returned as arable land. Or an ox or two would be turned out among a thousand sheep, and the land would be returned as land for the fatting of cattle, and not for the growing of wool. To prevent any appearance of vindictiveness, Hales had procured a pardon for all the offenders returned under this commission: the only result was that the offenders, as Hales says, returned at once to their old vomit, began immediately to enclose again, and were more greedy than they were before.

The same spirit appeared in the reception accorded to the bills promoted by Hales and the Protector in the ensuing Parliament of 1548-9. A few minor proposals were, indeed, passed: a tax of twopence was imposed on every sheep kept in pasture, and the payment of fee-farms was remitted for three years in order that the proceeds might be devoted to finding work for the unemployed. Another Act struck at rich and poor alike. It was complained that victuallers and others had conspired to sell their goods at artificial and unreasonable prices; in other words, they had tried to form corners and trusts, though we do not find mention of book-clubs. On the other hand, it was said, 'artificers, handicraftsmen, and labourers have made confederacies and promises, and have sworn mutual oaths not only that they should not meddle with one another's work, and perform and finish that which another hath begun, but also to constitute and appoint how much work they shall do in a day and what hours and times they shall work.' In other words, they wanted to establish trade-unions. It is important to notice that even this Parliament, which was not particularly sympathetic towards the poorer classes, regarded a ring and a combine as being just as reprehensible as a trade-union. Both were opposed to the public interest, and both were forbidden by law. It is one of our modern plutocratic notions that, while capitalists may conspire as much as they like to keep up prices or to limit output, or to fleece the public in any other way that seems convenient, workmen should not be allowed in the public interest to combine at all.

The bills passed by Parliament were, however, mere palliatives compared with those they rejected; and Hales, who was himself a member of Parliament, describes the fate of his measures to prevent the practice of gambling with the people's food. One was to arrest the decay of tillage and husbandry, by what expedients we are not told : it was introduced into the House of Lords, and there was slaughtered. Another was designed to prohibit practices similar, on a smaller scale, to the methods of the American beef-trust: graziers were, says Hales, in the habit of bringing both cattle and money to market, and then, if they could not get their price for their own beasts, they would buy up the market, and dictate their own terms. This bill, which was also brought into the House of Lords, was passed by them and sent down to the Commons. There it met with a stormy reception; it was tossed and mangled, impeded by dilatory motions, and referred to a committee of its enemies. It was, says Hales, as though a lamb had been entrusted to a wolf for custody.

The Protector was not turned from his course by these Parliamentary checks. He avowed that in spite 'of the Devil, private profit, self-love, money, and such-like the Devil's instruments,' he would go forward. He issued fresh instructions to the enclosure-commissioners in the spring of 1549; and, to provide speedy justice for the poor, which they could not obtain in the ordinary law-courts, he set up a Court of Requests in Somerset House, of which his secretary, William Cecil, afterwards Lord Burghley, acted as registrar. 'It is our duty and our office,' he wrote, 'to receive poor men's complaints.' And as a result of these complaints, he was often brought into conflict with his colleagues. Warwick's park had been ploughed up by the enclosure-commissioners, and Warwick took the lead in the opposition to Somerset's social policy.

K 2

The peasants, meanwhile, weary of waiting for redress which never came, made up their minds that, in Hales's words, they must fight it out or else be reduced to the like slavery that the Frenchmen were in; and risings began in nearly all the counties of England. In Devonshire and Cornwall the discontent was diverted into an ecclesiastical channel, and made to appear as a protest against the Prayer-Book and Act of Uniformity of 1549; but elsewhere it was seen in its true colours as a purely agrarian movement. In Norfolk Ket set up a commonwealth of peasants, in which no rich man did what he liked with his own. Troops, intended for the defence of English possessions in France or for the subjugation of Scotland, had to be diverted to the eastern or western shires. English strongholds in France and in Scotland fell into the enemy's hands, and their fall was used as a pretext for depriving the Protector of office in the following October. The real reason was the hatred of the majority of the Council for his social and constitutional policy. The Protector had tried an experiment in liberty: he had repealed all the heresy-laws and all the treason-laws of Henry VIII; he had deliberately repudiated the Tudor system, and endeavoured to govern by methods more suited to the eighteenth or the nineteenth than to the sixteenth century, while only an Independent Labour party would have heartily supported his social policy.

The Protector's fall was followed by the complete reversal of his schemes; the Parliament, which met in November 1549, was animated by a spirit of panic and revenge. It not only repealed the Protector's measures, but repudiated the whole Yorkist and Tudor policy with regard to enclosures. These had over and over again been declared illegal: they were now expressly legalised, and it was enacted that the lords of the manor might enclose wastes, woods, and pastures notwithstanding the gainsaying and contradiction of their tenants. It was made treason for forty, and felony for twelve, persons to meet for the purpose of breaking down any enclosure or enforcing any right of way. To summon such an assembly, or to incite to such an act, was in itself felony; and any copyholder refusing to assist in repressing it forfeited his copyhold for life. The same penalty was attached to hunting in any enclosure and to assembling for the purpose of abating rents or the price of corn; but the prohibition against capitalists conspiring to raise prices was repealed. The masses had risen against the classes, and the classes took their revenge.

This must be borne in mind when we try to account for the almost grotesque failure of Warwick's plot to place Lady Jane Grey on the throne. His government had been more arbitrary at home than that of Henry VIII, and feebler abroad than that of Somerset. It was hated as much by Protestants as by Catholics, and it was Protestants who decided the issue in favour of Queen Mary. But the fall of the conspirators, who had ruined Protector Somerset and his plans, brought little redress to the peasants; and half a century later a sympathetic divine lamented that the enclosure movement had turned merry England into sorrowful or sighing England. Some relief came by weary stages through the operation of natural causes; the development of home manufactures absorbed a certain amount of labour, and over-sea enterprise provided occupation for others. Eventually colonies supplied a home and subsistence for thousands left in the lurch by the economic march of events in England. But only the most robust belief in the dogma, that whatever has happened has been for the best, can blind us to the vast iniquity and evil of the divorce of the peasant from rights in the land which he occupies, tills, and makes fruitful. England could not have run the race for national wealth in the shackles of the Middle Ages, and perhaps national wealth could only be bought by the pauperisation of the poor. But, if absence of control means that the weakest goes to the wall, and national prosperity means that millions must hover on the verge of starvation, we are brought face to face with the question whether the product is worth the price, whether after all the feudal system was so very much worse than the present, and whether the social revolution of the sixteenth century was a very great step in the progress of man.

VIII

IT used to be said by an eminent professor of modern
history that it was a mistake to include more than one
definite idea in a single lecture, because that was as much
as the average audience could carry away. I have paid
you the compliment of neglecting this advice; but most
people find it very difficult to carry away more than one
idea of the sixteenth century, or to conceive of it as being
anything except an age of religion and theology. Yet the
political ideas of the century were at least as original as its
theology, and a great deal more apparent than its religion.
It is impossible to say whether they influenced religion
more than they were influenced by it; but both factors
have equally to be taken into our account of the time,
unless that account is to be a one-sided, unveracious affair.
If religion had been the supreme and only test, it would
have divided Europe into Catholic and Protestant parties,
and not into Protestant and Catholic nations. The
sixteenth was not in fact so religious a century as the
twelfth or thirteenth; there was no crusade; the
Armada, the nearest approach to one, did not sail until
Mary Stuart had bequeathed to Philip II her claims to the
English throne, and Philip would never have embarked on
that enterprise for the sake of religion alone. It can hardly
be said that religion was the sole concern of the Queen who
married the Protestant Bothwell according to Protestant
rites. Political as well as religious motives played their
part on the European chess-board; there were black
squares as well as white, and, while the bishops were

supposed to keep to their own colour, all the other pieces—
and especially rival queens and their knights—might move
upon either. It was not religion which fashioned the
Anglican church on a national, the Lutheran church on a
territorial, and the Helvetic churches on a congregational,
basis. It was political conditions which effected all these
things; politics had much to do with making Germany
Protestant and keeping France Catholic. Impartial
observers had some difficulty in determining whether the
War of the Schmalkaldic League was, or was not, a war of
religion; and one of the French wars of religion was also
called the Lovers' War. Secularisation, indeed, seems a
much more striking feature of the century; religious orders
were despoiled and not endowed, and in the wars of religion
there was more war than there was religion. Heresy was,
whenever possible, identified with treason; for treason was
more unpopular than heresy, because men were more
devoted to the State than to the Church. Wyatt's rebellion
enabled Mary to execute heretics on the plea that they
were traitors; and Elizabeth boasted that she did not perse-
cute for religion, because Campion and the others whom she
executed were disloyal to the State.

This predominance of the State is the all-pervading
political idea of the sixteenth century. It had complex
causes, some of which I have already tried to trace. From
the Renascence point of view its parent was Machiavelli,
who, it has been said, released the State from the restraint
of law. He only committed to paper, and made a theory
of, the practice of his time; and he has thousands of votaries
to-day who would indignantly repudiate his name.
He simply preferred efficiency to principle, and held in
the language of the Twelve Tables, that *salus populi* was
suprema lex. Bismarck and Mazzini thought the same;
tyrannicide and reasons of State are both Machiavellian.
The republican thought the tyrant might be slaughtered
for the common good, and the statesman believed force
and fraud to be legitimate means of serving his country;

both agreed that the individual might be sacrificed in the interests of the State. It is not easy to deny the proposition or to avoid the slippery slope which leads towards Machiavelli. An ambassador, said Sir Henry Wootton, is an honest man sent to lie abroad for his country's good. A diplomatist who told the truth, the whole truth, and nothing but the truth, would not be a diplomatist, except on the supposition that to tell the truth is the easiest method of deception, because the truth is what men least expect. But nowadays we begin to limit the sins one may legitimately commit in the interests of the State; and the late Lord Acton would have applied to States the same rigid code of morals which we commonly apply to individuals. We begin to perceive that the State consists only of individuals, and that the violation of individual rights and individual consciences in the interests of the State does more harm to the individuals than it can possibly do good to the State. Machiavelli and his models were less squeamish; in politics a blunder was worse than a crime; success was the only test of an action; expediency was more important than lawfulness; the end justifies the means; and the end was always the good of the State.

All this is pagan enough; it was left to Luther to sanctify it, and to become the putative inventor of the divine right of the State. The claim was not true, because consciously or unconsciously he borrowed it from the early Fathers. It was a natural reaction against the divine right of the Church, and part of the general appeal of the Reformation from the Middle Ages to the primitive days of Christianity. The Reformers set up the divine right of the State against the divine right of the Church; they did not advance, as is often supposed, to the divine right of the individual; we have scarcely got there yet, though the conscientious objector is making the effort in various spheres. The right had to be divine, or it was not much use in the ages of faith; for men had less reluctance then than now to saddle Providence with responsibility for their own creations. All legitimate institutions were regarded as of divine ordination. Once divine and once legitimate, it was always divine and always legitimate; there was no idea of progress or evolution, and, when men wanted to change an institution, they had to allege that it had never been legitimate. Hence all the talk about the 'usurped' authority of the Pope; it was abolished in England on that ground, and not on the more sensible plea that it had lost its savour, and become incompatible with national development. Providence, it was maintained, had never sanctioned the Papacy; that was a wicked invention of self-seeking Popes. But Providence had really ordained and sanctioned the State; the King was the Lord's Anointed rather than the Priest. Christ, by living and dying under the laws of the Roman Empire, had implicitly recognised its authority and explicitly required men to render unto Cæsar the things that were Cæsar's. St. Paul, the other Apostles and early Fathers continued in the same strain, and men invented a sort of Apostolic succession in the State. The authority thus sanctioned had descended through the ages to the emperors and kings of the sixteenth century. Luther saw in Charles v the successor of Augustus and Constantine the Great, and thought resistance was a sin. When circumstances induced him to abandon this view, he transferred the divine sanction to his territorial sovereign, the Elector of Saxony. Englishmen diverted the line of succession from the Holy Roman emperors to their own kings, and invented a legend to the effect that Constantine the Great had conferred imperial authority over the British Isles on King Arthur, from whom it descended to Henry VIII. Hence the King's imperial talk; it all fitted in with his designs on Scotland and Ireland and also upon the Church, for there was no ecclesiastical independence under the Roman and Byzantine emperors, whom Henry VIII tried to imitate. His ideas were perhaps Byzantine rather than Roman, for it was at Byzantium that the dependence of the Church was carried furthest and continued longest; and it was at Byzantium that the absolutist maxims of the Roman civil law were elaborated in theory and put into practice.

This imperial law made serious inroads upon the common law of England in the sixteenth century. Upon it was based the procedure of the Court of the Star Chamber, the Court of Requests, the equity jurisdiction of the Chancery, where all depended upon the expert opinion of a judge and nothing on the common sense of a jury. It was the foundation of the Council of the North and of the Council of Wales; 'if we do nothing but by the common law,' wrote a president of the latter, 'it will be long ere these things be amended.' The State required the latitude and discretion allowed it by the civil law, and emancipation from the bonds of common law. Henry VIII prohibited the canon law, but founded regius professorships of civil law at the Universities of Oxford and Cambridge; and a doctorship of civil law is still the highest honorary degree that Oxford can bestow. Protector Somerset wanted to establish a college at Cambridge devoted exclusively to the study of civil law : and Tudor officials were nearly all civilians, not canonists or common lawyers. Thomas Cromwell was the greatest advocate of this system; he recommended Pole to study Machiavelli,[1] who, according to Pole, had poisoned all England, and would poison all Christendom. Cromwell paid an English publisher to produce a translation of Marsiglio of Padua, the extremest champion of State against the Church in the Middle Ages; and he urged Henry VIII to adopt openly the theory that the Prince's will is law. It is one of the testimonies to Henry's common sense that he preferred the advice of Bishop Gardiner, who said it was safer to make the law his will than to make his will the law.

[1] This is the ordinary interpretation; but see Paul Vandyke, *Renascence Portraits*, 1906, App., where he gives good reason for believing that the book recommended by Cromwell to Pole was not Machiavelli's *Prince*, but Castiglione's *Courtier*.

There is no more striking illustration of the complete reversal of the medieval system than the fact that these maxims of the State were adopted by the Church. Convocation in England took up the cry about England being an imperial realm, independent of the Bishop of Rome, and dependent upon a monarch who was at once Pope, Emperor, and King in England. The King was admitted to be the supreme judge in matters of faith, and the 'King's Doctrine' was used as a synonym for orthodoxy. He had, it was maintained, been immediately entrusted by God with the whole governance of his subjects in spiritual as well as temporal things. Resistance to him was disobedience to God. So Cranmer informed the western rebels in 1549; and this contention produced his own difficulty in Mary's reign. He had unreservedly adopted the theory of the divine right of the State to determine all things, including matters of faith. Now in Mary's reign the State decided in favour of the Papacy, and Cranmer had no logical ground on which to withstand the decision; he had never admitted the divine right of the individual. Hence his recantations, which afford so easy a means of attack on his character. In justice to Cranmer it may be remarked that no one has yet found a logical answer to the dilemma which distressed his sensitive mind. If you admit, as all Anglicans did at that time, the right of the State to determine the national religion, and deny the right of the individual to choose his own, what are you going to do when the State establishes a form of religion repugnant to your conscience? Either your convictions or your conscience must go. Cranmer doubted between the two; his lifelong convictions at first proved stronger and he compromised with his conscience. Then his conscience triumphed, and he died in the flames with peace in his soul.

The divine right of the State or of Kings—for the two came to much the same thing in the sixteenth century, when, in the phrase attributed to Louis XIV but invented by Voltaire, the State was the King—became orthodox

Anglican doctrine; and, when Puritans and Parliament began to attack the Church, it had urgent reasons for putting its trust in princes. But there was all the difference in the world between this divine right and the divine *hereditary* right proclaimed by James I. The former was an ancient and a comparatively reasonable idea; the latter was new-fangled, and about as irrational a theory as was ever invoked to misinterpret history. The divine right of the sixteenth century was a theological counterpart of the Tudor claim to the throne; and that, if I may use a somewhat contradictory term, was a *de facto* theory, and not a *de jure* theory. When in 1485 Parliament recognised Henry VII as king, it admitted a fact rather than a right. It did not say that he ought all along to have been king: it merely recognised the fact that he was king. And you may remember that another statute of the same reign denied that obedience to a *de facto* king could be treason. That is the keynote of the Tudor period: the title of the Tudors really rested on their ability to govern, and not upon any theory of hereditary right. So the divine right of that age simply recognised the divine ordination of existing authority, without prescribing the way in which that authority was to be chosen; that was a matter for Providence and, sometimes, the God of Battles.

This was the doctrine asserted in the canons drawn up by Convocation in 1606. James I soon discovered a flaw; his mind was acute, and he was conscious that he had not, like the Tudors, established his throne in the hearts of his people. What, he asked in effect, would they do if some one treated him as Henry VII had treated Richard III?—this doctrine of theirs would compel them to recognise and obey the usurper as divinely ordained a *de facto* king. That was a horrible thought; for he was king *de jure;* not all the water in the rough, rude sea could wash the balm off from his anointed head; not all the canons of the Church or the pikes of a usurper could destroy his right to the Crown. For it was hereditary, an inalienable right of birth, something which even the sovereign himself could not destroy.[1] Providence had not only ordained the kings that be, but preordained the kings that ought to be; only through hereditary right could divine right descend: that was the divinely selected channel of royal prerogative. This theory was not an original discovery by James I, though it was he who introduced it in Great Britain. Henry of Navarre had asserted a claim to the throne of France which depended solely on hereditary right, against even greater obstacles than those which stood in the way of James I; and Stuart legitimists derived their reasoning from Bodin and the *Politiques* of France.

Now, there were good practical reasons why James attached so extravagant an importance to hereditary right; for that was his only title to the throne, and it had prevailed over almost insuperable obstacles. The greatest of these was perhaps the inveterate hatred between English and Scots, but there were also two legal impediments. By both common law and statute law James was debarred from the English throne. He was an alien; as such he could not by common law inherit one foot of English land; still less could he inherit England. By statute law he was equally excluded; Henry VIII's will had the force of a statute, and had been confirmed by statute. By it the descendants of Henry's younger sister, Mary, had been preferred in the line of succession to those of his elder sister, Margaret; and so, according to the law of the land, James was not Elizabeth's true heir. He was only so by hereditary right, and hereditary right was not the law of the land.

Now, the real reason why James succeeded in spite of these obstacles is, of course, to be found in the practical circumstances of 1603. The descendant of the Suffolk line,

[1] This also became the French monarchical theory, and Louis XIV maintained that he could not, if he wished, deprive the Dauphin of his hereditary right, which was divine. See Torcy, *Mémoires,* ed. 1850, pp. 710, 711.

Lord Beauchamp, was an impossible candidate for the throne : his legitimacy had been officially denied; his personal character was insignificant; and the advantages of a union between England and Scotland were felt to outweigh the defects in James's claim. But the king himself was too proud and too pedantic to owe his elevation to such mundane and transitory considerations; he attributed it to his hereditary right, which he erected into a divine dispensation and dogma. This again gives the keynote of the Stuart period; the dynasty claimed to exist *de jure,* not *de facto.* The Stuarts pretended that their abstract theory overrode all the practical necessities of government; that, whatever they did, they were kings by unalterable right. Parliament could no more repeal their divine hereditary right, than it could amend the constitution of the universe. Fitness to rule, conformity to the national will, had nothing to do with the matter. Their authority was something above the law; the law was derived from it, not it from the law. Theirs was the divine, the only right : all other things, like Parliamentary privileges, were matters of grace which had been granted, and might be revoked, by the Crown. The Stuart policy was throughout an attempt to force the English constitution into the narrow compass of this abstract system, to make facts conform to fancies, and to subordinate government to a theory. It was the reverse of Tudor policy, which had always considered the facts and left the theory to take care of itself; the Tudors were content with the substance of power, the Stuarts pursued its shadow.

This corruption of the Tudor into the Stuart theory, of the divine right of kings into the divine *hereditary* right of kings, ruined the Tudor system and spoilt the Tudor theory, for which originally there was a good deal to be said. Indeed, the ideas which underlay it have subsisted to this day, and form the fundamental difference between the English and Continental constitutions. Starting from the axiom that *salus populi* is *suprema lex,* and assuming that government is the embodiment of the State and the expression of national unity, political thinkers in the sixteenth century deduced the idea that special sanctions special immunities, privileges, and powers are required to protect the State and its servants. The common law could not provide for all contingencies; a wide discretion must be granted to the sovereign; he must in cases of necessity dispense with common law and make use of his prerogative The revival of the Roman civil law coincided with this tendency of thought; and the various prerogative court were practical expressions of the idea. The function of the Star Chamber was to deal with offenders and case with which the common-law courts could not deal; the Court of Requests administered to poor men a justice which they could not obtain elsewhere; the Council of the North and of Wales reduced to order turbulent districts which had defied ordinary methods; Chancery distributed equity where the common law failed to provide a remedy The special command of the King was a sufficient warrant for the arrest of a political suspect, whose guilt was known to the government but could not be stated in public, or conveniently proved in a court of law.

All this was tolerated so long as it was done in the national interests; but the system became intolerable when it was administered by the government, not on behalf of the nation, but against the nation on behalf of the government. It was only practicable so long as the nation consented, and the nation would only consent so long as it felt the need of special protection and agreed with the policy of the government. This condition began to disappear with the defeat of the Spanish Armada, and from that date the influence of Roman civil law, and of the ideas of prerogative government, began to decline in England, though the struggle between the two sets of ideas fills much of the history of the seventeenth century. On the one side we have Bacon, Cowell, Hobbes, the Chancery lawyers, and the Stuarts; on the other we have Coke

Selden, Prynne, the common lawyers, and Parliament, who insisted on the supremacy of the common law, and sought to restrict the operation of reasons of State and of the prerogative within the narrowest possible limits. They denied the necessity for what the French call *droit administratif;* they asserted that the servants of the government must be tried by ordinary tribunals even for offences committed in the discharge of their official duties; no one was to be arrested or imprisoned merely for reasons of State; there must be a definite legal charge. The Crown was not above the law; Parliamentary privileges were matters of right and not of grace; the executive must be controlled by the legislature, the popular representative.

The struggle was of world-wide importance. In 1610 Dr. Cowell's *Interpreter,* a book which asserted the prerogative in its most aggressive form, was burned by the common hangman at the order of Parliament. It was an indication of the coming victory of the common law. A year before, in 1609, the Virginia Company had been founded, and ten years later the Pilgrim Fathers set sail. The founders of England's colonial empire carried over the seas no despotic maxims, derived from the Roman civil law and embodied in Dr. Cowell's book, no ideas of the exemption of governments from the ordinary law and from the control of Parliament. They took with them, in their hearts and minds, the principle that there should be but one law, and by that law all men should be governed; and upon that foundation a hundred legislatures more or less are built and are building all over the world to-day. In 1619 elected burgesses met at Jamestown in Virginia, formed the first legislative assembly in the New World, and the first-born child of the mother of Parliaments saw the light. Those children are now spread over the earth, and every one has been nurtured and fed on the doctrine that the common law is supreme and not reasons of State or the will of the Prince.

That characteristic differentiates the English constitution, and those based upon it, from nearly all other constitutions in the world; and it may be worth while attempting to suggest a reason for this singular phenomenon. National character will not do as an explanation, unless no better can be found; and a better can be found in environment. Compare, for instance, the circumstances under which the last great constitutional changes took place in France and England. I refer to the establishment of the present French Republic in 1870, and the establishment of constitutional monarchy in England at the Revolution of 1688; and we shall see how those circumstances dictated one sort of constitution in France and another sort of constitution in England. In 1870-71 France was in the midst of the most disastrous war it has waged in modern times. German forces occupied the greater part of its territory; the capital underwent two sieges; the Commune established a reign of terror in its midst. Enemies from without devastated and dismembered it; enemies from within threatened it with domestic revolution. It was not a time when men were likely to think much about the liberty of the subject or the sovereignty of law. National existence was at stake; the supreme question was not how to guard with minute and scrupulous care the rights of the individual against the State, but how to save the State at any cost. A government had first to be organised and protected, and equipped with the means for crushing anarchy, before the individual could think of liberty. Reasons of State had to prevail over individual rights, and the government of France was hedged about with privileges, prerogatives, and powers of which the government of England did not feel the need.

Very different were the circumstances of what Burke loved to call the happy and glorious Revolution of 1688. The supreme question then was not how to protect England from invasion or from anarchy, but how to protect the liberty, property, and religion of English subjects against

he attacks of an arbitrary government. It was not the
State, but the individual, that was in danger. There was
no need to surround the government with special safeguards,
o protect it by administrative privileges, and entrust its
nterests to prerogative courts. And so the prohibitions
are addressed not to the people, but to the sovereign ; and
he Bill of Rights is a whole Decalogue of commandments
which the king was not to break. In this island the laws
were not drowned amid the clash of arms, nor individual
liberty sacrificed in the interests of the State. The simple
and obvious fact that Great Britain is an island has woven
itself in a thousand ways into the texture of English history.
f in England and nowhere else freedom has slowly
broadened down from precedent to precedent, it is because,
n Shakespeare's phrase, England is bound in with the
triumphant sea, because Nature had defined her frontiers
and thus relieved her of the greatest of national tasks ;
because, in working out her career and in developing her
constitution, she has not been hampered and beset by that
incessant fear of foreign foes which has interrupted and
retarded the growth of freedom on the Continent.

Hitherto we have been dealing with the more practical
aspect of political ideas, with that side of them which lies
nearest to actual history. But it is necessary to say
something about the two great writers of the seventeenth
century who regarded these questions from a more detached
and philosophic point of view. Of these two Hobbes is
he apologist of absolute monarchy, Locke of the Revolution
of 1688. But Hobbes, although he passed nearly the whole
of his life in the Stuart period, is really the exponent of
Tudor, and not of Stuart, ideals. He was a Freethinker,
and there was little divine in his idea of the State; but his
heory approached more nearly the divine right of the
sixteenth, than the divine hereditary right of the seventeenth century. His sovereign, while absolute in theory,
must be effective in practice; if he ceased to afford his
subjects protection, they might throw off his authority,

L 2

and this passage rendered Hobbes suspect to the Cavaliers. The *Leviathan* was begun about 1642 and was published in 1651; its demand for a *de facto* absolute sovereign would suit Oliver Cromwell much better than the King over the Water, who had nothing except the *de jure* claim of heredity; and Hobbes was accused of trimming his sails to catch the Cromwellian breeze. Another point about Hobbes's sovereign roused royalist suspicion; he must have the right of appointing his successor: that was the essential thing, but the successor need not be the eldest son, and divine hereditary right was unceremoniously thrown over. Again, Hobbes's sovereign might be an assembly; he need not necessarily be a monarch; but in all cases he must be absolute.

Hobbes's demonstration of this truth is his greatest contribution to political science, and it has been generally accepted in modern times. It is the philosophical expression of the maturity of the State which had grown from childish weakness into theoretical omnicompetence; and Hobbes is the great exponent of the idea, of which Luther and Machiavelli had been the god-parents. We do not to-day regard the State as divine or of divine ordination; but we practically admit that its authority is without legal limit. There are many things which it may be unwise for the State to do, and some would set up against it a divine right of the Church, and others a divine right of the individual; but these are abstract rights, the real existence of which is not open to practical demonstration. A legal right is the only right which can be legally enforced; and legal right can only be granted and sanctioned by the State, which can make anything legal that it likes. This power can be delegated, but it cannot be divided; no other authority can be admitted as co-ordinate with the sovereign State: and Hobbes was perfectly right in pointing out the impossibility of dividing sovereignty between Parliament and the King. But he failed to anticipate the modern refinement of a distinction between legal and political sovereignty. In Great Britain to-day the legal sovereign is Parliament, the political sovereign is the electorate. An Act of Parliament may be law in defiance of all the electors; and all the electors together cannot themselves make a law. But they choose their legal sovereign, and the authority of that sovereign is absolute. It is absolute over the Church in theory if not in practice, and Hobbes was especially severe against the Puritans who revived the medieval idea of divine right of the Church. Nor had individual conscience any rights against the State; the individual was bound to obey even against his conscience, and Hobbes quoted for his comfort the licence granted by Elisha to Naaman to bow in the House of Rimmon. There was only one class of men who were bound to go to the stake rather than to violate conscience, and that was the clergy. It is the only clerical privilege that Hobbes was prepared to grant.

The other great theory, embedded in Hobbes's *Leviathan*, is that the State is founded on an original contract by which every one is bound. The idea was not by any means new: it had been used both in England and abroad during the sixteenth century. It occurs in the 'judicious Hooker'; it was adopted in turn by the Huguenots and by the Catholic League in France. The Huguenots employed it to limit the authority of Catherine de' Medici and Henry III; the League to keep out Henry IV. According to them the contract was threefold, between God, King, and People; a breach of its implied terms on one part absolved the others from their obligations. Henry of Navarre had broken the contract with God by becoming a heretic; therefore the Catholic people, with divine concurrence, might elect another king, a Guise. In spite of the theological ends which this contract theory was made to serve, it seems to have really been an unconscious attempt to provide a more rationalistic origin for the State than that of divine ordination.

Hobbes, at any rate, had no theological ends to serve;

and his idea of the contract differed from that of hi
predecessors. They had conceived a contract betweer
sovereign and subjects, binding both of them. Hobbe
would not admit that the sovereign could be bound; the
contract, he said, was not between sovereign and subjects
but between all individual subjects to make a sovereign
The people simply agreed among themselves to set up ar
absolute sovereignty. Hobbes explains this complete
surrender of their liberties by the conditions of the State
of nature, in which men lived before the institution of civi
society. The State of nature is, he says, a state of war in
which every man's hand is against every one else's, in
which force and fraud are the two cardinal virtues, and in
which the life of man is 'solitary, poor, nasty, brutish
and short.' Men in fact had no option; they were in no
position to make terms with the sovereign. Any means o
escape was better than their existing condition; the mos
despotic government was an improvement on anarchy
There is some truth in this as an account of the abstrac
idea of sovereignty, though one must divest it of the
accidental characteristics of the seventeenth century. The
great objection to it as a description of the origin of the
State is that it is purely unhistorical; there never was any
contract at all; at no time did men meet together and
agree to set up sovereignty. Sovereignty was not made
it grew; like the State, it is a child at first, and Hobbes'
idea is a reflection of the State in its manhood. Historically
too, we know that in primitive times there could be no such
thing as a contract between individuals, for the individua
had no individuality; it was not he, but the family or the
tribe, which was the unit of society; and the developmen
of the individual is one of the latest growths of time.

The first reply to Hobbes did not come from Locke, the
apologist of the Whigs, but from Sir Robert Filmer, who
was a more orthodox Tory of the Stuart type than Hobbe.
himself; and in his *Patriarcha* he set himself to provide
a political theory which should not be capable of mis

interpretation in the interests of a Cromwell. It seems at first sight fantastic in the extreme. Sovereignty he deduces by hereditary descent from Adam and the Patriarchs, whose representatives the Stuarts were in Great Britain. But there is more in Filmer than appears on the surface. He perceives the unhistorical character of the contract theory, and tries to give sovereignty an historical basis, although his history is bad. He also perceives how both the theories of a contract and of absolute sovereignty could be used against the royalist and Anglican position in England. There was a fundamental agreement between the Jesuit and the Calvinist political theory. Both Parsons and Buchanan had asserted that kings might be deposed : Calvin and Bellarmine, writes Filmer, both look asquint this way; and the only protection against them was the divine hereditary right of James 1. This theory had in fact been adopted by the royalists and the Anglican Church, and it was their belief in it which produced the Nonjurors of William III and Mary's reign. Anglican divines of the sixteenth century would have had no difficulty in swearing allegiance to a *de facto* king like William III. It was the hereditary taint, introduced by James 1, which led the Church to abandon the canons of 1606 and led Sancroft into difficulties.

Locke's two *Treatises of Civil Government* were written in reply to Filmer, but he feels that Hobbes is the more serious antagonist, and the more solid portions of the book deal with Hobbes's theory. Locke had little difficulty in dealing with Filmer's history and with a sovereignty whose title was derived from Abraham. But in order to meet Hobbes, he abandons the historical argument and reverts to the theory of a contract. It is usually said that Locke supplied the Whigs of 1688 with a philosophical basis for their action at the Revolution : it is rather a philosophical *apologia;* for the *Two Treatises* were not published until two years after the event, in 1690. This circumstance is a reminder of the fact that political philosophy is not generally the parent of political action, but a deduction from the accomplished fact. The *Two Treatises* are, however, an embodiment of the principles of the Revolution, and were taken as a refutation and repudiation of the *Leviathan* of Hobbes. Locke does not, perhaps, reject the theory of sovereignty so much as readjust the *habitat* of that sovereignty. The State was just as omnicompetent after the Revolution as before; but the exercise of its sovereignty is not left at the uncontrolled arbitrament of the monarchy. It is entrusted to a composite entity; and the sovereign power is no longer the king alone, but the King in Parliament. Hobbes had imagined a contract by which all power was surrendered into the hands of an external authority; Locke imagined a contract by which certain powers were delegated to the monarch, while others were to be exercised conjointly by the monarch and a representative assembly. Men in fact had made terms with the sovereign, who was bound by those terms. They were not in the parlous condition fancied by Hobbes the state of nature was not a state of war; force and fraud were not the cardinal virtues before the institution of civil society. Those phrases only described the condition of wicked men; but men were not all wicked before the contract. Morals in fact existed before politics, and were not, as Hobbes seems to have thought, a deduction from politics. Before there was a law of the State, there was a law of Nature which kept men from the orgies imagined by Hobbes. Their condition was tolerable, they could afford to bargain with the sovereign, and set limits to his authority. The contract was made not for the sake of existence, but for the sake of a better existence, for the benefits of civil society. These benefits were endangered by absolute monarchy: the Stuarts had transgressed the original terms of the contract, and usurped more than their allotted share of power. The people were justified, therefore, in holding themselves quit of their engagement, and making a fresh contract elsewhere.

This is the theory of the English Revolution, but Locke was perhaps less important as its apologist than as the progenitor of Rousseau. He would not have recognised his progeny, but that is sometimes the case : and Rousseau put the contract theory to uses which would have horrified the Whigs. Hobbes had left sovereignty entire in the hands of the monarch, Locke associated monarch and people in its exercise, Rousseau restored it all to the people. They alone were the legitimate wielders of sovereignty, every other sovereign was a usurper. Man was born free, yet everywhere he was in chains because the people had been cheated of their heritage by priests and kings. The only way to reform the world was to restore the sovereignty of the people ; and on that basis the French Revolutionists went to work.

Rousseau was the last great exponent of the contract theory ; indeed, before his book appeared, the bottom had really been knocked out of it by Montesquieu, the parent of modern historical method in political science. Nothing could have been less historical or less true than Rousseau's dogmas. Man is not born free ; he is born helpless, and freedom is of little use to the infant. It can only be granted him gradually in exceedingly small doses. He is born into conditions which determine his life ; and Montesquieu sought to trace the influence, and show the importance of environment upon the development of man and his institutions. He rejected the abstract, *a priori,* method of the contractual school. It by no means followed that the same thing was true or beneficial in all circumstances. Mankind required different systems in different circumstances. Where only a few are capable of rule, the few must rule ; democracy is only possible where the many have attained a certain degree of intelligence, self-knowledge and self-control. Climate may make all the difference ; self-government does not flourish in the tropics ; nor tyranny in the temperate zones. Every political system must be judged with reference to its circumstances and not by abstract theories.

These are the contentions of the historical school, of which in England Sir Henry Maine was the chief exponent. He applied to political institutions the same kind of reasoning that Darwin applied to the natural world. Gradual evolution and not sudden creation was the history of both. The State did not originate in a single act, a contract; it developed from the family and tribe. Divine right, whether of the Church, the State, or the individual, and abstract rights derived from an imaginary secular contract, all disappeared from political science, though not from popular politics. States and constitutions have to stand on their own legs without the support of abstract rights, divine or other; they stand or they fall by their adaptability to changing needs, and the idea of development has supplanted that of fixed adherence to a prehistoric type. Theories of divine right, whether of Churches, or States, or individuals, have happily failed to petrify human institutions, and have all given way to a divine law of progress. The one immutable factor in human affairs is their infinite mutability.

IX

CHURCH AND STATE IN ENGLAND AND SCOTLAND

OF all the factors which have contributed to the making of the British Empire, none is more important than the Union between England and Scotland. It is difficult to imagine what the empire would be like without its Scottish ingredients; and it is a commonplace, that wherever in the British dominions there is a good thing, there you will find a Scot not very far off. Scots not only govern themselves, but others as well; no one ever dreams of making anybody but a Scot Secretary of State for Scotland; and soon, it would seem, no one but a Scot need apply for the post of Prime Minister; the present Premier[1] and both the living ex-Premiers are Scots.[2] Independence offers as few attractions to the Scots as the Zionist ideal does to most of the Jews; for it is poor sport ruling and financing yourselves when you can rule and finance other people.

But the mutual affection between English and Scots is of modern growth. During the two centuries with which we are dealing the blood-relationship between the two races showed itself in a somewhat sanguinary fashion; and English and Scots fought face to face, and not side by side, on the field of battle. Protector Somerset had the right object in view when he spoke of a united realm which, having the sea for its wall, mutual love for its garrison, and God for its defence, need not in peace be ashamed, or in war afraid of any worldly power; and he had some

[1] Sir H. Campbell-Bannerman.
[2] Lords Rosebery and Balfour [Mr. Bonar Law and Mr. Ramsay MacDonald are additions to the list].

155

notion of how these things were to be achieved when he said that the way was, not to win by force but to conciliate by love, to leave Scotland her own laws and customs, to establish free trade, to abolish the distinction of aliens between the two kingdoms, and to call the united realm the Empire of Great Britain. But even he fought the battle of Pinkie, and Pinkie is but one link in the chain which stretches from Flodden Field to Culloden Moor. Solway Moss, Dunbar, Killiecrankie, Sheriffmuir, and Prestonpans seemed to show that, whether England was ruled by Tudor King or by homespun Protector, by Dutch William or by German George, she would find insuperable antipathies north of the Tweed, or at least of the Forth.

This antipathy has been ascribed to a variety of causes, ranging from an inherent and mutual repugnance between Saxon and Gael to the effects of a single battle. One writer attributes to Pinkie, not only such immediate results as the revival of French influence in Scotland and the marriage of Mary Stuart to the Dauphin, but comprehensive phenomena like the divergence between the English and the Scottish Reformations, the refusal of both realms to complete the Union in 1603, and the hatreds which found expression in Dunbar and Worcester. It is rather a long list of fatalities to follow a single battle, but even greater results have been put down to the fact that Cleopatra's nose was of just the right length to fascinate Julius Cæsar and Mark Antony. Flodden Field and Solway Moss might perhaps have done as well as Pinkie, but for the fact that Somerset's statesmanship is a more conventional mark for critical arrows than that of Henry VIII; and, in any case, this kind of criticism mistakes the occasion for the cause and the cause for the effect. The divergence of the English and Scottish Reformations and the failure of the attempted union in 1603 were due to causes which went a great deal deeper than any single battle or series of campaigns.

To sum up this divergence, it may be said that England in the seventeenth century was Erastian, while Scotland was theocratic; and my object at this moment is to explain and illustrate this statement. Now, Erastianism is a vague word with many meanings; it is derived from a German doctor of the sixteenth century, Thomas Lieber, whose name, like that of Melanchthon and a host of others, was translated into a Greek form, Erastus. His view was that the State, and not the Church, should exercise coercive jurisdiction. But it has been denied that Erastus was Erastian, just as it may be maintained that Machiavelli was not really Machiavellian; and the modern use of the word seems to imply a right on the part of the State to set up any creed it likes and compel its subjects to acknowledge it. Erastus himself died in exile rather than admit this: and modern Erastianism is rather the policy adopted by Henry VIII and expounded by Thomas Hobbes. Without attempting any exact definition, we may perhaps say that a country is Erastian where the State, and theocratic where the Church, is the predominant partner.

Now in England in the sixteenth century there is no doubt that the State is the predominant partner. The Reformation is a naked and brutal assertion of that fact, which no amount of ingenuity can explain away. It was forced on the Church and against its will by the State, and it was not till late in Elizabeth's reign that the Church accorded a conscientious assent to a settlement extorted from it by force. In Henry VIII's reign the pretence of consulting the Church through Convocation and the pretence of electing Bishops by Chapters were kept up. But Chapters had to elect the royal nominee within twelve days under pain of *praemunire*. Even the taxes the Church imposed on itself could not be collected till Parliament gave its consent. The only check which Henry experienced from Convocation was when it inserted the qualifying phrase *so far as the law of Christ allows* in its recognition of the royal supremacy, and this has been represented as an act of courage. It was no more than a feeble effort of Convocation to save its face, and the Imperial ambassador pointed out that no one would venture to dispute with Henry as to where his supremacy ended and that of Christ began. Even these pretences were abandoned in Edward's reign, when Bishops were appointed merely by Royal Letters Patent, and when books of Common Prayer were enacted without reference to Convocation. 'Parliament establisheth forms of religion,' says Sir Thomas Smith, who was Dean of Carlisle as well as Secretary of State; and it was Parliament alone which gave legal sanction to the Elizabethan settlement.

Now the question we have to solve is, How came it to be possible to treat the Church in this cavalier fashion? In other words, why was Parliament so much stronger than Convocation? The answer is that Parliament represented the feelings of the predominant middle classes and Convocation represented only the clergy; it did not even represent the Church in our modern sense of the word. Nowadays we speak of a Churchman in distinction to any kind of nonconformist, and the Church party includes a number of eminent laymen. In those days no layman could be described as a Churchman; the Churchman was always an ecclesiastic, and only such were represented in Convocation; the rest of the people, who all belonged to the Church, were represented by Parliament. Convocation was thus the organ of a class, almost a privileged caste, whose privileges existed at the expense of the laity; and thus it could not be the organ of the mass of the people. Nevertheless, this privileged class had been able to hold most of what it called its own throughout the greater part of the Middle Ages, because it had represented all the education and almost all the intelligence and the enthusiasm of that time. That was no longer the case; enthusiasm had largely forsaken the Church; education was no longer its speciality; intelligence had spread to the middle and upper class laity; and even piety had ceased to be mainly professional. The solid foundations upon which clerical power and privilege had been based had disappeared, and with them went the acquiescence of men in clerical guidance and governance, in clerical pride and prerogative.

The monopoly of the Church had broken down long before the sixteenth century; but for that fact, the Reformation would not have been possible. The laity had invaded the professions; they had learned to read, to write, and to think. The greatest educator in the fifteenth century was Caxton, and the printing-press was no respecter of parsons; the greatest writer of English prose in the sixteenth century was a layman, Sir Thomas More; and the only clerical poet of note was the scandalous Skelton. The new forces of commerce, industry, and geographical discovery were in the hands of the laymen; and the enthusiasm was patriotism, a national spirit unsympathetic to cosmopolitan clericalism. Of this new public opinion Parliament was the focus and the voice. It represented a national feeling which had not existed before, although this representation was for a time concealed by the predominance of the monarchy and the union between King and Parliament. The alliance of these two representatives of the State was irresistible by the enfeebled Church. Hence Parliament prevails over Convocation, State over Church, and England becomes Erastian.

In Scotland the situation was curiously reversed. Parliament was weak, and the Church, as reformed by John Knox and Melville, was strong. To explain the weakness of the Scottish Parliament, we should have to go far back into the Middle Ages and into some intricate questions of legal and constitutional history. We can only indicate one or two points. Scotland did not achieve internal unity so soon as England; she had no Henry II to create a native common law strong enough to resist the inroads of the Roman law; and the victory of Roman law across the Border is at the bottom of the divergence between the present English and Scottish legal systems. This lack of common law was inimical to Parliamentary development; and Parliament in Scotland was only a system of Estates similar to those which sank into impotence on the Continent. There was no shire representation as in England, and only tenants-in-chief could exercise the vote : the freeholder, that backbone of the English Parliament, was unknown ; and there was no co-operation between the various social classes. The boroughs stood alone, and only boroughs on the royal demesne were represented at all. Legislation was enacted by the Privy Council and not by the Estates. It was a mere *simulacrum* of a Parliament ; and, when it met, it delegated its functions to a committee or clique known as the Lords of the Articles. No strong monarchy had fashioned this feudal assembly into a modern Parliament ; a series of infant kings and disputed regencies had prolonged the feudal agony into the sixteenth century, and Ruthven raids and Gowrie plots were still the custom of the country. Kings are kidnapped as of old, and 'bands' are formed against a Queen, though the feudal 'band' has been converted, and calls itself a Covenant. We hear much of these things, but little enough of Parliament ; for Parliament is weak, and is no organ or no trumpet on which a middle class can play..

The ultimate reason, of course, was that Scotland had no middle class requiring an organ to express or to relieve its feelings. Scotland had been poor and pastoral : only industry and commerce can make a Parliament. When Russia has a middle class proportionate to its size and population, it will also have a Duma which will not be dismissed. But Scotland in the sixteenth century was developing a trade, and consequently a middle class. 'During no previous period,' says a Scottish historian, 'had the Scottish people taken such a forward stride at once in material well-being and political importance. Mary's reign saw the end of feudalism in Scotland and the appearance of a middle class, which was thenceforward to determine the development of the country. It is the sensational events of Mary's reign that have drawn attention to it beyond every reign in Scottish history ; but, in truth, its highest interest and importance lie in this transference of moral and political force from the nobles to the people.' Scotland, like England, was achieving national consciousness with the progress of its people in wealth and education ; and this new national feeling was trying to find a voice and clamouring to be heard.

Parliament did not and could not respond : some other organ had to be provided, some other vehicle and outlet for public opinion. It was found in the Assembly of the Presbyterian Church; it is there, and not in what has been called 'the blighted and stunted conclave of the three Estates,' that you hear the voice of Scotland in the sixteenth and seventeenth centuries. There you have the secret of the strength of the Church in Scotland. The Church had reformed itself in spite of the State : it had not been reformed by the State in spite of itself; the reformer in Scotland is a minister of religion and not a minister of State, a John Knox and not a Thomas Cromwell. The Reformation was adopted by the Church in Scotland as a matter of faith and conviction, not one of convenience and submission to the monarch. The wrath of the King might mean death in Edinburgh as well as in London, but John Knox never used that plea of Warham's. 'Here lies one,' said the Regent Morton at Knox's grave, 'who never feared the face of man' ; and there was no hang-dog look of defeat and a conscience ill at ease among the new presbyters of Scotland. The Kirk could hold up its head in a fashion impossible for ecclesiastics who accepted Henry VIII, Edward VI, Mary and Elizabeth in turn as orthodox defenders of the faith, and who did not know whether to call themselves Protestants or Catholics. 'Throughout all the troubles of that anxious time,' a modern high Churchman has written of a Tudor turncoat, 'he remained unshaken in his fidelity to the national religion.' The Vicar of Bray, you may remember, was equally staunch to the national religion. That sort of fidelity was rare in Scotland, and the Church had the strength of its convictions and the consciousness of the national support. It reaped the reward of its boldness: it did not halt between two opinions; it rode the whirl-wind and directed the storm of religious revolution. The Reformation in Scotland is the triumph of the Church; and the Church is vastly stronger after than before the change, because it made itself the mouthpiece of the nation, and fulfilled a function abandoned by the Parliament.

That is not the only, or, perhaps, the most essential point. The great cause of the weakness of Convocation in England was its exclusively ecclesiastical composition; it was a conclave, in which the laity had no part nor lot. The Kirk in Scotland avoided that mistake; its assemblies were not composed of ministers alone. In the kirk-sessions of the parish, in the presbyteries, in the General Assembly itself, laymen sat side by side with ministers as deacons or lay-elders. In the gatherings of the Kirk, from the lowest to the highest grades, the Scottish layman found a sphere of activity and self-government, which was denied him in the Scottish Parliament.

Hence Scotland becomes theocratic and not Erastian. The voice of the people sounds through an ecclesiastical, and not a secular organ; and every popular movement in Scotland takes an ecclesiastical colour. Is a popular protest to be made? It does not take the form of a Grand Remonstrance or a Petition of Right, but of a National League and Covenant. Is a tyrant to be murdered? The victim will be an Archbishop Sharp and not a Duke of Buckingham. Are guarantees to be extorted from a King? Charles II will have to sign the Covenant in Scotland, while William III accepts the Declaration of Right in England. Instead of a Speaker being held in his chair in a House of Commons at Westminster, a stool will be hurled at a preacher in St. Giles', Edinburgh. Scotland calls its civil wars the first and second Bishops' Wars; its revolts are Covenanting raids, and even its generals are

ometimes preachers : it was they who appealed to the God
of Battles at Dunbar and ruined the campaign.

The real Parliament of Scotland is the Congregation, and
ts real platform is the pulpit. Scotland is more anxious
or the freedom of the pulpit than for privilege of Parlia-
nent. While Peter and Paul Wentworth were fighting for
reedom of speech in the House of Commons, Andrew
Melville was claiming in 1584 that a seditious harangue
vas privileged because it had been delivered from the
pulpit; and in 1596 the ministers laid down the principle
hat in the pulpit they were free to say what they pleased.
Privilege was needed to combat the divine right of kings
ust as much in Scotland as south of the Border; for
ames VI's pretensions were as high as those of James I,
nd he was less controlled by the Roman law of Scotland
han by the common law of England. Parliament in
cotland was unequally matched with the King, and
cottish servility was concentrated in the three Estates.
Divine right of Kings is opposed in Scotland, not by common
aw and Parliamentary privilege, but by divine right of the
Church. The opponents of the Crown are not Parliamentarians like Pym or common lawyers like Coke, but
Presbyterian ministers like Melville and John Knox. .

And here we come across one of the singularities of the
cottish Reformation. While the Scottish Church assimi-
ated Calvinistic dogma and adopted the extremest possible
ntipathy to Roman ritual and doctrine, it took up, in its
elations with the State, the identical position which the
apacy had assumed from the eleventh century onwards.
Melville talks of the two kingdoms, Church and State, in
anguage which might have been borrowed from Hilde-
rand : the Church was a visible kingdom, the rival if not
le superior of the State. Another minister threatens
ames with the fate of Jeroboam, just as popes threatened
ings with the fate of Nero, Sennacherib, and any other
monarch who happened to have come to an evil end.
Melville told James to his face that he was but 'God's

silly vassal.' Kings might be deposed for their sins by the people. 'Cardinal Bellarmine and Calvin,' says Filmer, 'both look asquint this way'; and one Scottish minister took it upon himself to excommunicate Charles II by his own authority. The second Book of Discipline asserted that the civil magistrate ought to 'hear and obey' the voice of the minister; the Church claimed the right of inflicting penalties and of demanding that the State should carry them out : just as in medieval times the ecclesiastical courts had condemned men to the fire and handed them over to the secular arm to be burnt. 'New Presbyter,' says Milton, 'is but old priest writ large.'

This is the fundamental antagonism between England and Scotland in the sixteenth and seventeenth centuries. Against this theory of dual control of Church and State, against these claims to a coercive jurisdiction exercised by the clergy, the English Reformation was a protest. The men who supported Henry VIII had no idea of toleration, and no hatred of persecution in itself; but they wanted the persecution done by the State and not by the Church, and they would tolerate no divided authority, no organisation competing with the State for men's allegiance. On this issue the Pope and Calvin were at one against Luther, Erastus, and Cranmer, not to speak of Machiavelli, Filmer, and Hobbes; and to this antagonism between Protestants is largely due the success of the Counter Reformation. That is why we find Lutherans preferring to fight for Catholics in France against Calvinist Huguenots; it is why Presbyterian and Independent fight one another at Dunbar and Worcester. From this point of view, the Reformation in Scotland was a reaction to medieval ideas against the modern conception of the State. It was not permanent, and even the Papacy has implicitly abandoned its medieval position. The Pope no longer tries to deprive heretics of their thrones; he merely defines the faith. From being lord of lords he has become merely a teacher of teachers. The Church has ceased to trespass on secular domains, and has retired for the most part into its more proper spiritual sphere. So, too, Presbyterian ministers do not as a rule resort to excommunication, nor expect the State to execute their judgments. But, while these pretensions lasted, they caused much friction between the sister-kingdoms, which might have been avoided had Scotland found a secular voice in her Parliament of the sixteenth century.

On the other hand there is something to be said. However highly we estimate the courage and tenacity of the English Parliament in resisting the divine right of kings, it may be doubted whether the Kirk was not a more stubborn obstacle in the path of the Stuarts; and it is difficult to see how that divine right could have been overthrown in England in the seventeenth century without the help of the Scots and their divine right of the Church. Charles I's eleven years' tyranny might have gone on indefinitely, but for the need of money to maintain an army against the Scots. The financial expedients of Noy and his colleagues sufficed for the King's ordinary needs, and it was the Scots who compelled him to summon the Short and then the Long Parliament. The Scottish Kirk had struck before the English Parliament, and divine right rebelled before the common law.

Even in England itself the backbone of resistance to the Stuarts was ecclesiastical. Laud was brought to the block as well as Stafford and Charles I; and Parliament would not have been either so determined or so ferocious, had it not also been Puritan and Presbyterian. The old priest writ large was not confined to Scotland; his voice was heard in the mouth of Cartwright, Travers, and Wilcox, though their note is not so clear as that of Knox and Melville. They were Puritan rather than Presbyterian; and, in spite of their theological views, they could not escape the national atmosphere. Parliament was more to them than it was to the Scots, and the divine right of the Church was less. They were ready enough to appeal to Parliament to establish their religion, and said more about the popery of the Church than about its independence. The reason was that they had expectations from Parliament, which Knox and Melville had not from the Scottish Estates. The English Parliament reflected national sentiment in all its forms, and thus it sometimes spoke in ecclesiastical tones. English Puritan ministers had more to hope from Parliament than from the Crown, or from the Bishops and Convocation; and so, although ecclesiastics themselves, they appealed to the lay, and not to the ecclesiastical assembly. Hence it was that Puritanism in England did not foster theocracy, as it did in Scotland, and England is less theocratic than Scotland, even when Puritanism is dominant in both.

Nevertheless, the English Presbyterians were more theocratic than the mass of Englishmen liked, and it was their efforts to impose a Presbyterian system upon England which divided the Roundhead party, led to the military rule of Cromwell, and finally to the Restoration of Charles II. From the first, indeed, there were opponents of the Crown and the Bishops who were not Presbyterians. Most of these were independents or Congregationalists, who believed that the original *ecclesia* or church was the congregation, and that each congregation had the right to manage its own affairs without interference from the State, from bishops, or from synods. The names of their leaders, such as Cromwell and Milton, are familiar household words, and the part they played in history is known to all. But there were other enemies of the Anglican Church, as represented by Laud, whose hostility arose, not so much from theological antipathy, as from dislike of the political pretensions of the prelates : and these men were hostile to ecclesiastical claims from whatever quarter they proceeded. They detested the new presbyter just as much as they did the old priest, and their main concern was to uphold the supremacy of State over Church, whether the Church was Catholic or Protestant, Anglican or Presbyterian. They were Erastians, pure and simple.

Of these men the chief was the great lawyer, Selden, who had made a sensation and fame early in his career by writing a book on tithes, in which he attacked the divine origin of that institution, and denied the divine right of the clergy to receive them. For even after the Reformation, the Church claimed a divine right, though it took a financial form. This was not the only contention which brought Selden into collision with the Anglican Church. 'All is as the state pleases,,' he says in his *Table Talk*. And again, 'every law is a contract between the king and the people, and therefore to be kept.' Such principles were destructive of the claims to *jus divinum* alike of kings, bishops, and presbyters; and they were as distasteful to the Scottish divines at the Westminster Assembly as they had been to Charles 1 and Archbishop Laud. During those famous discussions, Selden employed his immense learning to humble, as Fuller says, the *jure-divinoship* of Presbytery; but a rift in the Puritan union of hearts had appeared before the Westminster Assembly met. When Pym threw the Scottish sword into the balance between King and Parliament, the Scots demanded, as the price of their alliance, that there should be a religious covenant between the two nations as well as a civil league; and they wanted to pledge the English Parliament to a remodelling of the Anglican Church ' according to the example of the best-reformed churches,' that is to say, their own. But, through the skill of Sir Henry Vane the younger, there was added the clause 'and the Word of God.' The Scots could not very well resist the addition of this clause, for that would be to admit that their own Church was not according to the Word of God; at the same time, its adoption opened the door for Independency, and, indeed, for any other form of Christian church, for no one would admit that his own particular church was not according to the Word of God. The Scots, doubtless, trusted to the influence of their military and political strength to make their interpretation prevail; and, assuredly, it would have done so, had it not

been for the unforeseen development of Cromwell's Iron-
sides; and the issue, which had been debated at the
Westminster Assembly, was fought out at Dunbar and
Worcester.

Dunbar was the death-blow to the theocratic and
presbyterian system. The Covenanters had done everything which could, according to their principles, insure
success. They had sought to purge their army of every
taint which might bring down the wrath of Heaven upon
the chosen people of God; Charles II had been forced to
declare that he was 'deeply humbled and afflicted in spirit
before God because of his father's opposition to the work
of God.' Even so, he was kept at a distance from the
army, let his presence involve it in the condemnation of
Achan. With the same object a commission was appointed
to weed out from the army every soldier who did not come
up to the requisite standard of godliness. Some four
thousand troops were thus cashiered on the eve of the
battle of Dunbar, and, in the words of a royalist historian,
the army was left to 'ministers' sons, clerks, and such
other sanctified creatures, who hardly ever saw or heard of
any sword but that of the Spirit.' This army made texts
do duty for tactics; Leslie was overruled, and Cromwell
snatched victory out of the tightest corner he ever was in.
Before the campaign had opened, Cromwell besought the
divines to think it possible that they were mistaken, and
Dunbar must have caused many searchings of heart. From
it may perhaps be dated the decline of the Covenanting
spirit in Scotland. The ministers, it is true, continued to
strive as before, and the Covenanters split into two factions,
the Remonstrants and the Engagers, one attributing their
failure to their connection with a godless king, the other
ascribing it to the folly of the zealots. But this distraction
only weakened the Kirk, and facilitated the work of
Cromwell's government in Scotland.

It would be absurd to pretend that Scotland was content
with the English domination; but that rule gave it a

period of prosperity, sound administration, and peace, such as Scotland had not known before. In particular, it was not a persecuting government itself, and to some extent it prevented persecution by others. Fanaticism was thus deprived a sustenance, and materially abated. A secular spirit of compromise begins to appear, and to soften the rancour of theological debate; and it was this spirit of compromise which alone could make possible any real union by consent between the English and the Scottish peoples. The union effected under the Commonwealth and Protectorate lacked this essential condition of consent; the Scots considered the thirty M.P.'s allotted them on the basis of wealth and population to be a ridiculously inadequate recognition of their moral and intellectual importance. These members were generally the nominees of the government, and the legality of their position was challenged on that score. They were, said one member, a wooden leg tied to a natural body, and that kind of grafting is not, as a rule, successful.

The Restoration dissolved this union, undid all the work of the last ten years, deprived Scotland of the benefit of the free trade enjoyed with England under Cromwell's union, exposed her to the operation of the Navigation Laws, and plunged her back again into the political and religious bitterness which the tolerant rule of Cromwell had to some extent allayed. When Monck, amid almost universal acclamation, set out to cross the Tweed and restore the Stuarts, he opened the most pitiful chapter in the whole of Scotland's history. The revival of the theories of divine right of kings renewed the necessity for a divine right of presbytery to combat them; and the restoration of persecution as the policy of the government inevitably produced a recrudescence of fanaticism. Hence we get the execution of Argyle, the Pentland rising, the excommunication of Charles II by Craig, the murder of Archbishop Sharp, the battle of Bothwell Brig, and the martyrdom of Margaret Wilson and scores of others The Parliament of

Scotland, as of yore, is no bulwark against the encroachments of the Crown, and the task of saving Scotland's
liberties is left once more to the stubborn temper of the
Kirk, which, like other churches, could stand any test
except that of prosperity.   But the secular spirit had
affected even the Kirk; its resistance to Charles II and
Lauderdale is less national, less unanimous than it had
been to Charles I and Laud.   It is more sectional, more
irresponsible; while some resort to murder and ill-prepared
revolts, others seek favour with the Court. The Cameronians
are a section, the Covenanters of 1638 were a nation.   Part
of this sectionalism was due to the attraction which the
Anglican Church exercised over the higher faction of the
Scottish clergy, the majority of whom had become Episco-
palian by 1688, part to the effects of Charles II's Declara-
tions of Indulgence, but a great deal to a growing immersion
in commercial pursuits, which weakened the theological
bond of union.

One illustration of the fanaticism of this period
has generally been neglected, for obvious reasons, by
Presbyterian historians; and that is the belief in, and
persecution of, witchcraft.   This superstition seems to have
been a particular weakness of extreme Protestants, and we
hear far more of it after the Reformation than we do in the
Middle Ages.   It was not, of course, unknown before the
sixteenth century; Charlemagne had legislated against it,
and the Inquisition had been actively employed against
witchcraft in the fifteenth century.   But it was not until
1563 that the penalty of death was first prescribed for this
offence in Scotland.   This remained the law until 1736,
and it was during the period between the Restoration and
the Revolution that the fury against witches reached its
height.   In the year 1662 alone no fewer than one hundred
and twenty women were burnt as witches in Scotland, and
the total number of victims to this barbarous delusion must
be reckoned by thousands and not by hundreds.   Scotland
was exceptional in this respect, but only in degree, for in

England witches were burnt as late as the eighteenth century, and at Salem, in Massachusetts, there was an appalling outburst of fanaticism against witches in 1692, in which several eminent and esteemed Puritan divines were disgracefully involved. But, as witchcraft has not yet become a respectable creed, these victims of religious persecution have not been honoured with a martyrologist, and occupy but little space in the voluminous pages of ecclesiastical history.

This recrudescence of the theological spirit in Scotland threatened to revive the antagonism between the two kingdoms, and they were only bound together by a common resistance to a despotic government. Not that England herself was without her theological disputes. A German historian carries on his account of the period of the Reformation in England down to 1688; and there is much to be said for the view that the predominant interest in English politics is religious throughout the seventeenth century, and that it is not until the Revolution that the Reformation has worked out its full effect. Not until 1688 are Roman Catholics debarred from the English throne, and, although some High Churchmen would have us believe that the English Church was Protestant before the Reformation, and Catholic after it, the Church was really more Protestant during the eighteenth century than at any other period of its existence. However that may be, there is no denying the power of religious feeling in the reign of Charles II. The so-called Clarendon Code, the Test Act, the rabid fury of Titus Oates's Plot, are ample proof. Anglican fanaticism rules the roost under Clarendon, Protestant fanaticism under Shaftesbury, and Roman Catholic fanaticism under James II. One of the two great aims of Charles II was religious; he wanted to make himself an absolute monarch, but he also wanted to re-introduce the Roman Catholic religion; and it was not until he had realised the impossibility of this second object, and abandoned it, that he succeeded in making himself

absolute for the last four years of his reign.   Had not
James II been a more zealous Romanist, as well as a more
stupid man, and had he not tried to make England Roman
Catholic, as well as to make himself absolute, he might
have made permanent the temporary success of Charles II.

Yet there was, despite this religious atmosphere, a
difference between the England and the Scotland of the
Restoration.   Charles II and Shaftesbury do not strike
one at first sight as natural leaders of religion.   They may
have been leaders of religious parties, but that, after all, is
another matter.   And, even if leaders of religious parties,
they were politicians first and sober leaders of religion last.
Shaftesbury himself, 'a daring pilot in extremity,' as
Dryden calls him, was as inferior in moral character to
Pym as Charles II was to Charles I.   The pagan spirit of
the Restoration pervaded politics and religion, and in the
religious passions of the time there was a good deal more
passion than there was religion.   The contention is not
about doctrine or theology, but about the political power
and privileges to be enjoyed by the members of the various
churches.   The Puritans are not hated because they refuse
to subscribe the Thirty-nine Articles, but because they
had cut off the head of a king, and had closed the theatres.
Romanists are not feared because they believe in Tran-
substantiation, but because they were thought to be in
league with Louis XIV.   The motive was, in fact, largely,
if not mainly, political; and the party leaders use religious
passions for political purposes.   James II was enthusiastically welcomed on his accession, in spite of the fact that
every one knew that he was a Roman Catholic; indeed,
his staunchness to his faith was reckoned one of the points
in his favour.   It was not until he began to dispense with
the laws and with Parliament, and to show an inclination
to set up a military despotism, that the nation began to
distrust him.   The Revolution, while its religious aspect
looks back to the past and consummates the Reformation,
has also its political aspect, which looks forward to the

future and points towards the Reform Bill. It rang out the old religion, but it also rang in the new politics. The curtain came down upon the Reformation, but it rose upon Reform, and a secular, latitudinarian spirit takes the place of the old theological passion.

A similar transformation was coming over Scotland, though it was not by any means so marked. Ever since the battle of Dunbar, religious interests had really been declining in Scotland; and the revived importance of them after the Restoration was a fictitious importance due to the misgovernment of the Stuarts. This becomes evident upon the accession of William III; he was neither an Englishman nor a Scot; coming from abroad, he looked at both countries from a more detached point of view, just as an Englishman sent out to govern India takes a more comprehensive and impartial view of Indian politics than if he had been born a Mahratta, a Sikh, or a Bengali. William was anxious for the maintenance of the existing episcopal organisation of the Church in Scotland, but so liberalised as to comprehend all the Presbyterians. This scheme of comprehension broke down through the unexpected fidelity of the Scottish Episcopalians to James II, and Presbyterianism became the State religion. But the settlement was very different from that of 1647. The Covenants were not renewed: indeed an Act of 1662, which condemned them as unlawful, was allowed to remain in force. Excommunication was deprived of its civil penalties, and the oath of allegiance was adopted, in lieu of all religious tests, as the passport to political office. The majority of Scotsmen were, in fact, turning away from theological disputes, and concerning their interests on that expansion of Scottish commerce which is a marked feature of Scottish history during the latter part of the seventeenth century. The prominent Scotsmen of the reign of William are no longer Presbyterian divines, but financiers, like William Paterson, who founded the Bank of England, or John Law, who sought to revolutionise the French finance. The events which make a stir are not Covenants, but the Darien scheme and the Massacre of Glencoe.

This decline of the theological spirit smoothed the path to Union in 1707. Scotland's consent was largely bought by the prospect of free trade with England, a motive which would not have appealed to a nation entirely immersed in religion and theology. The same inducement had failed to work throughout the seventeenth century, and it was only effective now because the spread of latitudinarianism had undermined the strength of theological antipathies. As it was, Presbyterian Scots accepted union with an Episcopal country, and sat cheek by jowl with Anglicans at Westminster, braving the contagion of prelatical poison. Anglicans connived at the establishment of heresy as a State religion across the Border. The old priest, not writ so large as before, and the new presbyter, looking somewhat small, lay down together, and Walpole led them in the paths of peace..

X

CROMWELLIAN CONSTITUTIONS

Of the many interesting and important questions connected with the history of the Commonwealth and Protectorate, none are of more permanent significance than the various expedients to which recourse was had to solve the constitutional problems created by the destruction of the monarchy, the dissolution of the House of Lords, and the undisguised predominance of the army. These phenomena were revolutionary enough, but perhaps they were not really so radical as the attempts to give England a written, rigid constitution, embodying certain fixed and fundamental principles which should be unchangeable even by the Legislature itself. For the great characteristic of the British Constitution, which distinguishes it from all foreign constitutions, is that it is not and never has been, except for temporary aberrations, a written, or a rigid constitution, or one in which there was any fundamental law.

These phrases, perhaps, require some explanation, especially as they represent the principles upon which some political philosophers would classify and distinguish modern constitutions. The old classification derived from Plato and Aristotle into monarchy, aristocracy, and democracy, and the several perversions of these forms, has long ceased to have any practical application to modern conditions, although it still retains its place in text-books as the starting-point of all political wisdom ; and political writers have long been casting about for some more satisfactory method of classification. What, then, is meant by saying that a constitution is written or unwritten? When a great French political philosopher, De Tocqueville, was asked about the English Constitution, he said, 'Elle n'existe point.' It does not exist, in fact, in the same sense that the French or Belgian constitution exists; for these are definite written documents. Most educated men in France have a copy of the French Constitution on their bookshelves, and can point to it and say, 'That is the French Constitution.' Now that is not possible for an Englishman : there is no one document, or series of documents, called the British Constitution. For him it is a much more complex thing, and sometimes he finds himself in the law-courts before he finds out what the British Constitution is : and even the mere repetition of the words is, I believe, sometimes used as a test of sobriety. The British Constitution is a miscellaneous, uncollected, undigested mass of statutes, legal decisions, and vague understandings or misunderstandings, some of which have never been put down in writing. No book contains them all; and there is nothing—not even the House of Lords— to which we can point and say, 'This is the British Constitution.' That is what De Tocqueville meant when he said that the British Constitution did not exist; and that is what we mean when we say that the British Constitution is unwritten. That phrase does not, of course, imply that no parts of it are written; for Magna Carta, the Habeas Corpus Acts, and the Bill of Rights are all parts of the British Constitution; but there is no one document which can be described as such.

Now, what do we mean when we say that the British Constitution is not rigid but flexible? We mean this : that no part of the Constitution is unalterable by the ordinary legislative methods. Parliament could at any time repeal the Habaes Corpus Acts, the Bill of Rights, and even Magna Carta itself; it could prolong its own existence indefinitely by repealing the Septennial Act : it could abolish trial by jury, and set up a Star Chamber or the Inquisition, and none of these things would be illegal. There is, in fact, nothing fundamental in the British

Constitution; for although we loosely talk of things being fundamental which are merely more important in our eyes than other things, the word properly means things which cannot be altered by the ordinary legislative machinery. But in the French, or in the American Constitution, there are many things which cannot be altered by the French or American Legislatures : both are bound and limited by the powers conferred upon them by the original, written Constitution. That Constitution is beyond the reach of the legislative bodies, and can only be touched by calling into play a special and cumbrous constitutional machinery. The reason for this in America is, that the framers of the Constitution were forced to safeguard the interests of the individual States against the possible encroachments of the Federal authority, and consequently they embodied in the Constitution a number of prohibitions and limitations on the powers of the Legislature, and they entrusted the Supreme Court of Judicature with the duty of seeing that these limitations were observed. Any law passed by Congress may be brought before the Supreme Court, and its legality contested. If the Supreme Court decides that the enactment contravenes any of the limits imposed by the Constitution, that enactment becomes *ipso facto* void. Thus, a few years ago, Congress found that it had no power to impose an income-tax upon the American people; and one of the great difficulties in dealing with the Trusts is, that the law of Association is as much a matter for the individual States as for the Federal authority, and Congress cannot dictate the conditions upon which individual States shall permit associations and combines to be formed within their borders. So, in the same way, the American Constitution rigidly defines the limits between the Legislature, the Executive, and the Judicature. No judge in America can be removed by an address of Congress, as he can in England by an address of both Houses of Parliament. No vote of censure by the Senate or the House of Representatives can terminate, or even shorten, the existence of an American administration.   On the other hand, the President cannot dissolve the Legislature one hour before its appointed time; he cannot appeal from a hostile Congress to a friendly country.   In England the Prime Minister can, if he likes, turn out the House of Commons, and the House of Commons can, if it likes, turn out the Prime Minister.   In America, neither can remove the other; they can only annoy one another, and impede one another's action until the period pre-ordained by the Constitution has elapsed.   The whole Constitution is fixed and rigid and consequently there is a good deal of friction.

There is nothing corresponding to all this in the English Constitution, where all the more important parts of the Constitution are flexible; and, perhaps, the greatest advantage, of this flexibility is that it has permitted the Constitution to be shaped and moulded by those who have had to work the machine, without the necessity of appealing for approval to the ignorant and prejudiced.   Let me take the Prime Minister as an example.   I do not, of course, refer to any particular Prime Minister, but to the species.   The Prime Minister is the pivot of the whole constitutional system; yet until the other day he was unknown to the written law of the Constitution: no Act of Parliament has ever been passed to create, to regulate, or to modify his office or his functions.   He does not occur in the Statute Book, he is unknown in the courts of law.   In fact, he has grown, and not been made.   It would not have been possible to make him by Act of Parliament; for the prejudice against such an office throughout the eighteenth century was so great that no House of Commons, and probably no House of Lords, would ever have passed the bill.   Walpole, who was a Prime Minister if ever there was one, had to repudiate the title; but a Prime Minister was felt to be necessary by those who had to govern England; and so, gradually, imperceptibly, and in spite of the prejudices of the Houses of Parliament, the office of Prime Minister was evolved, thanks to the flexible and unwritten

character of our Constitution.   If the practice of writing
Constitutions, set by the Commonwealth and Protectorate,
had been followed, we should never have had a Prime
Minister at all.

So it is with the Cabinet; that body, which rules the
Empire, is as unknown to the written law of the Constitution
as the Prime Minister.   It, too has grown without the
help of legislation.   It is an organic growth and not a
manufactured article.   Therefore it has been able to adapt
itself to the changing circumstances of its being silently
and gradually, without the intervention of the written law.
Nor, again, would it have been possible to create the
Cabinet by statutory enactment; for Parliament was
bitterly jealous of all such bodies.   It even did its best to
make a Cabinet permanently impossible by prohibiting all
holders of paid offices under the Crown from sitting in the
House of Commons, a prohibition which still survives in
the obligation on ministers to seek re-election on their
appointment to their office.   We may be sure that
Parliament in such a frame of mind would never have
passed an act creating the modern Cabinet.   So the Cabinet,
again, was left for the statesmen of the eighteenth century
to work out by a slow and gradual evolution.   Similarly,
the whole process of the modification of the powers and
position of the House of Lords has been achieved without
legislation.   No statute has deprived the Upper House of
the power of amending or rejecting money-bills sent up by
the House of Commons; no Act prohibits it from rejecting
as often as it likes measures approved by the constituencies.
Again, no statute requires a Government to resign when it
has forfeited the confidence of the majority of the House
of Commons; no direct law enjoins the summons of
Parliament every year; and there would be nothing illegal
in the disbandment of all the military and naval forces of
the Crown.   All these things are left to the operation of
public opinion, or of what are called the conventions of the
Constitution.

These conventions are the most characteristic and perhaps the most important parts of the Constitution; they are simply understandings, upon which statesmen may be trusted to act, but which are not written, and could not be enforced in any court of law.   They are as flexible as usage cares to make them, and they are always being formed and modified day by day.   The British Constitution is thus a living organism, ever adapting itself to the changing needs of time, and ever avoiding that friction which a rigid Constitution inevitably involves. For you cannot keep things as they are; and if your Constitution is based on the assumption that they will not change, it is bound sooner or later to prove inadequate or ineffective.   The most stable Constitution is that which ensures the readiest adaptation to the change of circumstances.

This somewhat lengthy preface has seemed advisable in order to bring out the importance of the attempts which were made during the Commonwealth and Protectorate to divert the stream of English constitutional development, and to provide England with a written, rigid Constitution. It may also be worth remarking that the character of the American Constitution has been attributed to conscious and deliberate imitation of these Puritan and Republican constitutions of seventeeth-century England; though other influences must also be taken into account.   For one thing, the American colonists had always lived under a system of written, rigid constitutions, namely the charters by which the various colonies had been founded. Secondly, the fact that the new State was bound to be a federation compelled the authors of the Constitution to define in a written document the relations between the individual States and the central power.   Thirdly, the Americans had obviously been frightened by Hobbes's doctrine of sovereignty.   They saw George III in every possible sovereign; and they came to the conclusion that this sovereignty was much too dangerous a thing to be left at

large. Consequently, they put it under lock and key, or
rather a triple lock and triple keys. And they gave one
key to the Executive, one to the Legislature, and one to
the Supreme Court; and it is only with the connivance of
these three that sovereignty can be let loose in the United
States. Rousseau said that the English were free only
once in seven years; and it is true that only at a general
election do the constituencies exercise political sovereignty.
But only about once in a generation does the American
people assert its mastery over the Constitution, which at
all other times controls and limits its action.

Now, why was it during the Commonwealth and
Protectorate that attempts were made to tie up the English
Constitution in a somewhat similar manner? The answer
will be found in the circumstance that the dominant party
wanted to place certain political principles out of the reach
of the ordinary Legislature, which was pretty certain to be
hostile to those principles. And this arose from the logical
quandary in which the nation was landed by the result of
the Civil War. The whole struggle from 1603-1649 had
centred round the question whether the Executive or the
Legislature, Parliament or the Crown, was to be the supreme
authority in the State. In that contest the Crown was
defeated, but Parliament did not reap the fruits of victory;
in fact it had not won the victory. Had Parliament been
left to its own genius and to its own resources, the victor
would have been the King. It was Cromwell and the
army which had saved England from a Stuart despotism,
and Cromwell and the army were resolved to have a voice
and a share in the distribution of the spoils. But both
soon found themselves as much out of sympathy with the
majority of the House of Commons as Charles 1 had ever
been. They were equally out of sympathy with the mass
of the nation; the appeal to arms had meant, as it always
does, the triumph of military efficiency over political
principle: success in the barborous arbitrament of war has
no relevance to the validity of civil argument, and the

victor in a war is just as likely to be wrong as right, and almost certain to be despotic. In this case neither Cromwell nor the army had much sympathy with the principles for which Parliament had contended. Cromwell believed in a strong executive, at least so long as he controlled it; and, indeed, the possession of power makes even the most radical anxious to avoid at least one change, just as being in opposition converts the most conservative to the necessity of one political alteration. Cromwell was not so purely an opportunist as this : his constitutional ideas were not so very far removed from those of the Stuarts. He had objected to the things they did, rather than to the way they did them, and he was convinced that an executive, to be strong, must have a wide discretion. He had little patience with the talking-shop at Westminster; that was why he appealed so strongly to Carlyle, who once said to Lord Wolseley that he hoped some day to see him treat the House of Commons as Cromwell did the Rump. There is, however, no occasion to denounce him as the destroyer of a constitutional *régime* : for from that point of view, there was little to choose between him and Parliament. Both were bent on ruling in defiance of the wishes of the majority of the people; and it was the determination of the Rump to prolong its own existence by its own illegal fiat which provoked its violent expulsion by Cromwell's troops. So, too, there is an answer to the common charge against Cromwell that he ruled by the sword; and that is, that there was nothing left to rule by, other than the sword.

The crux of the situation was the fact that government by consent was for the moment out of the question. It was not in human nature for the victors to give up the spoils of victory, and quietly submit to be ruled by the majority they had conquered. Therefore a despotism was inevitable, and, Englishmen being averse from naked despotism, the question was how to clothe it with a decent constitutional garb. That was the real, though perhaps unconscious, motive of the rigid, written constitutions of the Commonwealth and Protectorate. There were so many efforts to fix a legal wig upon the point of the soldier's sword. The covering was somewhat scanty and the effect was not all that might have been desired. The sword remained too obviously the important part of the concern, the wig was difficult to adjust, it was always falling off, and the two things did not really harmonise.

The all-important thing, then, was to secure the government, which the army had set up, against attack from the Parliament, which this government desired to create as a cloak for its military nature. The powers of Parliament must, then, be limited and defined; certain things must be placed beyond its reach. Now, Parliament could not be trusted to do this definition itself; it could not be expected to pass two self-denying ordinances in one generation, more especially as the first had led to that very supremacy of the sword which it now so much resented. So there must be a bold assumption of fundamental law existing by its own authority, and circumscribing and defining the legislative authority of Parliament. You may remember that law, which is originally no more than custom, is afterwards regarded as a sort of treasury of Divine or natural wisdom which human rulers may apply to the countries over which they rule; and only in the latest stage of the development of human thought is it a command of the State. The Fundamental Law of Cromwell and the army seems to belong to the second of these stages, and they regarded themselves as more or less divinely commissioned to employ force in the application of this law.

Cromwell himself described the doctrine of Fundamental Law in a speech to the Parliament of 1654. 'In every government,' he said, 'there must be somewhat fundamental, somewhat like a Magna Carta, that should be standing and be unalterable. Some things are fundamentals, they may not be parted with; but will, I trust, be delivered over to posterity as being the fruits of our blood and travail. The Government by a Single Person and a Parliament is a fundamental.. . . . That Parliaments should not make themselves perpetual is a fundamental. . . Again, is not liberty of conscience in religion a fundamental; So long as there is liberty of conscience for the Supreme Magistrate to exercise his conscience in erecting what form of church-government he is satisfied he should set up, why should he not give it (the like liberty) to others; Liberty of conscience is a natural right; and he, that would have it, ought to give it, having himself liberty to settle what he likes for the public. . . The magistrate hath his supremacy, and he may settle Religion, that is church-government, according to his conscience. . . . This, I say, is fundamental. It ought to be so. It is for us and the generations to come. . . . Another fundamental, which I had forgotten, is the Militia. That is judged a fundamental, if anything be so. . . What signifies a provision against perpetuating of Parliaments, if this power of the Militia be solely in *them*? . . And if this one thing be placed in one party, that one, be it Parliament, be it Supreme Governor, they or he hath power to make what they please of all the rest. Therefore . . . it should be so equally placed that no one person, neither in Parliament nor out of Parliament, should have the power of ordering it.'

These fundamentals of Cromwell anticipate much of later English history, and Dr. Gardiner speaks enthusiastically of his 'power of seeing into the heart of a situation'; for, 'whilst the Instrument of Government, with its many artificial devices for stemming the tide of Parliamentary supremacy, perished without leaving its mark on the Constitution, his four fundamentals have been accepted by the nation, and are at this day as firmly rooted in its conscience as Parliamentary supremacy itself.' Some qualification seems necessary before we can accept this as a literal statement of the fact. Government by a single person and a Parliament is not accepted as a fundamental in the sense in which Cromwell meant it, for the single

person does not really govern in the sense that Cromwell
governed.   He may not 'settle religion, that is church-
government, according to his conscience.'   Indeed, he is
prohibited by Act of Parliament from indulging his
conscience to such an extent, at any rate, as to become a
Roman Catholic.   The same interpretation has to be put
on Cromwell's 'magistrate' as upon Hobbes's sovereign to
make them applicable to latter-day conditions; they must
both be given a composite and not an individual personality;
the king must be the king in Parliament, and so must be
the magistrate.   Even then, as a matter of practical
politics, he cannot settle religion according to his conscience.

Moreover, these things, so far as they are accepted to-day.
are accepted as fundamental ideas rather than as fundamental laws.   It is quite true that Cromwell's conception
of the functions and objects of the State is singularly
modern, but his conception of the methods, by which those
objects were to be achieved, has never been adopted since
his time.   Even Magna Carta, which Cromwell quoted as
a fundamental, was not really fundamental law, though
the barons had tried to make it such by legalising armed
rebellion and civil war if the king refused to carry out its
provisions.   Fortunately they failed in their attempt to
perpetuate Magna Carta as fundamental law; for it was
really a feudal document drawn up in the interests of the
barons and designed to protect their private jurisdictions,
privileges, and monopolies against the rule of common-law.
There would have been little liberty or justice in England
had the barons secured the privilege, promised them in
Magna Carta, of trying their dependants for almost all
offences in their own manorial courts; and there would
have been little law and order had they retained the right,
also promised them in Magna Carta, of settling their
disputes by recourse to trial by battle.   The modern
conception of Magna Carta is, in fact, a myth invented in
the seventeenth century; and the only serious use made
of it in the sixteenth was the attempt, by an appeal to it,

to stop the Parliament from legislating for the Church and to perpetuate the Roman jurisdiction.

The whole conception of fundamental law was alien to the spirit of the English Constitution, and the attempt of Cromwell to make it fundamental was in itself a revolution, the magnitude of which the Protector did not himself perceive. And it was not more likely to prove palatable because it was dictated solely by the interests of the ruling military faction and not by the interests or desires of the nation as a whole. Cromwell, conscious of this antagonism, was driven to take up a position hardly distinguishable from that of the Stuarts. 'Though some,' he says in his fourth speech, 'may think it is a hard thing without Parliamentary authority to raise money upon this nation; yet I have another argument to the good people of this nation . . . whether they prefer the having of their will, though it be their destruction, rather than comply with things of necessity?' He claimed the right to levy money without the consent of Parliament, he claimed the right of controlling the militia. Yet he had voted for the Petition of Right, which prohibited taxation without the consent of Parliament; and in 1642 he had taken part in the struggle of the House of Commons to deprive the king of the right to control the militia, which he now claimed to exercise as Protector.

But, in spite of the unfortunate circumstances which attended the birth of these Cromwellian constitutions and condemned them from the first to a short and unhappy existence, there was much in their nature which entitled them to a better fate. They were not merely the expedients of an army embarrassed by lack of consitutional clothing; they were also great measures of reform and constructive statesmanship. The *Instrument of Government*, which was drawn up in December 1653, contained in it two, if not three, Acts of Union, a Franchise Act, an Act for the Redistribution of Seats, an Act for the Settlement of the Revenue, besides the establishment of the Protectorate and Council of State, and the definition of the functions, the duration and the powers of Parliament. The provisions with respect to the office of Protector, the composition of the Council of State, the revenue, and the machinery for securing triennial sessions of Parliament may be omitted, because they anticipated nothing of importance in subsequent English history.

But it is important to remember that the *Instrument of Government* was the most comprehensive Act of Union in English history. Both Scotland and Ireland were included at the same time; thirty members were to represent Scotland, and thirty Ireland, in the United Parliament. The numbers seem small compared with the four hundred members allotted to the predominant partner; but, apparently, they were not unfairly based upon a calculation of the respective wealth and population of the three countries. Nor were Scotland and Ireland the only spheres which were now for the first time brought within the Parliamentary system. Wales had received Parliamentary representation at the hands of Henry vin, who had also extended the same boon to Cheshire, to Calais, and to Berwick-upon-Tweed. But the County Palatine of Durham and the Channel Islands still remained unrepresented in the Parliament of England. Durham was the last of those great medieval franchises which had been guaranteed by Magna Carta, and long resisted all efforts to incorporate them in the national system; it had its own courts of law and other regalia, or royal rights, such as the right of coinage; but the dangers of the system in the case of Durham were mitigated by the fact that the earl was also bishop, and could not found a feudal dynasty. The Channel Islands were originally part of the Norman duchy, and claim to have conquered England rather than to have been conquered by England. They had been left to their own legislative devices, probably because they were distant and their common-law was widely different from that of England. In the sixteenth century they were declared to be directly subject to the Privy Council, but with the brief exception of the Protectorate, they have never been subject to the British Parliament. And even Cromwell did not incorporate that other outlying island, the Isle of Man, of which the Earls of Derby were the sovereign lords.

The most important feature of the *Instrument of Government* is its aspect as a Reform Bill, including a redistribution of seats and a revision of the franchise. The redistribution was on a drastic scale. We often hear talk about the change which has converted England from an agricultural into an urban community, but the remark seems singularly inapplicable to Parliamentary representation. In the Middle Ages the county members numbered only seventy against nearly three times that number of borough members. In the Long Parliament of 1640 the disproportion was even greater, and there were about four hundred and thirty borough members to about a hundred county members. Of course, we must remember that the boroughs of those days were more agricultural than they are at present, but even so, there seems to be a striking inequality ; the county of York, for instance, only returned two shire-members, while the boroughs in Yorkshire returned twenty-eight. This anomaly the *Instrument of Government* now proceeded to remedy. The borough-members were reduced from about four hundred and thirty to one hundred and thirty-nine, while the county-members were increased from a hundred to two hundred and sixty-one. The total number of English and Welsh representatives was reduced from five hundred and thirty to four hundred. This was the most sweeping change ever effected at one blow in the history of Parliamentary representation. And it was accompanied by a regular slaughter of rotten, or rather insignificant, boroughs ; for they did not become really rotten until late in the eighteenth century. The representatives of Cornish boroughs sank from twenty-eight to four; Newport, Newtown, and Yarmouth in the Isle of Wight lost their members; and the island, which had returned six representatives to Parliament, had now to be content with two. Old Sarum disappeared, Gatton, Grampound, and a host of other hoary antiquities. On the other hand, Yorkshire was divided into its three Ridings for the purposes of Parliamentary representation; and the West Riding was given six members, and each of the other Ridings four. Essex was allotted thirteen county members instead of two; Devon, Kent, and Somerset eleven each; and Lincoln, Norfolk, Suffolk, and Wiltshire ten apiece instead of two. These reforms were all annulled at the Restoration of Charles II; every insignificant borough was restored with him; and among the benefits which we owe to the Restoration are the weakness and corruption of Parliament down to 1832, the dominance of George III, perhaps the loss of the colonies of North America, and the postponement till the nineteenth century of the real supremacy of the House of Commons and all that is involved therein. For George III and the Whig and Tory landlords could not have pocketed the great county constituencies created by Cromwell, as they did the tiny boroughs restored by Charles II. Nabobs could not have bribed the West Riding of Yorkshire as they did Old Sarum; and without these aids at his disposal, George III could not have kept Chatham out of power and Lord North in office.

The question of the franchise was not treated in so radical a manner. In fact, the borough franchise, with all its absurdities and anomalies, was left alone; probably it was thought too thorny a subject to be tackled in the time at the disposal of the framers of this Constitution. But a thorough-going change was effected in the county franchise. As I have said before, the qualification for a Parliamentary vote in the counties was the possession of a forty-shilling freehold. This sum had originally represented something like forty pounds of our present currency, but by the middle of the seventeenth century it had sunk to considerably less than a quarter of that value, so that it was quite possible to be a poor man and yet to have a county vote. On the other hand, the vast majority of the rural population was shut out altogether, because copyhold and leasehold were more plentiful than freehold, and no amount of copyhold or leasehold entitled its holder to a vote. This anomalous discrimination was abolished by the *Instrument of Government,* and the county franchise was made to depend on the one uniform qualification of a real or personal estate to the value of £200. This would, of course, exclude all agricultural labourers, but it probably enfranchised a great many more voters than it disfranchised.

There is one other point about this Constitution which should, perhaps, be noticed. It left out the House of Lords, and the omission was assuredly not accidental. The Long Parliament in 1649 had declared that the Commons of England assembled in Parliament had found by too long experience that the House of Lords was useless and dangerous to the people of England, and had decreed that it should thenceforth be wholly abolished and taken away, while individual peers might, if they could, get elected to the House of Commons. This decision, after five years' experience, was respected by the *Instrument of Government*; but it is no part of my business in this place to express an opinion whether this was or was not like other provisions of that document, an intelligent anticipation of future reforms. You may either lay stress on the fact that England had since 1649 prospered, especially in its repute abroad, in spite of its lack of hereditary and noble councillors; or you may emphasise the fact that Cromwell, nevertheless, saw fit three years later to restore a Second Chamber; or you may, thirdly, combine the two observations, and deduce some conclusion from the fact that, although Cromwell restored a Second Chamber, it was not exactly our House of Lords.

But this Constitution, admirable though it may have been in some or, perhaps, in most respects, was marred by its conscious want of trust in the people, for whom it was intended.   To start with, it embodied a vast number of penal disqualifications. Every one who had aided, advised, assisted, or abetted in any war against the Parliament since the first day of January 1641 was disqualified from voting or being elected for the first four triennial Parliaments after the *Instrument* came into force; all who professed the Roman Catholic religion, or had taken part in the Irish Rebellion, were disqualified for ever. For the first three Parliaments, moreover, the returns were to be made to the Council of State, and members of Parliament were only to be admitted if the Council approved of them. And in the returns there was to be a stipulation that the persons elected should have no power to alter the government, as settled by the Instrument, in one single person and a Parliament.

This last provision at once proved a bone of contention. The arbitrary exclusion of a hundred members by the Council had not been sufficiently drastic a purge, and others began to impugn the validity of the restrictions imposed on their liberty of debate and powers of action. By what authority, they asked, had these things been done? Who had the right to set up fundamental law beyond their reach?   And they set to work to discuss the *Instrument of Government,* which, according to Cromwell's idea of the Constitution, they had no power to alter. They insisted on debating this Constitution instead of passing the measures Cromwell wanted. He possessed his soul in such patience as he could muster until the five months had elapsed within which he could not, by the *Instrument,* dissolve the Parliament; and then he himself went down to the House and made a speech. He spoke rather in sorrow than in anger. Never had his hopes beat higher than when he first met this Parliament, never had they been so keenly disappointed. 'Instead of peace and settlement, instead of mercy and truth being brought together, righteousness and peace kissing each other, by reconciling the honest people of these nations, and settling the woeful distempers that are among us—which had been glorious things and worthy of Christians to have proposed— weeds and nettles, briars and thorns have thriven under your shadow.　Dissettlement and division, discontent and dissatisfaction, together with real dangers to the whole, has been more multiplied within these five months of your sitting than in some years before.　Foundations have also been laid for the future renewing the troubles of these nations by all the enemies of them abroad and at home.' Instead of construction, they had been bent on destruction ; they had sought the overthrow of the *Instrument* ; they had endeavoured to make the Army discontented by refusing to provide its arrears of pay, and to make it odious to the nation by compelling it to live at free quarters. The partisans of Charles Stuart made capital out of the Parliament, and laid plots of all kinds.　And worse than the Royalists in Oliver's eyes were the Levellers or Common- wealth's Men, who 'have been and yet are endeavouring to put us into blood and into confusion—more desperate and dangerous confusion than England ever yet saw.　And I must say . . . it is some satisfaction, if a Commonwealth must perish, that it perish by men, and not by the hands of persons differing little from beasts.　That if it must needs suffer, it should rather suffer from rich men than from poor men, who, as Solomon says, " when they oppress, leave nothing behind them, but are as a sweeping rain." Now such as these have grown up under your shadow.' Cromwell was a very middle-class and bourgeois revolu- tionary, and with this fear and detestation of the lower classes, there is little wonder that he limited the franchise in the counties to the possessors of a £200 property qualification.　He made no appeal to the poorer classes, and this must be taken into account when estimating the causes of the failure of the Puritan system.　Better, thought Cromwell, the Stuarts than the Levellers ; better, thought the Levellers, the Stuarts than Oliver Cromwell.

Both dangers were attributed by the Protector to the folly of his Parliament. ' You have wholly elapsed your time,' he exclaimed, ' and done just nothing '; and the concluding moral of his speech was a dissolution.

The legal wig had fallen off; there was only left the naked sword; and England was divided up into eleven districts, ruled by Major-Generals. Nothing could have been less likely to conciliate public opinion, and this, after all, was Cromwell's earnest desire, if only it could be done without a Restoration of the Stuarts and their ways. It was quite obvious that the nation preferred government by a King and Parliament to government by a Protector and the Army; and it was determined to try the desperate expedient of a Cromwellian dynasty. ' They are so highly incensed,' wrote a member of Parliament, 'against the arbitrary actings of the major-generals, that they are greedy of any power that will be ruled and limited by law.' Hereditary monarchy was also to be a protection for the Protector, as well as for those who served him. They would be protected by Henry vii's statute providing that obedience to a *de facto* king should not be treason; he would be protected from assassination by the consideration that his removal would only place his son upon his throne. But the Army would not have a king; and Cromwell himself had in his speech dissolving the last Parliament quoted from Ecclesiastes the query, 'Who knoweth whether he may beget a wise man or a fool? ' So the proposed Royalty was reduced to the power of choosing a successor. But the *Humble Petition and Advice,* as this second constitution was called, had some advantages over the *Instrument of Government.* It was drawn up by an elected Parliament; it was the work of lawyers and merchants, and not of Cromwell's officers. And, although there was to be fundamental law, that law was not to be merely assumed without Parliamentary authority. There were to be two Houses of Parliament; the ancient and undoubted liberties and privileges of parliament' were declared to be the birthright and inheritance of the people, wherein every man is interested'; they were to be preserved and maintained. Elected members were not to be excluded except by the decision of a parliamentary commission. The ' other House ' was to be chosen by the Protector with the consent and approval of the House of Commons—a provision somewhat similar to those in force in New Zealand and Canada at the present moment. The great officers of State were to be appointed with the approval of both Houses of Parliament; no taxes were to be levied without its consent, and it was to meet once in three years or oftener. The questions of the franchise and the redistribution of seats were left for Parliament itself to settle—if ever it got to business.

This it never did. Cromwell seemed to have almost obtained what he wanted by the *Humble Petition and Advice*. His authority rested at last upon a constitutional basis; he was no longer the mere nominee of the Army, but the elect of the people's representatives. He had moreover, obtained an increased revenue and augmented powers by the *Humble Petition*, and he opened this Parliament in January 1658 with a speech which reads like a pæan of thanksgiving. Four days later his tone was changed, and his hopes had given way to fears. His chief partisans had been called up to the ' other House,' to which the Republicans refused to give the title of the House of Lords, and the balance in the Lower House was almost even between the Republican opposition and the Government. The members, who had been excluded while the *Humble Petition* was being elaborated, insisted on making the speeches which they would have made then had they been present. They made a dead set at the new House of Lords. The providence of God, said one, had delivered the people from an authority which could exercise a veto on their resolutions. 'What was fought for,' he asked, 'but to arrive at a capacity to make your own laws?' The House of Lords was the weak part of the

Constitution; to the Republicans it was the thin edge of Royalty; it was disliked in the Army, and schemes were afoot for a monster petition calling on Fairfax to take the command instead of Cromwell.   On the 4th of February 1658 the Protector summoned both Houses to him.   ' I would have been glad,' he said, ' to have lived under my woodside, to have kept a flock of sheep, rather than undertook such a government as this is. . . .   You have not only disjointed yourselves, but the whole nation. . . . These things tend to nothing else but playing the King of Scots' game (if I may so call him) : and I think myself bound before God to do what I can to prevent it. . . ..   It hath been not only your endeavour to pervert the Army while you have been sitting, and to draw them to state the question about a Commonwealth ; but some of you have been enlisting persons, by commission of Charles Stuart, to join with any insurrection that may be made.   And what is likely to come upon this, the enemy being ready to invade us, but even present blood and confusion?   And if this be so, I do assign it to this cause : your not assenting to what you did invite me to by the Petition and Advice, as that which might be the settlement of the nation.   And if this be the end of your sitting, and this be your carriage, I think it high time that an end be put to your sitting. And I do dissolve this Parliament.   And let God be judge between you and me.'   ' Amen,' responded the defiant Republicans.

It was the last of Cromwell's Parliaments.   Seven months later Oliver himself was dead and Richard his son reigned in his stead.   ' Who knoweth,' Oliver had asked, ' whether he may beget a wise man or a fool? '   And there followed eighteen months of bewildering revolution.   Then, amid the drunken frenzy of a delirious people, there dawned the golden days of good King Charles—a monarch who had no heart and knew no shame, who debauched a whole generation, who swindled national creditors and sold himself and his country to Louis of France for gold.   The

Restoration meant a good deal else : it meant the disintegration of the United Kingdom and the dismemberment of the Imperial Parliament. It meant the restoration of legislative independence to Scotland, Ireland and the Channel Islands, the revival of rotten boroughs, the restoration of the House of Lords on its ancient and antiquated basis, and the restitution of that 'veto on the people's resolutions.' It meant a hideous moral reaction, an orgy of open shame. Sin sat enthroned on the sovereign's seat and vice was crowned king at court, while the author of *Pilgrim's Progress* lay twelve long years in Bedford county gaol; and up the Thames there rolled the roar of the Dutchmen's guns to where Oliver's head gazed, a ghastly sight, from a pole over Westminster Hall.

Against this mass of corruption, cruelty, treason, and shame there is this to be set. The Restoration was not only the restoration of a King with a foul mind and an evil heart; it was also the restoration of Parliament, unfettered by rigid law and freed from the fear of the force of arms, a Parliament which, if not yet sovereign, was soon to make its title good, and slowly earn the envy of the world. If the Restoration banished the Ten Commandments from high places in the land, it also banished the sword from the High Court of Parliament. A mighty fall was there; but the nation fell back from arduous paths which led towards barren heights, and resumed the truer ways of peaceful progress towards the goals of liberty, self-government, and law.

XI

COLONIAL EXPANSION

PROBABLY all of you are familiar with that well-known quip of Horace Walpole's when he wrote in 1759 that it was necessary to ask each morning at breakfast what victories there had been, for fear of missing one. It was the year in which the French fleets were beaten off Lagos and Quiberon Bay and the French army at the battle of Minden, the year in which Guadeloupe was captured and Havre was bombarded; and finally, the year in which Wolfe stormed the heights of Quebec and laid Canada at England's feet. I think it has been described as the birth-year of the British Empire. But it was only one in a series of wonderful years of victory. Its predecessor, 1758, had brought the capture of Louisburg, Cape Breton, and Fort Duquesne; its successor, 1760, brought the battle of Wandewash, which secured Madras and completed the downfall of the French power in India; and 1762 saw the capture of the capitals of Cuba and of the Philippine Islands. If the year 1759 was not actually the birth-year of the Empire, it would at least seem that we could not date its advent into the world very far from the Seven Years' War.

But we are all inclined to attach a somewhat excessive importance to our birthdays—until we reach a certain age, when we go to the other extreme and like to ignore them altogether; and the emphasis laid upon the events of the year 1759 has unduly diminished in our eyes the importance of the processes and developments which preceded that year and which alone made possible its striking triumphs. The fall of the French dominion in Canada, the establishment of what was practically a British monopoly over the continent of North America, would not have been achieved, at the middle of the eighteenth century, had it not been for the colonial and naval developments of the seventeenth ; and the significance of seventeenth-century colonial history has been obscured by the dramatic interest of the domestic history of that time.   It is to the importance of these germs of empire in the seventeenth century that I wish to call your attention.

It was, in fact, during that century that the political changes which followed upon the Seven Years' War were pre-ordained.   In the same way gradual causes, silently working through many years, pre-ordain which trees will weather the storm and which will be laid low.   The superficial observer is content with the outward manifestation, and only remarks that the tree fell because the wind blew.   But the scientific student, the man interested in forestry and in the preservation of trees, wants to know why some trees fell, while others survived.   He knows that storms must come, and his business is, by taking thought, to see that they do as little damage as possible.   He is not content to take the storms and their effects as things entirely beyond his understanding and control.   So, the real student of history is not content to attribute the creation of the Empire to the storm and stress of the Seven Years' War.   That war raged over many spheres ; it only produced far-reaching results in some.   Nearly every country in Europe took part in it, but it is not a great landmark in the history of Russia, of Sweden, or of Spain.   Even the principal actors were only affected in parts of their dominions.   The boundaries of the European States were hardly altered ; Austria failed to recover Silesia, but that result was merely a recognition of the *status quo*.   Outside Europe the consequences were, of course, more serious, but even in America there were vast dominions belonging to the protagonists of the war which remained almost unaffected by its results.   South and Central

America continued predominantly Spanish, and the French settlements on the west coast of Africa were for the most part left alone. Why was the Seven Years' War fatal to some and not to other dominions?

That is the question which we have to answer, and, in seeking a solution, we shall be led to the conclusion that more than victories on land and sea is needed in the building of an empire. Even a battle is only the summing-up, in a striking and dramatic way, of a series of causes. Nelson could not have won the battle of Trafalgar had it not been for the administrative work of Earl St. Vincent at the Admiralty. Indeed, the British Empire has not been really won by military conquest; there has been no great conqueror in British history like Alexander, Hannibal, or Napoleon, none of whom, it may be incidentally remarked, succeeded in founding a permanent empire. Military skill of course is needed, but it can only work on materials and conditions provided for it, and these are more important than the military skill. Dominion acquired by the sword can only be maintained by the sword, and ultimately the sword always fails unless it is reinforced by the arts and crafts of peace. The essential factor in the building of the British Empire, the factor which distinguishes it from the jerry-built empire of Napoleon, is the colonist, not the colonel, the settler, not the sergeant. He has wielded the spade and trowel, and not the sword and spear; he has scattered seeds, not blows, and has returned bringing his sheaves with him—sheaves of good grain, and not the tares of human tears and curses.

The soldier and the sailor in 1759 were, then, only putting the final touches to a process which had been going on for a century and a half; and,, before a blow had been struck, or a victory won in the Seven Years' War, it had been determined that North America should belong to English-speaking races, and to no one else. This is clear enough if we mentally look at a map of North America, as it was in 1756, and consider the relative position of the rival

claimants to the inheritance. The sparse trading-posts in
the far north, Hudson's Bay, New North Wales, New
South Wales, and New Britain, as these territories then
were called, did not bulk very large in the eyes of European
statesmen; but they all belonged to Great Britain, and
they shut in the French dominions to the neighbourhood of
the great lakes and the River St. Lawrence. South and
east of them came the solid block of the Thirteen Colonies,
stretching all along the eastern sea-board from Nova Scotia
down to Florida. Now, the French population numbered
eighty thousand, but the population of Virginia alone was
two hundred thousand, and the total white population of
the British North American colonies was a million and a
quarter. There were fifteen Britons for every Frenchman,
and it is on that fact that I base my statement that before
a shot was fired in the Seven Years' War, the future of
North America had been already ear-marked for the British
race. Of course, the numerical proportion is not everything; if the Britons had been blacks or Red Indians,
the French might still have won, though the policy of
the old *régime* in France discouraged the development
of colonies; and the slow growth of Canada, while it was
French, did not hold out the prospect that the French,
if left alone, would very quickly colonise the rest of
North America. But, as those million and a quarter
were British settlers, the conclusion was foregone.
Whether there were a Seven Years' War or not, the
million and a quarter were destined to prevail over the
eighty thousand.

Now, the all-important question to solve in American
history is this : How came there to be in 1756 a population
of a million and a quarter British subjects occupying the
whole, or almost the whole, sea-board of the present
United States; this result had not been achieved without
serious trouble, or as a matter of course. There had been
numerous competitors, and a century before the Seven
Years' War no one could have anticipated such an over-

whelming preponderance of Britons in North America as had been established by 1756. Let us take a glance at the map of North America about the middle of the seventeenth century. The solid mass of British colonies does not exist; and the territory which they afterwards occupied presents a variegated political appearance. To the north there are, it is true, the New England colonies, but they stand alone. Their southern as well as their northern neighbours are foreigners; while on the north they have the French, on the south they have the Dutch. There is no such place as New York; it is called New Amsterdam, and is peopled by the Dutch, and is part of the New Netherlands. Pennsylvania does not exist; and the future States of New Jersey and Delaware are a Swedish settlement. Then at length we come to British territory again in Maryland and Virginia. But they are isolated, and south of them lies the vast and ill-defined district of Florida, belonging to Spain, and west is the still vaster and vaguer territory of Louisiana, which is French.

What will be the final colour of this mass of patchwork? No one can tell in Cromwell's time, but it is fairly certain that the power which can paint that country red will dominate the whole North American continent. And the question is really decided in the reign of Charles II, not a period with which one usually associates the idea of imperial expansion. We have heard a good deal lately about Cromwell and the Empire, and attempts have been made to set him up as the patron-saint of Liberal Imperialism. It is the irony of fate that far more extensive and important additions should have been made to the Empire under the rule of the monarch who let Dutch guns blaze away in the Medway and the Thames. The cession of New Amsterdam and the New Netherlands was a handsome compensation for that insult The seventeenth has thus some claim to stand beside the eighteenth century as an important era in the making of the Empire.

Let us consider for a moment how it compares with the sixteenth, which is, I suppose, next to the eighteenth century the most important era, according to the popular notion, in the history of the Empire. But, if we examine the extent of the Empire at the death of Queen Elizabeth, we shall be astonished to find how slight it was, and how meagre had been the achievements of the Elizabethan era, when measured in the number of English colonists and in the number of square miles covered by their settlements. Henry vii had, indeed, encouraged Cabot, who had discovered Newfoundland; and in 1536 a person called Armagil Waad visited Newfoundland, Cape Breton, ,and Penguin Island, for which somewhat slender achievements his admirers dubbed him the 'English Columbus.' Later on, Frobisher explored the coasts of Greenland and Labrador, and Sir Humphrey Gilbert did actually found a colony at St. John, in Newfoundland in 1583. This was the earliest British colony founded in North America; but the colonists were many of them taken from English gaols, and the better class, which consisted of sailors more useful on sea than on land, sought to be taken home or anywhere rather than be left on that scene of disorder and crime. Gilbert was drowned on the way home. 'We are as near Heaven,' he was heard to say shortly before his vessel foundered, 'by sea as by land'; and it was the spirit, rather than the achievements, of the sea-dogs which gives them the title of builders of empire. Raleigh was hardly more successful as a founder of colonies than his half-brother, Humphrey Gilbert. His first attempt to colonise Virginia in 1585 failed owing to quarrels between the English and the natives, and among the English leaders themselves. A second and larger expedition in 1587 did leave eighty-nine men, seventeen women, and two children behind it; but the reinforcements sent out in the following year turned pirates; and when, in 1589, tardy relief did actually reach America, the original colonists had disappeared, and no trace of them was ever afterwards found.

So that, in 1603, the net English achievement in the way of a colonial empire was practically nil.

Nor, indeed, had these expeditions gone forth as a rule with any idea of founding a colonial empire at all. It may be doubted whether any successful colonial empire ever has been founded with that as the original idea. It is much talked of, but it has never been a very powerful motive, and those who talk loudest about expanding the Empire generally return to the haven of Park Lane as soon as they have made their pile. Colonies designed under stress of the imperial idea, like those of Germany in South-West Africa, or those of France in North Africa, do not flourish, and are not really colonies at all. Some more definite and practical motive than imperial sentiment has to be found before men will undergo the hardships involved in the establishment of new communities in distant lands. In recent times the real basis of imperial sentiment has been the commercial instinct; the flag has been valued as a commercial asset, and some pronounced imperialists have been found to have made not inconsiderable, and sometimes improper, profits out of their country in times of war. On the eve of the War of American Independence Horace Walpole writes that Birmingham was enthusiastically in its favour because it had a small-arms manufactory. But this kind of spirit has been more apt at breaking up than at founding empires; and the signal failure of the Elizabethans to found colonies must be ascribed, in part at least, to the fact that their motive was gain, either from gold mines or from commerce. They wanted, not the white man's burden, but the white man's percentages; they were more concerned with interest than with principle; their ideal was, not Empire, but Eldorado. They preferred coloured labour to white because it was cheaper, and so they started the negro slave trade. That curse has come home to roost; and it has been calculated that by the end of the present century there may be a population of a hundred million negroes in the United States. That means a race war, of which the lawless lynchings and burnings of to-day are but a faint and distant rumble. Repentance has come, of a sort; but it has not wiped out the effects of the original crime of thinking that dividends exalt a nation more than righteousness.

The negro slaves were intended for the mines of Mexico and Peru, which were in Spanish hands, and even the trade in them was English in only a minor degree. Nor is the piracy charged against the English sea-dogs a very disgraceful accusation. Piracy was the only form of trade with the Indies open to Englishmen, for the Spaniards and Portuguese tried to exclude the traders of all other nations but themselves from American commerce. They based their claim to monopoly on the award of Pope Alexander vi and the only right the Pope had to decide such a question was derived from the Donation of Constantine, and that was forged. There was no reason why the English, who had repudiated the authority of the Pope in religious matters, should respect it in a far more doubtful sphere. For all that, their motives were anything but lofty; fortunately, they did not find the gold they sought, or England would probably have adopted the strange delusion of the Spaniards that gold and silver were the only forms of wealth. But gold and silver were their object, and Queen Elizabeth's imperial enthusiasm always waxed or waned according to the booty brought into her coffers by Drake or other bold, bad buccaneers. As early as the reign of Edward vi, one Richard Eden had pointed out that, if England had only been awake to her interests, the bullion in the royal warehouse at Seville might have been reposing in the Tower.

Next to gold-mines, trade-routes were the object of discovery; and it was their desire to find a short cut to the Indies which led Willoughby and Chancellor towards the White Sea, Frobisher, Baffin, Davis and Hudson to the straits and bays which bear their names to-day. Even the earliest settlements of Gilbert and Raleigh were perhaps

designed as outposts against the Spaniards rather than as
colonies; and the French were, curiously enough, in
advance of the English in their ideas of colonisation.   In
1506 a Frenchman had first entered the St. Lawrence, and
named the island at the mouth of it Cape Breton—a
puzzling name, which so struck the Duke of Newcastle that,
when as Secretary of State he first learnt that Cape Breton
was an island, he rushed off to communicate the astonishing
intelligence to Pitt.   Then, in 1534, Jacques Cartier of
St. Malo sailed up the river, and determined to found a
colony in the country.   In 1540 he led a band of two
hundred French colonists thither, and they formed the
nucleus of the Canadian nation.   Next the great Huguenot
leader, the Admiral Coligny, took up the idea of forming
colonies as a refuge for persecuted Protestants; but the
wars of religion in France absorbed his energies, and that
idea came to nothing for the time, though other Frenchmen
sought and gained a temporary footing in the Spanish
Florida.   On the conclusion of the Civil Wars in 1598,
Henry IV again took up the idea; in 1603 Champlain
founded Quebec, and a few years afterwards Montreal.
Canada was under weigh before the United States; and
the spacious times of Queen Elizabeth did not include
colonial expansion.

The foundations of empire were, in fact, laid in the
seventeenth and not in the sixteenth century; and they
were laid by men who would never have been called, or
have called themselves, imperialists.   Their motive was
not to expand, but to escape, the England of James I, and
these pioneers and colonists had no wish to reproduce the
conditions they had left behind.   They wanted something
different, and something better.   They went for something
which they prized more highly than gold or silver; they
would not turn back because they did not see a dividend
in sight; their minds were stayed on religious conviction,
and not puffed up with imperial pride.   'Lest we forget'
was their daily thought; it was not reserved for show at

a Diamond Jubilee, and then drowned in a greater debauch than ever. They were of the stuff of which nations are made; power came to them in the fulness of time, and prosperity in good measure, not because they sought it, but because they sought first of all righteousness according to their lights.

It was the Pilgrim Fathers and their children who made the New England across the sea; but they were not the earliest colonists in America who went out in the reign of James I. Indeed, colonisation of Virginia, on the lines suggested by Raleigh, had been attempted by various people since 1589, but misfortune dogged their steps; and even when the Virginia Company was fairly started in 1606, and a band of settlers established under Captain John Smith on the James River, the colonists proved unsatisfactory, and the colony was more than once on the verge of breaking up. The principal cause was that the settlement was regarded as a speculation, to be exploited entirely in the interests of the Company. The settlers had no property in the land they tilled, and their profits were to go to swell the wealth of the promoters. It was not until this system had been altered, and the merits of Virginia tobacco realised, that the colony began to take root and flourish. Nor did it ever show the robust and stubborn vigour of New England, which within a generation had begotten four of the original thirteen United States. The tobacco planters of Virginia, with their large estates, their slaves, and their comparatively luxurious existence, would by themselves have been a poor protection against the French and Dutch rivals of the British colonists. The Puritan settlers were the backbone of the English power; they were organised in townships, not plantations; and they were a democratic rather than an aristocratic society.

Not that there was anything idyllic about these New England colonies. They soon showed that they conceived of liberty as being a privilege, and not a common right to be enjoyed by all alike. Religious toleration was a thing they wanted for themselves and not for others; and uniformity was to be as rigid in the New England as it had been in the Old. The difference was, that they were to do the persecution instead of being persecuted; and Roger Williams had to flee from them as they had fled from Laud. Their ideal was borrowed from Geneva of the Calvinists. where Church and State were one; where only the orthodox were entitled to a vote; where every ecclesiastical offence was an act of civil disobedience; where obstinate refusal to communicate and continued or frivolous absence from church were punishable crimes; where the creed was a law of the State, and heresy as much an offence as immorality. It was no place for any one but a Puritan; and when Roman Catholics also sought an asylum from English persecution. in America, they wisely set up for themselves. Their leader, Sir George Calvert, afterwards Lord Baltimore, as early as 1612 had obtained a patent of Newfoundland from James 1; but the rigour of the climate and the attacks of the French in Canada during the war of 1626-9 induced his followers to remove to Maryland, named after Henrietta Maria, with its capital called Baltimore, from the title of its founder.

Meanwhile rivals from other European countries had appeared upon the scene. In 1614 the Dutch, relieved by the Twelve Years' Truce from their war with Spain, turned their attention to the New World, and founded the New Netherlands, with their two chief settlements at New Amsterdam and Fort Orange, between New England and Virginia. On the river Delaware, too, Sweden established a colony called New Sweden, which was doomed to a brief and undistinguished career. More important was the development of the French power in the north. In 1604 the foundation of Quebec and Montreal had been followed by the settlement of a colony of fishermen and woodcutters at Port Royal, now called Annapolis, on the Bay of Fundy —a settlement which was destroyed by an expedition from Virginia in 1613. This exploit was followed up in 1621 by

James I's grant to Sir William Alexander, afterwards Earl of Stirling, of practically the whole of Canada, under the name of New Scotland or Nova Scotia. The patent conferred enormous rights upon Alexander—on paper; but to induce colonists to settle was another matter, especially when the King wanted also to make money out of the transaction. James's favourite bauble was dangled before men's eyes : every one who would pay the King a hundred and fifty pounds should receive a grant of land three miles long and two miles broad, and a baronetcy. Thus that slighted order of Nova Scotia Baronets came into existence, and a barren land was to bloom with baronets.

But this grant might have had important consequences. In 1626, owing to the foolish policy of Buckingham and Charles I, England was involved in war with France. With both countries claiming the greater part of Canada, it was natural that the war should spread to North America ; and then a little-known event took place. Wolfe was not the first Briton who conquered Quebec for the British Crown. He was anticipated in 1628 by an Englishman of Derbyshire, named Gervase Kirke, who has not even found a place in the *Dictionary of National Biography.* Kirke had lived at Dieppe, and had there married a Frenchwoman ; but in spite of all temptations he remained an Englishman, and used whatever knowledge he had acquired from his French connections in the interests of his native land and of himself. In 1627 he obtained letters of marque from Charles I, fitted out three ships, commanded by his three sons, and sailed for the St. Lawrence. There were many Huguenots among the crews who, having been expelled from New France as settlers, returned as enemies. There Kirke captured or sank the whole French naval force in the river. Sailing back to England with their spoil, they returned in the following year to complete their conquest. The French garrison had been reduced almost to a state of starvation, and the governor could no nothing except arrange the terms of a dignified surrender. Quebec and the whole of New France passed into English hands, and remained under English control for three years. Then came peace, and all was given back to France. Charles and his advisers had no notion of a colonial policy at all, or of the potential value of Canada. His financial necessities were much more important in his eyes, and they were caused by his attempt to rule in defiance of his Parliament. The motive which induced him to surrender the greater part of North America was the payment by France of the residue of the dowry of Henrietta Maria—some sixty thousand pounds—which would relieve him of the immediate necessity of appealing for Parliamentary grants. The Kirkes and their associates, who had conquered Canada at their own expense, were not repaid, except by the grant of a barren knighthood to David Kirke, which cost Charles nothing. That was his idea of empire-building.

The services of Charles I to the American colonies were, however, great, but they were undesigned. The idea of New England as a refuge from the Old had by this time taken root, and the more unbearable Charles and Laud made things at home, the greater numbers flocked abroad ; and fortunately the Stuarts were unable to exclude religious dissidents from their colonies as the French government did the Huguenots from theirs. Over twenty thousand colonists are computed to have sailed from Old to New England between the accession of Charles I and the opening of the Long Parliament in 1640 ; and one of the unrehearsed effects of the activity of that Parliament was to check this stream of emigration. These colonists formed a number of almost independent municipalities, which were a peculiar feature of New England, but resembled the municipalities of the United Provinces; for those provinces not only formed a federation, but each province was itself a federation of towns and cities. So in New England each municipality was sovereign in itself, and stood to the colony or State in much the same relation as the individual State now stands to the American Confederation.

But in 1643 the need was felt of a wider union. There had been differences with the Dutch; the Indians were supposed to be hostile; there was always the French danger in the north; and there might be advantages in presenting a united front to the authorities at home. So at Boston in May 1643 a confederacy called the United Colonies of New England was formed. Two commissioners from each of the four federating colonies were to meet annually, or oftener, if necessary, and to chose a President from among themselves. No war was to be declared by a colony without the consent of the federal commissioners, and the expenses were to be apportioned among the colonies according to their population. Mutual arrangements were made for the surrender of fugitive criminals and for the recognition of the judicial decisions of the contracting colonies; and the maintenance of ' the truth and liberties of the Gospel' was declared to be the object of the Federation. Not a few of these provisions were anticipations of the famous American Constitution of a hundred and fifty years later; but more important was the fact that these colonies should be claiming to act and acting just as though they were sovereign states, without the least reference to the powers from whom they had derived their existence and authority. Of course, it must be remembered that at this moment no English government was in a position to intervene and restrain this independent tendency. But it should be noted that this tendency to confederate and claim the right of almost independent powers of self-government was an early and a gradual growth; it was not, as is sometimes represented, the sudden outcome of the Seven Years' War, which relieved the English colonies from all fear of molestation on the part of the French, and by thus rendering them independent of home protection made them more impatient of home control.

There was little need of protection against the home

overnment during the Commonwealth and Protectorate; or Puritan called unto Puritan and both responded. In 642 Parliament had passed a resolution freeing New England from the import and export duties levied on other colonies; and in 1644 Massachusetts made a law that any one seeking to raise a party for the King should be treated as an enemy to the State. Massachusetts, too, was wonderfully accommodating with regard to the question, which was raised at that time, whether the English Parliament had any authority over them, as they were not represented in it. They had not disputed their subjection to the King, but the abolition of the monarchy raised a different question. They recognised, however, that Parliament was their best friend and made a curious admission. All land in America had at the original grant been treated as detached portions of the manor of East Greenwich; and the colonists now conceded that, as they held their lands of that manor, they were really represented in Parliament by the knights of the shire for Kent. They were of another mind in 1775.

With the Restoration this harmony was broken up. The first dispute arose over the Quakers. The English Privy Council forbade the colonists to inflict any bodily punishment on those peaceful people, and ordered that they should be sent to England for their trial. The colonists refused, not entirely from bloodthirsty motives, but because concession would have meant the surrender of their right to try all offences in the colony. There were differences also with respect to the King's demand that churchmen should be admitted to the franchise, and about the extradition of two regicides who had escaped to the colonies. But colonies outside the New England Confederation had a happier time than the stubborn Massachusetts; Rhode Island and Connecticut had their charters confirmed and extended; and the planters of Virginia had more in common with the government of Charles II than with their fellow-countrymen in Puritan New England.

P 2

These southern lands were indeed more suited to the royalists, and in 1663 the colony of Carolina was founded to the south of Virginia and named after Charles II. It was apparently intended to compensate those royalists who had suffered during the Civil War and had found the Act of Oblivion and Indemnity passed at the Restoration to be an act of Oblivion for the King's friends and Indemnity for his enemies. The Lord Chancellor Clarendon, Shaftesbury, and others were interested in the movement, and the philosopher, John Locke, was associated with Shaftesbury in drawing up a fundamental constitution for the colony. In spite of the eminence of its authors, the Constitution was never put in force, and, indeed, it had been drawn up on theoretical principles with little reference to, and without any knowledge of, the practical requirements of the colony for which it was intended. By the time that the colony was settled enough for a constitution it had developed ideas of its own as to what that constitution should be like, and the colonists expressed a decided preference for the institutions they had developed without the assistance of political philosophers. Carolina, which was soon split up into North and South Carolina, marks the furthest extension of the English southwards in the seventeenth century; and only one more colony was added in that direction before the great disruption came. That one was Georgia, founded in 1732 by General James Oglethorpe, partly as a military outpost against the Spaniards, but chiefly as a benevolent institution. For Oglethorpe, driven, as Pope expressed it, 'by strong benevolence of soul' and by a survey of crowded debtors' prisons, founded Georgia as an outlet for those who would otherwise have spent their lives in the workhouse or the gaol.

But the greatest colonial achievement of the reign of Charles II was the filling up of the gulf between the northern colonies of New England and the Southern colonies of Carolina, Virginia, and Maryland. The Swedes had already facilitated this process by succumbing to the Dutch in

1664, but the Dutch left deeper marks upon the history of America. Among the mayors and aldermen of New York we early find the names of Roosevelt, Bayard, Schuyler, and Wendell, reminding us that not a few of the presidents, ambassadors, generals, and men of letters of the United States are descendants of the Dutch founders of the New Netherlands. ' Boss' and 'Bowery,' neither of them pleasant terms, are both of Dutch derivation, and suggest that there was a legacy of evil as well as one of good. The acquisition of these Dutch colonies was one of the most barefaced instances of the policy of 'grab' in the history of the Empire. The Dutch commanded the finest harbour on the eastern coast of America, and their river Hudson was the most convenient waterway for the fur trade with the interior; but they had enjoyed these advantages unmolested and unchallenged for fifty years, when in 1664, while both nations were at peace, the English government suddenly discovered that priority of discovery entitled it to claim them, and resolved to put the claim in execution. The Dutch could only answer with a declaration of war, but the New Netherlands were in no condition to defend themselves against the expedition sent out under the auspices of the Duke of York, then Lord High Admiral; and New Amsterdam became New York and Fort Orange was converted into Albany. In the Second Dutch War of the Restoration these colonies were recovered by the Dutch, but the recovery was only temporary, and at the Treaty of Breda in 1674 they became permanently parts of the dominions of the English-speaking world. The acquisition of the New Netherlands was, it has been truly said, a turning-point in American history. It made it possible for the English colonies to become one united dominion. But for it, there would have been no solid mass of English settlements stretching from Florida to Nova Scotia, and hopelessly outweighing in the balances the colonies of France and Spain; but for it there would have been no War of American Independence and no United States.

There remains to be said a word as to the form in which these new acquisitions were fashioned by the conquerors, and the expiring effort of the Stuarts to crush Puritanism and liberty in the New World. New York became the property of the Duke, who had full power to legislate for it on his own authority without the participation of any popular representative; and a design has been attributed to the Government of Charles II to centralise the administration of all the colonies under the control of the Crown. But in 1683 a constitution was granted to New York, and no serious attempt was made to interfere with it during the reign of James II. Another part of the New Netherlands was sold to Lord Berkeley and Sir George Carteret, and was called New Jersey, in honour of the gallant defence of Jersey made by Carteret against the Parliamentarians. All religious sects were to enjoy liberty of worship and equal political rights in this colony, and it afforded a refuge for the Quakers. But it was threatened in 1686 with an attack by James II upon its charter, and was only saved by the Revolution. One of the proprietors of New Jersey was the famous Quaker, William Penn, who desired to improve upon the religious liberty existing in New Jersey by founding an exclusively Quaker colony. With this object he obtained a grant from Charles II of the land now known as Pennsylvania. The distinguishing feature of the colony was its decent treatment of the Indians, but it had internal troubles, and in 1703 the discontented section seceded to found the little State of Delaware.

It was the Puritan colonies of New England which excited the animosity of the Stuarts, and they were threatened with the fate which overtook their co-religionists at home. Their strongholds had been the corporate towns, whose representatives in the House of Commons had made themselves so obnoxious to the Court during the latter part of Charles's reign. When that king won his victory in 1680, he turned at once against these corporations, and by writs of *Quo Warranto* succeeded in annulling their charters, and filling their places with royal nominees. The same policy was then tried in North America. Massachusetts had given additional offence by secretly purchasing what is now the State of Maine, which Charles intended to bestow upon the Duke of Monmouth. It had also undoubtedly turned its charter to purposes which had never been intended. In 1683 the charter was annulled on the ground that the colony had systematically violated the Navigation Acts, and had illegally set up a mint and coined money on its own authority. Rhode Island was induced to surrender, and in 1686 the charter of Connecticut was likewise declared forfeit. All these colonies, with New Hampshire and Maine, were to be united in one State, and to be ruled despotically by a Governor and Council nominated by the King. The Governor, Sir Edmund Andros, was as incompetent as he was arbitrary ; and when, in 1688, there came news of the revolution in England, there was another revolution as bloodless and complete in the New England across the sea.

The objects of the two revolutions were much the same, their achievement was very different. The legislatures of the American colonies wanted the same powers of self-government as were secured by the English Parliament. The Bill of Rights prohibited the levying of taxes, the raising or keeping of a standing army in the kingdom without consent of Parliament; in 1692 the legislature of Massachusetts passed an Act declaring that no tax should be levied in the colony without its own consent. The Bill of Rights received the royal assent, the Massachusetts bill did not. The revolution in England had made the English Parliament master in its own house ; the revolution in the colonies left them at the arbitrament of another. There you have the root of the War of Independence. And so the causes of the one disruption of the Empire, as well as the causes which made that Empire, may be traced back to the seventeenth century ; and we are brought back to the thesis with which we started, that there is nothing really sudden in the great developments of history. Nothing can be explained in human affairs without reference to the past.

Hence the value of history; it contains the causes which have produced the men, the nations, and the empires of to-day; it supplies the only means whereby we may understand the present, and the only solid ground on which we can base our forecasts of the future. It is the strangest educational phenomena of the time that educational authorities, governments, universities, some county-councils, and most headmasters should be under the delusion that they can turn out efficient citizens without the glimmering of an idea as to the causes which have made them what they are. The Duke of Newcastle, who did not know that Cape Breton was an island, has his counterpart in the Government departments of to-day; and it is neglect of historical studies which often makes the brilliant man of science as inefficient in the sphere of politics as is the politician in the world of science. No one, however, is called upon to deal with scientific matters without some scienific training; but every one is called upon to play his part as a citizen of the Empire, and every one should possess some mental qualification for the duties which his country expects him to perform.

XII

HISTORY AND CITIZENSHIP

THE last chapter ended with the suggestion that the claims of history to an important place in education rest upon the facts that modern civilisation presupposes for the most part a democratic political organisation, in which the ultimate decision of vital questions depends upon the popular vote; and that wise decisions cannot be expected from electorates ignorant of the causes which have produced the world in which they live, its nations, churches, classes, parties, states; its problems, policies, failures, and achievements; its affinities and discords, its order and disorder, its ideas and its illusions, its science and its superstition, its poverty and wealth. The following remarks, or their substance, were addressed to the Eighteenth Annual Conference of Educational Associations in January 1930 as a contribution to a discussion on 'History as a Training for Citizenship.' The word 'training' suggests, perhaps, a teleogical conception, a definite motive and aim, somewhat alien to the spirit of scientific history and incompatible with a term so ambiguous as citizenship. Children can hardly be taught citizenship as they can reading, writing, or spelling, and certainly not by means of history. What is taught systematically tends to sink into doctrine and then into dogma, and to produce what are called the facts of history rather than to stimulate understanding. If we could restore to politics their Aristotelian sense and regard them as the rarest form of science dealing with the highest activities of man, 'History and Politics' might have been a happier indication of the questions at issue.

Citizenship is, however, useful in that it raises by its very ambiguity vital problems of politics. *Civis Romanus sum;* what has Roman citizenship meant in the many and diverse ages of Roman history? What does it mean to Pius XI or Sig. Mussolini now that Rome is shared between two independent States? Is the 'city' of our allegiance and our 'civics' a Little Pedlington or a London; an England, Scotland, Wales, or a United Kingdom; a State or a Commonwealth of Australia; a Dominion or the British Empire; the British Empire or the League of Nations? Or do we think of man 'that will live and be a citizen of the world' as Bacon predicted of his Latin *De Augmentis Scientiarum?* Nor can we stop with citizens of the world; we have also to reckon with those who hold that here we have no continuing city and who would take as their first text-book of civics St. Augustine's *De Civitate Dei.* These are no idle questions, for most wars have in the past been conflicts between these different kinds of allegiance and citizenship, and most problems of modern politics are akin thereto. Is not class consciousness the latest form of 'citizenship'? Do we or should we weigh in equal balance our professional claims as teachers and our civic duties to the State? What part would the 'Burnham scale' play (*a*) in our vote at the polls, (*b*) in our teaching of civics, and can we reconcile the two? Where does citizenship begin and where does it end?

Obviously a discussion on citizenship would never end if it branched off into an examination of the relative claims of local particularism, class-consciousness, union in the trade or union of the trades, professional solidarity, nationalism, imperialism, congregationalism, secular and religious catholicism. The problem can only be here discussed in its simplest, which is also its most vital form, namely, the relation between the individual and any kind of community, whether it be a social class, a professional or trade union, a church, a parish or a county, a national, federal, imperial, or world State. For the individual is the fundamental element in every association, and upon the terms of his relation to it depend both the nature of the association and its strength or weakness, weal or woe. However communistic man's politics may be, he is born and dies, eats and drinks, sleeps and wakes, an individual : he may not have much of a soul or a mind of his own, but he has at least his own physique, and his physical needs determine to no small extent his reactions to the community of which he is part.

That community varies with the scope of his sympathies or imagination; it may consist of the neighbours among whom he has been born or whom he has selected by migration, profession, taste, or ambition. He may take the whole world for his neighbour as John Wesley took the whole world for his parish; or he may dig himself into his native village, his clique or his class, his club or his college, and think everyone else an outsider. The greatest common outsider to the common man is the Government. It used to be thought his natural enemy, and the suspicion still survives, tempered with the growing popular view of the State as a friend indeed when in need of money—a miraculous agency possessed of limitless funds on which democracy can draw for paying wages, salaries, doles, insurance, making roads, relieving rates, protecting and subsidising industries without any cost to one's neighbour that need be felt or counted. It was, and is still, easier to accept the command of the old dispensation to love one's neighbour than the answer of the new dispensation to the question, 'Who is my neighbour?' And training for citizenship would be simpler if our 'city' could be seen as our fellow-citizens, and defrauding or raiding its treasury revealed as picking our neighbour's pocket.

Whatever the form of our city, the essence of citizenship consists in the relation to it of its individual members, and its component groups, whether classes, professions, or parties. It is a public spirit moderating, controlling, and subordinating our lesser loyalties to the common weal, a sense of responsibility to the State for what we do as individuals or partisans, and a sense of responsibility for what the State does as our representative. Democracy does well to watch and criticise and, on occasions, to dismiss its government agents. It used to be said that the price of liberty was eternal vigilance; the same might now be said of other things, economy for instance. But it is idle for democracy with an adult suffrage to place the ultimate responsibility on any other shoulders than its own; for who but democracy makes the governments which do the things of which democracy complains? Does it wish, by its denunciation of its agents, to admit that it is not itself competent to choose them, and return—as some have already done—to the selection of governments by other than democratic methods? It was an excellent thing to make governments responsible to the peoples they govern : it would be a greater but far more difficult reform to make peoples feel a real responsibility for their choice of governments.

It was once a maxim that the tax-collector was the best political schoolmaster, and George Washington remarked that people could never see what they did not feel. The tax-collector, indeed, makes men feel the effect of the policies they approve; but that applies mainly to the payers of direct taxation, and what shall we say of those who are not? It is of course idle to pretend that only those who pay income-tax feel the effects of national policies : the killed and the maimed in a war are not, most of them, payers of income-tax, and comparatively few of those who pay it are unemployed. The point is that the absence of direct taxation removes the most direct and effective means of bringing home to the voter the connection between his vote and its consequences. Hence perhaps the reason for the conjunction of history, rather than any other subject, with citizenship at this conference of educational associations; for, in the absence of personal experience of cause and effect, what but history can prove by examples the consequences of men's political action and their responsibility for them? What may happen is always a disputable proposition : what has happened is not, indeed, always indisputable, but it is less uncertain than the future ; and history is full of warnings from people who have treated their common wealth as a joint stock bank into which they paid as little as possible, but from which they drew out as much as they could. There is no surer sign of bad citizenship than to talk much of the rights of man—that institute and digest of anarchy,' as Burke called them—and say little about his duties.

These are the common sense and the commonplaces of the commonwealth ; and, whatever his conduct in practice, no one disputes them in principle. The real difficulty is not in the conflict between what is clearly right and what is clearly wrong, but between things that appear to be right from different points of view. What are the limits of conscientious objection to the community? To what extent can professional claims be allowed to obstruct the course of justice? If the soldier may not plead his military code in bar of the common law, why should the common lawyer plead professional etiquette to conceal his knowledge of a client's guilt? If the priest may plead the sacred seal of the confessional to save a murderer, may not a physician do the like, and indeed any other profession that has established an equally close and binding code of its own? And what becomes of the communal oath to 'the truth, the whole truth, and nothing but the truth,' when each group or profession claims to contract out of it so far as concerns its own practice? To what extent can the community tolerate 'cities' which are laws unto themselves? In what precisely does the citizenship we are to teach consist?

Most of these questions lie outside the scope of education, as it is usually conceived, and certainly outside any school curriculum. Nevertheless there are certain basic considerations which must intrude into the most elementary treatment of citizenship; and enough things have been said in this conference and elsewhere to show not only that the problem is much in teachers' minds, but that no monopoly, on the part of history or any other subject, of the things that make for citizenship would be admitted. It was claimed, for instance, the other day at the Science Masters' Association that 'the constant application of scientific methods in the laboratory should develop in the people a readiness to suspend judgment until adequate information was available,' and that 'no boy in whom interest in science and its application had not been awakened was properly equipped to play his part in life, whatever his occupation or profession might be.' Simultaneously, on the other side of the Atlantic an eminent physicist in his presidential address to the American Association for the Advancement of Science was pleading that the path of peace lay through science, and predicting that science could save the world from war and its future inhabitants from starvation : war, he said, would disappear owing to changes in the world situation being brought about by science.

Professors of natural science, unfortunately, agree no more among themselves than professors of any other science except in the persuasion that the only proper science is their own; and since this optimistic American forecast of the effect of science on war, a most eminent surgeon has acclaimed war as 'Nature's pruning-hook.' This is not exactly a happy illustration of the scientific method. combining as it does confusion of thought with mixture of metaphors. A pruning-hook is not a product or weapon of Nature; it is devised and made and used by man to check the redundancy, waste, and harmfulness of Nature which, left to herself, turns gardens into jungles and chokes fruitful soil with weeds. Man with his pruning-hook. like the surgeon with his scalpel, selects with care and skill the harmful growths to be excised : war, if it selects at all. chooses for its victims precisely those whom wisdom would preserve. Is the world richer, stronger, or more fruitful for the surgical operations of Nature's pruning-hook in the Great War? Chaos, says Karl Pearson, is the law of Nature, order the dream of man. Civilisation and citizenship are the exact measures of man's success in taming, controlling, and turning to beneficent uses the riotous, reckless, barbarous, physical passions and forces of Nature. To reverse the process and take Nature as man's master and model is not a means of education : the natural man receiveth not the things of the spirit, for they are foolishness unto him; neither can he know them, for they are spiritually discerned. We cannot ascertain the rudiments of justice or law, of politics, ethics or economics, of logic, language, or literature, or even of 'Nature's pruning-hook' by the most 'constant application of scientific methods in the laboratory.' For they teach us nothing of human nature, and there is no more certain or prolific source of mental confusion than the application of physical formulæ to the study of human affairs.

The pruning-hook theory of war, however, recalls another scientific presidential address which brings us nearer to the heart of our subject. A year ago, Professor (now Sir) Leonard Hill referred at the annual conference of the Sanitary Inspectors' Association to the recent discovery of a deadly bacillus which, he said, was easily cultivated. 'And,' he continued, 'if men were as susceptible as guinea-pigs to the toxin produced by this bacillus—and there was reason to think they were—it would appear that one gramme, say a saltspoonful, of the dry toxin would suffice to kill a million. . . . If men set out to prepare such a toxin and scatter it by aeroplane, what would be the use of the panoply of war?' Here indeed is a prospect of peace, whichever alternative method mankind might prefer. It might forswear war for fear of the toxin; but if it did not, there would still be 'peace through science,' only it would be a peace without the human race. They make a desert and they call it peace. Neither the name nor the nature of this bacillus was revealed, and that silence was golden. But history holds out little hope that it would be always observed. As Lord Randolph Churchill remarked in 1887, the possession of a powerful weapon puts an irresistible temptation into the mind of its possessor to use it; and for a thousand years no peace and no war has stopped the incessant progress in the scientific invention and improvement of methods of human destruction. Man's capacity for destruction, like his capacity for making noise, is ever on the increase. In the old days of hand-to-hand fighting no man, not even Achilles, could kill more than a select handful of foes: it was far too exhausting. Now, apart from bacilli, we hear of a bomb which will destroy without an effort everything within a hundred miles of the spot on which it falls; and it seems likely that, if not already, mankind will soon, for the first time in its existence, have acquired the power to wipe itself off the face of the earth—on a Day of Judgement in which it would have condemned itself as unfit to live because it could not keep the peace.

Who would have been responsible? Surely not the eager discoverers of bacilli, the zealous inventors of high explosive, the altruistic men of science who discover or make these things in the interests of preventive and therapeutic medicine or of constructive mining and engineering. No responsibility for the use to which an invention is put need attach to the inventor; the value of his discovery may to him be purely scientific, but the value to others will consist in the uses to which they can put it. Armament firms and war departments are not concerned with pure science, but with its application to practical warlike purposes, and they are always on the look-out with tempting offers to simple inventors. Nor are inventors always quite simple; it was a scientific discoverer of gases who first suggested their use as poison in warfare; and patriotism seconds other inducements to convert discoveries into judicious revelations. The innocence or excellence of intentions cannot quite solve the problem of responsibility for the undesigned consquences of our acts : few of our thousands of motor fatalities are due to ill-will, and even those in haste to save life are responsible if they incidentally kill on the way.

The dilemma, put bluntly, is that the survival of the human race might depend upon the suppression of scientific truth unless we could rely upon a world-wide civic sense strong enough to prevent the perversion of science to destructive purposes.   The discovery of a virulent toxin may be a great scientific achievement and yet its concealment a civic duty.   But the man of science will contend that he must go on discovering as much scientific truth as he can, irrespective of the uses to which his discoveries are put ; and his plea is within limits irrefutable.   Nevertheless his disclaimer of responsibility subordinates his citizenship to his science.   For responsibility is the essence of citizenship, and its denial the ruin of States.   Throughout its constitutional history our country, at least, has maintained as its vital principle that there should be no power without responsibility : that is why Ministers now govern through the Crown and not the Crown through Ministers ; for Ministers are legally and constitutionally responsible for all the Crown does, while the Crown itself is not.   That, too, is the answer to a formal complaint made in 1915 that eminent men of science were not included in the Cabinet or given high executive office during the war.   We cannot claim power and disclaim responsibility, and any Minister who pleaded that he was not responsible for his acts because he did not foresee or intend the consequences of what he did, or even said, would find his plea laughed out of court. The scientific expert, whether his science be biological, physical, medical, economic, historical, or even political, will probably play an increasing part in human government. General Smuts has recently declared that democracy is not enough, that universal suffrage has to be tempered with universal science, and that the scientific political expert is

a necessary institution in national government. That i
undoubtedly true; but the scientific expert can only be ai
adviser to Ministers who have the power to accept or rejec
the expert advice because they alone will bear the responsibility for giving it effect. The alternative was tried by
Germany before the war: it took the form of a bureaucratic
despotism tempered by expert advice which provoked the
war with suicidal results to its authors.

But this scientific dilemma is the dilemma *in excelsis* of
teachers in general, and Bury, the historian, has given the
same 'scientific' answer: 'History,' he declares, 'must
be studied as if it had no reference to anything beyond
itself." History, indeed, is not commonly reckoned a
practical science; yet Thiers' history had much to do with
the revival of French imperialism which led to Sedan, and
Treitschke's with the German imperialism which provoked
disaster in the Great War. Knowledge is power—for good
or for evil—and the increase of knowledge is the general
purpose of education from the most elementary stages
upwards. Must not teachers, like the man of science, teach
children to read and write, irrespective of the uses to which
some of them may put that knowledge and skill? Yet
there would be no forgery without that elementary
education, no burglary without some mechanical training,
no falsification of accounts without some arithmetical skill.
It is obvious that ignorance cannot be fostered lest
knowledge should be misused, nor education denied to the
mass because it provides criminals with their equipment.
Nor does the cause of the trouble lie in what we teach but
in what we do not: the sin, if it be one, is a sin of omission.
In other words, we spread knowledge and power like heat
or electricity without any adequate safeguards, without
sufficient protection or warning that these things are
excellent only under certain conditions and proper control.
The knowledge of virulent toxins and high explosive should
clearly be insulated at least as rigorously as an electric
current, and restricted to those who can be trusted to use

t only for good. Aye, there's the rub: what is good? Is it good to prepare toxins or high explosive for use against a possible enemy when it is sure in the long run to be used against a certain friend? Or is it good in any case?

When Bacon taught that the 'sovereignty of man lay hid in knowledge,' he thought that scientific discovery would ensure the 'fortune of the human race.' He calmly assumed that man would know how to use his knowledge, and thus left the Prince of Denmark (or of darkness) out of his prophetic *Hamlet*. Do we not make the same mistake, and take it for granted that somehow or other the 'training' of children to write and of youth to fly will automatically teach them to write what is right and to flee what is wrong; that in the knowledge of good and evil nheres an instinctive preference for good; and that man is born not merely free and equal but with a native or natural sense of citizenship and of responsibility for his actions and an aboriginal mastery of that quintessence of wisdom the knowledge of how to use knowledge? So our worship of youth descends into superstition: 'the worst thing of all,' says Bacon, 'is the apotheosis of error.' Herbert Spencer, a childless old bachelor, thought that children were best left to learn, without teaching, that fire burns by burning their fingers in the nursery of experience. Experience is, however, a painful and sometimes a fatal experiment; and we do not, for the sake of its educational value, habitually leave our poisons unlabelled, our railways unfenced, and our nursery fires unfended. Nor do we leave our children at school to learn exactly what they like or do exactly what they please. But we tend too much in our curricula to limit ourselves to teaching them how to do things without explaining what they should do or why they should do it, to increasing knowledge without understanding, and power without responsibility. Hence the stress on linguistic studies and means of expression, as though the purpose for which we speak and the wisdom of what we say were less important than the tongue or

Q 2

the grammar in which we speak it. Greater is he that prophesieth than he that speaketh with tongues; but we are content with providing the tongues and leaving the rule of those members to chance.

This abdication of education in favour of experience has the further defect that only the few and the wise learn much from any experience but their own. Here, however, the child has the advantage over the adult : much of the value of school life consists in seeing and learning from the penalties others suffer for ill-conduct. But in Dame Europa's adult school one nation learns little from the experience of others : it does not really feel because it does not see what or how or why they suffer from their conduct. It discerns little enough the reasons for its own discomforts, because when the fathers eat sour grapes, it is often the children's teeth that are set on edge; and cause and effect are spread over from one generation to another. Here is where history comes in : it is the sum of the past experience of our own and other nations, and if it is studied and taught to any purpose, it is not a mere tale that is told, but a relation of cause and effect, and a treasury of responsible citizenship.

That doctrine used to be left to the schools of the Church which taught the child in admirable terms of citizenship his duty to do to all men as he would they should do to him. But that injunction was followed by others enjoining submission to all his governors, teachers, spiritual pastors and masters, and lowly and reverent behaviour to all his betters. A further exhortation to do his duty 'in that state of life, unto which it shall please God to call' him was and is, widely misquoted as an exhortation to do his duty in the state to which it *had* pleased God to call him. Democracy could not stomach conservative doctrine like that; and as the State grew more and more democratic, and education became more and more a State affair, any kind of instruction which inculcated duty was discountenanced lest it should rest on particular doctrines and

lead to sectarian bias. The religious basis of civic responsibility was undermined, and pure science and simple
knowledge were taught without any regard to the fact that
the ensuing power without a concomitant sense of responsibility is an unmitigated evil. The religion of the Church
was barred because it was that of a particular church; the
religion of the State did not succeed because, while it was
the religion of no particular person, it was often the religion
of a very particular State.[1]

How is the gap to be filled? If the need is to be supplied
at all effectively for democracy, it must be supplied in the
schools which provide nine-tenths of our future voters with
whatever school-education they receive. Direct lessons
would probably defeat their own object. I have been told
by an old pupil, now one of H.M. Inspectors of Schools,
that where he received his 'training' as a teacher there
was every degree of variety in the order kept in the different
classes; but if you went down a corridor and heard a
special pandemonium, the sounds were almost certain to
proceed from a class which was being taught how to keep
order. So one heard long ago at Oxford that, if there was
profanity anywhere, it was in a college where special stress
was laid on religious teaching and observances. No one
would relish the task of teaching the whole duty of man to
students of any class or age; and if the problem confronts
the teacher of history, it is not because he claims it as a
privilege but because the nature of his subject seems to
impose it on him as an obligation.

For history comprises, among other things, the politics
and the civics of the past, and one of its definitions is that
it is philosophy teaching by means of examples. Its proper
study is man; and, while the contention that human
nature does not change is a sheer denial of progress and
civilisation, human nature provides fundamentally common
ground between history and politics such as does not exist

[1] The Fascist and the Bolshevist States are the most obvious
examples.

between citizenship and physical science, mathematics, or even linguistic studies. History deals with men of like passions as ourselves struggling with problems much the same as our own. The problems of peace and war, poverty and wealth, Church and State, concord and discord, conscience and authority belong to all time and confront all generations of men : they are always with us. They may change their form and vary their incidence ; but in principle they remain the same, and that is why text-books like Plato's *Republic,* Aristotle's *Politics,* St. Augustine's *De Civitate Dei,* Machiavelli's *Prince,* Hobbe's *Leviathan* or Rousseau's *Contrat Social* are still live wires. And history demands for the understanding of these problems the same qualities as statesmanship requires for their solution—sympathy, imagination, insight, the capacity for seing the unseen things that last more clearly than the bubbles which burst and the shadows which pass away. The *imponderabilia* of human affairs are the raw material of the historian and the statesman ; and the very fact that they cannot be weighed, seen through microscopes, tested in tubes or reduced to formulæ sets a deep gulf between them and the materialistic schools of physical science, and makes wholly unscientific the application of the principles of the one to the study of the other. Insight and imagination have, indeed, played a great part in the mental equipment of every great man of science ; but it is insight into other nature than man's, and there is not much sympathy—or shall I say compassion—between the chemist and his elements, the geologist and his strata, the physicist and his forces. It is easy to be dispassionate in one's natural history ; it is not so easy in dealing with Whigs and Tories, Catholics and Protestants, Capitalists and Communists, Bolsheviks and Fascists. But the touch of human nature is needed to make the essential kinship between the study of history and the problems of scientific politics.

Imagination and insight are no less indispensable. The other day at an International Congress on the History of

Science an eminent physiologist deprecated school-time spent on such things as battles between England and France in the fifteenth century (involving Joan of Arc); they could not, he thought, be of any moment to us to-day. Possibly not, if one thinks Joan of Arc and her achievements a simple problem of physics or physiology; if one has no interest in how or why things have happened in the past, and how or why they might conceivably happen or be prevented in the future; and if one has no understanding of the issues involved. But is not a knowledge of why wars happened of some importance to those who are anxious that they should not recur and are seeking better means of prevention than improving the weapons and increasing the deadliness of war? As for the triviality of the issues involved, one of them was whether there should be a France or an England, as we know them, at all. England was fighting to establish the claim of her Lancastrian kings to the throne of France and to reproduce the Anglo-French empire of Henry II. If successful, the attempt would have involved England in perpetual European wars which would have destroyed the chance of a British empire overseas. France would have disappeared, but a Germany might have established itself on the Somme, the English Channel, and the North Sea, and there would certainly have been no great war such as that which was fought in 1914-18. This is not history; but history is a comparative study which loses most of its value if deprived of its comparison with the background of what might have been had men thought and acted and succeeded otherwise than they did. But the facts of history seem often to the man versed only in physical science merely fortuitous events, without rhyme or reason; to him they have no more meaning than helium has to a Hottentot, and history itself is a tale of sound and fury, told by an idiot and signifying nothing. Absorption in the task of explaining what man is as an animal appears to preclude any wish to understand what he is as a man, or why he became what he is as a citizen.

History itself, as taught fails often and sadly enough both in its sympathy and its understanding. It loses sight of the whole in the part, the general in the particular, time in the period, the world in the nation, claiming some knowledge of Englishmen, Frenchmen, Germans, Americans, but disclaiming mankind in the mass. Yet some appreciation of the unity of time and of man is essential to the understanding of any part of history and to the foundations of any real citizenship. Independence has almost passed out of the sphere of effective political (and economic) science; and interdependence has taken its place. Neither nations nor individuals are, or ever have been, completely independent : each one's action has always depended upon the actions of other people. One of the idlest contentions about the origin of the war is the argument whether or not our hands were 'free' in July, 1914 : our action depended on what was done by other people, and the simplest and best explanation of what England did after Belgium's invasion was given by King George himself when he asked the American ambassador, 'Good God, Mr. Page, what else could we have done?' The history of the most self-contained nation, church, or other group depends upon that of their neighbours. Hence our national history cannot be confined to the history of one nation, our ecclesiastical history to that of one church, our social history to that of one class; and, if we are to deal with other men's history, we must be able to put ourselves in other men's places. That is why we have to visualise things we have not seen, and understand feelings we have not ourselves experienced.

For history is a matter of sense as well as of science, of feeling as well as of fact; and it is no use thinking we understand why men acted unless we know what they felt.

> Show me what angels feel : till then
> I cling, a mere weak man, to men.

Let history show what men in history felt : till then the

public will cling to the sensational Press and to fiction parading itself as such or masquerading as history or psycho-analysis. It is because history is not felt that citizenship is feeble. That is also why wars recur : they are, indeed, felt, more or less, for a time ; but the feeling is soon forgotten, and the facts remain only as food for romance. So Ruskin could dwell on the 'beauty' of war because he had never seen a shot fired in anger, and had forgotten or never known what Wellington said was 'hell.' A surfeit of war has always produced a passion for peace, and each of the last four centuries began with a scheme to make it perpetual. We ourselves hope to cement its foundations ; and out of their stony griefs the bereaved of the War are striving their Bethel to raise in a League of Nations. But feeling descends into sentiment ; and memory of the war recedes into the poetic background of 'old, unhappy, far-off things and battles long ago.' Science holds in its hands the future and, while pleading pacific intentions, provides the new weapons of war : there are others, still 'heathen folk, who put their trust in reeking tube and iron shard.'

Meanwhile, generations of children grow up who cannot feel, without our help, what they have never seen. Let us then help them, if we can, to realise what men felt in history, and why they fought, and where they failed in sympathy and understanding, because they could not grasp what others felt and therefore knew not what they did themselves. Thus may we hope to be teaching them not only the realities of history, but some of the elements of good citizenship, and guiding their feet perhaps into the way of peace.

XIII

THE UNIVERSITY OF LONDON AND THE STUDY OF HISTORY[1]

(i) IN 1904

IT may seem a bold and hazardous thing to have put two such topics as the University of London and the Study of History into the title of an hour's lecture; for either of them might well afford material for at least a dozen discourses. But I have no intention of attempting to deal with either in its general aspects; it is only of the University of London in its relation to the Study of History, and of the Study of History in relation to the University of London, that I propose to speak at the present time. If there be presumption on my part in approaching these subjects at all, a few facts will, I think, justify the view that it is none too soon for some one to call attention to the position which the study of history at present occupies in the University of London.

An eminent member of the Senate of the University, in a recently published book on London Education,[2] refers more than once to what he describes as 'the dwindling Faculty of Arts.' Now I am not prepared to defend or dispute the general truth of that phrase; but those of us who are interested in the study of Modern History cannot conceal from ourselves the fact that that school is not in a

[1] This lecture was originally delivered at University College in October 1904. During the two and a half years which have elapsed since that time some progress has been made. The footnotes will indicate how considerable that progress has been, and how many of the suggestions here discussed have been actually adopted, or are in the process of adoption (1907).

[2] Sidney Webb, *Problems of London Education*, 1903.

healthy condition. The University Calendar itself bears mournful testimony to the truth of this statement. I take the Class Lists for recent years. It was in 1896, I believe, that the separate examination in History for the B.A. Honours degree was established. In that year there were three candidates who obtained a class; in 1897 there was one; in 1898 there was one; in 1899 there were none; in 1900 there were five; in 1901 there was one; and in 1902 there were five again. The total for seven years is thus sixteen, or an average of just over two a year. That does not strike one as a particularly brilliant result; but, when these lists are scrutinised somewhat more closely, the result for London itself is still more distressing; for, of those sixteen candidates, only six were produced by the various institutions which now make up the teaching University of London; and of those six only one has been granted First Class Honours—one candidate a year, and one candidate in seven years of First Class standing[1]— surely extraordinary figures for a university which aims at providing the highest possible education for a population numbering some seven millions of souls, a population many times more numerous than that which produced the Art and the Literature, the Science and the Statesmanship of Ancient Athens, a population more numerous than that which made the Roman Empire, a population more numerous than those of the Holland, the Belgium, the Switzerland of today, each of which countries maintains several universities, each with a vigorous school of Modern History.

The conditions, I know, are totally different; and the more decisive of those conditions are beyond the power of

---

[1] This condition of things no longer exists. In 1905 the first B.A. Honours Examination in Modern History for Internal Students (*i.e.* students who have had three years' instruction at some recognised school or under some recognised teacher of the University) was held. There were five candidates, of whom one was placed in the first, three in the second, and one in the third, class. In 1906 the number of candidates increased to nine, of whom two were placed in the first, five in the second, and two in the third class. There will probably be further increases in 1907 and 1908.

any university, and even of any government, to alter; but some of the existing obstacles are more amenable to treatment and may be removed in time. Among such is the fact that London University has few scholarships and few exhibitions to give for Modern History, while older establishments count these attractions by the score and even by the hundred; so that a London youth with a taste for history is pretty sure to be tempted elsewhere. A second obstacle, which has been painfully brought home to my mind by six years' experience as a Matriculation Examiner, is the fact that the most promising history candidates almost invariably fail in elementary mathematics or in some other uncongenial subject;[1] and a third consists in the fact that no one can pass the intermediate examination in Arts without a knowledge of Greek,[2] a prohibition which warns off the history course most of those who have not learnt Greek at school; and those who have not learnt Greek at school inevitably constitute no small proportion of the undergraduates of London Universtiy.

But, whatever the causes, the fact remains that Modern History is at present the Cinderella, perhaps I should say one of the somewhat numerous Cinderellas of London University who await the advent of some fairy prince to raise them to their proper station in life; and, roughly

---

1 The remedy for this is not easy to prescribe. The difficulty, which is partly natural and inevitable, is magnified by the lack of guidance from which candidates suffer. Often they have no one to point out their weak subjects and make them concentrate on those; and there should be greater facility in the communications between examiners and teachers, a facility which has been established for the higher examinations on the Internal side, but is lacking for Matriculation and the External side.

2 This has now been altered; an Arts candidate must take two languages at least, of which one must be either Latin or Greek. Any candidate may take both, but they are not compulsory. Historical students can now take those two indispensable modern languages, French and German, which was practically impossible before; and professors of Greek are no longer compelled to turn their Intermediate classes into Fourth Forms.

speaking, there is no such thing at the present moment as a History School in the University of London.[1] The question then arises whether there should or should not be such a school. Well, I suppose that that question is settled for us here in a vague theoretical way by the definition of University College as 'a place of teaching and research in which wide academic culture is secured by the variety of the subjects taught in different faculties.' For I imagine that no one would exclude Modern History from that variety of subjects; and I assume that the University of London will not be content with a narrower ideal than University College. Supposing, however, that a young man were to come and say, 'It is all very well to talk about academic culture, but what is the *use* of history? what tangible advantages can you hold out if I take up the study of history, spend weary hours in attending your lectures, and precious money in paying your fees?' Well, I suppose it would not be in accordance with professorial practice or with professional etiquette, but I should be inclined to reply, taking the words in the current conventional sense, that history is of absolutely no *use* whatever. Yet it is precisely on that assumption—that history is of no use whatever—that I would base its claim to a prominent place in the curricula of every University under the sun. It is of no use according to the popular notion of education; because education is vulgarly thought to be valuable mainly, if not solely, as a means of increasing our individual or our national wealth; and it is to be feared that, if education were to be stripped of that glamour and of its theological delights, there would be little popular interest left in the subject. At any rate, from a point of view of those who regard education as a path to prosperity or even to moderate comfort, the study of history holds

[1] This is happily no longer true; there are over half a dozen students doing post-graduate research in Modern History, and some have already published original work of no slight value. One was awarded the Royal Historical Society's Alexander Prize last year (1906).

out only the feeblest attractions. One of the most brilliant and popular of English historians, James Anthony Froude, declared that he would not bring up a son as an historian, because the pecuniary rewards for the writing of history did not suffice for even a modest living. Another historian recently dead, more learned if less brilliant than Froude, for writing one of the greatest of English histories received less per hour than the wage of an unskilled manual labourer. Gibbon could not have written his *Decline and Fall of the Roman Empire* nor Macaulay his *History of England* if they had not possessed independent means; and the first requisite for an historian in England is neither skill nor industry, neither knowledge of documents nor a faculty for turning them into literature, but the command of financial resources independent of those which can be derived from the writing of history. These are the giants of the world of history; as for the lesser folk, I am told they eke out a scanty subsistence by trouncing each other's books in the newspaper press, and spoiling each other's market by selling their review copies below cost price. One of them not long ago published a book at his own expense, and after a time went to inquire how many copies had been sold. The publisher, a humane man, tried to parry the question; but the author was persistent and at length extorted the answer 'Four.' 'Four,' he exclaimed, 'four! Well, I made my family buy three, but who in the world could have bought the fourth?' There is a pathetic side to the picture. I have heard tell of an historical student who has spent years on a piece of research, without hope or desire of profit, and now that it is completed is unable to give it to the world because he cannot afford to pay for its publication himself and cannot persuade a publisher to take the risk. I do not refer, of course, to the authors of school books, which are often a re-hash of old facts flavoured only with an original spice of error, and are generally popular and profitable in inverse ratio to their merits.

I cannot therefore hold out the study of history as an easy or pleasant method of making a fortune. It is in fact of little use as technical instruction; but is that fact a bar to its use as a means of liberal education? I think not. For it seems to me that there is a deep and vital distinction between technical instruction and education in the true sense of the word; and the tendency to ignore and gloze over the difference is one of the greatest perils in the path of our universities to-day. With technical instruction a university has primarily nothing to do; its main object is to educate. It should limit itself to the ascertainment and propagation of knowledge; the *application* of that knowledge to industrial and manufacturing processes lies outside its proper sphere and should be left to other agencies. For surely the whole justification of endowments is this : that they enable professors and others to pursue knowledge and investigate problems quite irrespective of the question whether the results of their researches are convertible into terms of hard cash or not. The application of this ascertained knowledge should be a matter for commercial or industrial enterprise which would bring its own reward. One of the worst features in our higher educational circles is that the true *raison d'être* of endowments is constantly being lost sight of, that they come to be regarded as a right and not as a trust and a privilege, as property without conditions and duties attached to it, and that the leisure which its possession affords is employed not in the pursuit of unremunerative research but in the acquisition of gain.

But what is the difference between technical instruction and education proper? Perhaps it is something like this : the function and object of technical instruction is, for instance, to make a brewer a better brewer; the function of education is to make him a better man. Technical instruction regards the means of living, education regards the end of life. It seeks to make men, not money, to develop to the utmost possible extent the faculties, mental, moral, and spiritual, of mankind, and to enable them not merely to exist, but to live the fullest life of which they are capable. It used to be said in the old days of the struggle for the extension of elementary education and of the franchise, that no amount of education and no number of votes would enable the ploughman to drive a straighter furrow or the dock-labourer to heave a heavier load. It was the function of the ploughman to follow the plough and the cobbler to stick to his last. To which it was replied that the ploughman does not live in order to plough, but ploughs in order to live; and that hard labour is not an end in itself, but only a means. The old fallacies still survive, and popular indifference to education, as distinct from technical instruction, is largely due to the idea that no amount of it will enable a man to add one cubit to his financial stature. But surely it is no part of the business of a university to lend itself to errors like these. A university should set its face against the encroachments and usurpations of technical instruction. The State has more than once taken upon itself to raise the limit of age at which children may be taken from school and put to earning a livelihood; in the same way a university should endeavour to postpone, not accelerate, the limit of age at which bread-and-butter considerations come in to dominate, narrow, and check the growth of the youthful mind. Not that I wish to depreciate technical instruction; the more of it the better—in its place. It is excellent to have a Charlottenburg, provided that your Charlottenburg does not usurp the place of a university.[1] It is excellent to have technical instruction, provided it does not oust liberal education; it is excellent that ploughmen should be taught to plough, and dairymaids to milk, provided that such

[1] The safest way of guarding against such encroachments would be to place both under the same control. At any rate to establish in London a vast Technical Institute, side by side and independent of the university, and to give it the power of granting degrees, would simply be the destruction of the newly created teaching University of London. The Charlottenburg should be a supplement to, and not a rival of, the university; and a university qualification should be made compulsory for all Charlottenburg students.

instruction is not allowed to take the place of education. I know that there are difficulties in the way of liberal education here; the practical as well as the ideal must always be borne in mind, and the undergraduate of London has on an average to think of earning a living earlier than the undergraduate elsewhere; but *that* is an evil to be diminished and not a good to be encouraged.

Another cause of popular indifference to education and comparative zeal for technical instruction is the impression that England is being outstripped by her rivals, and particularly by Germany and the United States, in the race for commercial prosperity, because she has in the past, and does still in the present, stand too much on the ancient ways, and devotes to liberal education the time and energy which her competitors spend in technical instruction and in the application of science to commerce and industry. This assumption, I believe, is entirely erroneous. Germany at any rate does not neglect higher education because it is zealous in the cause of technical instruction. The Germans are at least as efficient in pure scholarship as they are in mixed mathematics or in applied science. Take, for example, the University of Berlin; I am told by my scientific colleagues that that university is perhaps the best equipped university in the world from a scientific point of view, and one would therefore hardly select it as the type of university in which the study of Arts was the most highly developed. Yet what do we find? Berlin has its six professors of Modern History, and, perhaps even more important, its professor of the methods of historical research; and there is scarcely a university in Germany which does not possess two or three professors of Modern History; that appears to be the minimum without which a German university dare not look the world in the face. America is not far behind; Chicago, I believe, has seven professors of Modern History, and for an elucidation of the most important problems in English Constitutional History one has to send one's pupils to books written and published under the auspices of American universities. Nor is the German interest in Modern History confined to universities; nearly every State has its royal or ducal commission for the publication of its historical materials, and the same object is energetically pursued by numbers of local associations; most districts have their *verein* or *gesellschaft* for the purposes of research; and practically no one in Germany dreams of giving or seeking a doctor's degree unless his thesis is based upon the study of portions of unpublished material. In Germany there are to-day some two hundred regular periodical publications exclusively devoted to historical research; in England there is one. Now I do not fancy all the German's methods; what he has won in intensity of gaze he may have lost in broadness of outlook; his zeal may not always be tempered with wisdom, but of his zeal the facts I have mentioned leave no doubt. And they might be multiplied indefinitely, but I have said enough to show that there is no inherent incompatibility between the keenest pursuit of efficiency in commerce and industry and the keenest devotion to pure scholarship; a nation or a community is not bound to choose between the two. Rather their existence side by side—both developed to such an extent as they are in Germany—indicates that there may be some subtle connection between the two, and suggests that what makes the Germans such formidable rivals is not their preference of technical instruction to a liberal education, but the intellectual keenness which enables them to pursue both with success.

These facts, then, show that foreign universities are not blind to the value of history as a subject of education. Testimony as to that value is, indeed, superfluous; it is not disputed that you cannot understand what man is to-day unless you know what he was yesterday and the day before, that the past has produced the present, and is the only guide for the future. Down at the bottom—even in London—we admit the value of history, though at times we dissemble our appreciation, and at times express it in curious ways. Some three years ago a committee was formed in London for the purpose of establishing a chair of Modern History at Cape Town in South Africa, and it was urged with some force and some truth that it was of the highest importance that the future citizens of the Empire in South Africa should be made acquainted with at least the outlines of the history of their own and of other countries. I believe a fair sum was collected for this excellent project; but the odd thing was that it did not seem to have occurred to any one that charity begins at home, and that if it was essential for the youth of Cape Town to know something of history, it was, at least, as essential for the six millions who live at the heart of the Empire. For when, about the same time, an effort was made to establish a university professorship of History in London, in memory of the late Bishop Creighton, the magnificent sum of £300 was all that was realised, a sum just sufficient to pay one lecturer £100 a year for three years, which have now expired.[1] That fiasco[2] seems to have damped the ardour of those who hoped to see a school of history established in London University; and I have been told that there is no demand for history teaching in London, and that it is of no use for the university to appoint teachers or professors until such a demand has been created.

Admitting, then, that we have no history school at present, and assuming that there ought to be such a school, we must next ask what prospect there is of its ever taking shape. And here it is necessary to distinguish between an undergraduate and a post-graduate school of Modern History. I have already alluded to various obstacles in

[1] Another £300 was subsequently collected, and Mr. Passmore Edwards gave a similar sum to found a second lectureship. Both are associated with the School of Economics, and even they depend for existence to some extent on their appeal to the economic rather than the educational motive.

[2] The attempt was revived last year (1906) with no better success.

the way of an undergraduate school of Modern History, the rival attractions of numerous and substantial scholarships and exhibitions elsewhere, the enforcement of Greek in the Intermediate Examination in Arts, and of other subjects at Matriculation. To these must be added the somewhat inadequate provision for teaching at various schools of the university, the difficulty of arranging intercollegiate courses, owing to the geographical distribution of the various centres,[1] the want of good libraries, and the necessity of keeping down the standard of the Honours Examination to the level attainable by External students dwelling in lonely villages inaccessible to any culture except that which comes by post. In all these respects London has had to contend with infinitely greater difficulties than other universities. Yet they are not insuperable, and they do not absolutely forbid the creation of an undergraduate school of Modern History. Granting that many of the best students are, and always will be, drawn off elsewhere, surely there is a sufficient residuum among the six or seven millions residing within the university radius, most of whom could not, even with the help of scholarships, spend three or four years at Oxford or Cambridge. London, it is said, engages about fifteen hundred new teachers for its schools in every year; surely some of these should have undergone a course of university instruction in Modern History, a course which, for the vast majority of them, is only possible within the London radius. There are, moreover, a few scholarships in the University of London; and it is a matter for regret that the very existence of these scholarships appears to be unknown, alike to teachers and to pupils. With regard to books and libraries, there is now a fair nucleus for a University Library at South Kensington;[2] and there is a most

[1] This difficulty has not been found insuperable. The present writer has had at his lectures, students from King's, Bedford, and Westfield Colleges; and has sent pupils of his own to all colleges from which they were not debarred by sex.

[2] The difficulty about the location of the university buildings

admirable library here in this college, the advantages of which are not sufficiently appreciated, although it has been thrown open to every Internal student of the university, whether he or she be a member of University College or not. Finally, the differentiation of the External and the Internal Examinations for the B.A. Honours Degree opens up at least the possibility of raising the standard of the Internal Degree to a considerably higher level. It has, I know, been suggested that, owing to the paucity of candidates and the expense of conducting two sets of Examinations, it may be necessary once more to amalgamate the two. There is no objection to that step, provided that the External Examination is raised to the level of the Internal, and not the Internal reduced to that of the External, and provided that there be no ruling-out of subjects on the ground that Little Peddlington does not afford adequate facilities for their study. A university purchases increased numbers at too great a cost when it lowers its standard in order to increase its size.

I turn to a vastly more promising topic—a post-graduate school of Historical Research in London; and here the stars in their courses have fought in our favour; here we have a monopoly of advantages which no other city in the whole Empire can boast. To begin with, at present there is no competition; for there is no real school of research in History in any English university.[1] Not that competition would matter; for the special opportunities which London enjoys should enable it—if it is wise—to outdistance its rivals with ease. Undergraduates may be tempted in that and in this and in every direction; but graduates who aspire to research in Modern History are compelled to

at South Kensington is their inaccessibility to London undergraduates. Youths who live in South Kensington go to Oxford or Cambridge, if they go to any university at all, and the Engineering and other technological students at the Imperial Institute do not frequent the University library.

1 Cf. Professor Firth's inaugural lecture, *A Plea for the Historical Teaching of History*, delivered at Oxford five weeks after this one

resort to London. For here in the Record Office, in the British Museum, and in other Government Departments are stored the vast bulk of materials on which they must base their work, if their research is to reach that standard which other countries have set, and which we now have a right to demand. It is true that the Bodleian has considerable manuscript collections unused, untouched, unseen; it is true that there are archives at various noblemen's seats, like those of Lord Salisbury at Hatfield, or those of the Duke of Portland at Welbeck, and of course the materials for local history must always be sought in various localities. But from the point of view of national history all these are a drop in the ocean of records existing in London. Of course, some of these have been printed or calendared, and thus made accessible in any respectable library; and, indeed, I read in a review the other day the statement that the materials for the history of the sixteenth century had been worked over so often and scrutinised so closely that nothing now remained to be learned or to be said on the subject. That only illustrates the unfathomable ignorance of reviewers—I speak as a fairly frequent reviewer myself. For, as a matter of fact, no human eye has so much as glanced at all the materials for the history of that century, and the same may be said with even more certainty for every succeeding age. To mention one class of material, —the despatches of English ambassadors abroad : those extending from 1509 to 1579 have indeed been calendared under the direction of the Master of the Rolls. But, except for these seventy years, they remain for the most part unprinted and unread; and even when calendared it takes about a generation for their contents to be digested, and at least two generations for the truth that is in them to filter down into the history that is taught in our schools and universities. Of the extant materials for English history not one-tenth has yet been calendared or printed, and the whole of English history, as it is written and read or known, is like an edifice built on foundations which do not occupy one-tenth of the possible area. Here is a void clamouring to be filled; herein lies the unique opportunity for a post-graduate school of research in London University.

Circumstances, too seem to mark out beforehand the lines on which this post-graduate school should run. As the materials existing in London are mainly concerned with English History, it is obvious that this school should be mainly, though not exclusively, a school of research in English History. But even within the limits of English History there are certain subjects which pre-eminently demand our attention; and first and foremost among these I place the subject of Naval History. For, considering that this Empire is the greatest naval power the world has ever known, considering it has had the longest and most glorious naval history on record, considering further that it has been built up and rests upon sea power, that its very existence therefore depends to a large extent upon the true interpretation and appreciation of the lessons of naval history, it is surely an astounding fact that there is not, and never has been, a professorship or a lectureship or a readership in naval history in any university whatsoever within the limits of the British dominions.

Fortunately there has been of late years no great naval war to test how much the nation may have risked by this neglect; but it is not a fact of which we can be proud that we are even now indebted to the individual enterprise and researches of a distinguished American author for the best exposition of the influence of sea power upon history. In London alone can this need be adequately supplied, for here in the Record Office we have, in enormous masses, materials of every description, hundreds of volumes of despatches from Admirals in command on the various stations, letters to them from the Home government, proceedings of courts-martial, and logs of ships recording the individual history of most of the vessels of which the British Navy has from time to time been composed.

Closely connected with naval history is a study for

which the present provision is equally insufficient. I am no great admirer myself of what J. R. Green used to call the ' drum and trumpet ' style of history; but at the same time no nation can with impunity neglect the teachings of the history of war; and, indeed, I suppose it is generally admitted that a better appreciation of those lessons on the part of the nation and of its rulers in recent years might have saved us some thousands of lives and some millions of money. I know that we, as a people, hold the student and the theorist cheap compared with what we call the practical man; but we often forget that the man who won the Franco-Prussian War was firstly a student and a theorist, and that Napoleon himself knew almost by heart every great campaign recorded in history.

A third topic which would claim the particular attention of a school of research in this university would naturally be the history of London itself. I stated above that a moderate-sized city or town in Germany, or for that matter in France as well, would blush if it did not possess some association for the study and publication of its own historical records. I know of no such society in London; perhaps the subject is too vast. And when I speak of the history of London, I would not exclude the most recent times; for a course of study of London history should be the first introduction to the scientific investigation of its present-day problems of local government, the vastest problems of the kind with which human intellect has ever been called upon to deal.

A fourth branch of history of which we should naturally make a speciality is the history of the nineteenth century, partly because that vital period is deliberately cut from the historical curricula of other universities,[1] and used to be universally ignored in schools; so that of no period is the ordinary British citizen so ignorant as of that which immediately preceded, and therefore most powerfully influenced, the age in which he lives. The other day I set

1 This defect, again, has been remedied to some extent.

a question in the Matriculation Examination upon the origin and growth of the idea of Imperial Federation. Incredible as the fact may seem, about half the candidates who attempted that question had not the ghost of a notion what Imperial Federation meant; many thought it was equivalent to Colonial self-government, and at last I came to regard it as a sign of unusual intelligence when a candidate stated that in 1867 Imperial Federation was granted to Canada, and in 1900 to the Australian Colonies. Yet Dr. Arnold of Rugby regarded contemporary history as more important than either ancient or modern, and in fact superior to it by all the superiority of the end to the means. In France, such is the weight attached to the study of our own times, that there is a specially organised course of contemporary history with expert teachers and appropriate text-books; and London University never did a wiser thing than when it extended the modern history of its curricula down to the death of Queen Victoria.

With all these departments there would naturally be associated competent instruction in the meaning and use of original sources such as hitherto English scholars have had to pick up for themselves or go to the *Ecole des Chartes* at Paris to learn. The other day I was asked by a history tutor of twenty years' standing (not in this university), ' Can you tell me what an original authority is? ' and a university magazine recently described a living scholar as an original authority on the history of Ancient Greece ! Yet the definition of an original authority is the most elementary axiom of historical research, and the basis of all historical criticism.

These are some of the measures which might be taken to build up a school of Modern History worthy of the capital of the Empire and of its university. But the function of a university is not exhausted when it has collected and trained a number of youths in various arts and sciences. That is its internal duty, its duty to itself; it has also an external duty to the nation which does (or should) provide it with funds. ' It is not my business to make chemists,' an eminent professor of chemistry is reported as saying, ' but to make chemistry.' It will not be the business of a School of History merely to make historians, but to discover and spread historical truth.   A university should be a focus of national intellect, and a source of national inspiration; and it fulfils its function badly if it does not help to expand the national mind.   Centuries ago there used to be sung a jingle to the effect that when Oxford draws knife, England is soon at strife, a boast that Oxford stood not so much upon the ancient ways as in the van of national movement.   It can hardy be said, I fear, that English universities have maintained their hegemony of the national intellect; they certainly do not contribute so much to our intellectual prestige as German universities do to that of their Fatherland; and it has often been a subject of comment abroad that such men as Darwin, Huxley, and Spencer should never have occupied chairs in an English university, as though there were a great gulf growing. if not fixed, between the universities and the leaders of the nation. That reproach does not of course lie at the door of London, and one may hope that, when London has its properly appointed staff of professors and teachers, it will do something to recover the lost national lead.

One at least of the services which our History School might render its day and generation would be to broaden the meaning and increase the uses of history. For history should record the whole life and not merely the political life of nations; it should devote as much space to the evolution of thought as to the development of events. A hint of the way in which it might be studied and written is given in a book by an able Cambridge historian entitled *The Annals of Politics and Culture,* where on one page is recorded the progress of politics and on the other the simultaneous advancement of science, of art, and of literature; a more elaborate hint may be found in the *Dictionary of National Biography,* where as much space is

given to Newton as to Marlborough, and twice as much to
Shakespeare as to Queen Elizabeth; and if there be any
one here with abundant means and a few score years of
time to spare, he might employ them worse than in
re-writing those sixty-six volumes in the form of a national
history; he would be able to trace not merely the growth
of the British people in politics, but their achievements
in arts, philosophy, science, commerce and industry.
Seriously, I should like to see a history which gave as
much space, for instance, to the story of the foundation of
the Royal Society as to that of the Popish Plot, as much
to the discoveries of Joseph Priestley as to the speeches of
Edmund Burke. For in this way history could be made
profitable not merely to the politician and to the publicist,
but to the philosopher, the scientist, and the physician.

Further, our School of History might perform not merely
an academic, but a national service in raising the standard
of taste and criticism. I referred above to the inadequate
appreciation which makes the work of so many scholars
disheartening and unremunerative. It is not that there is
no popular interest in history; the hundreds of books on
historical subjects which are published every year are
sufficient evidence of this. But it is because that popular
taste is ill-educated and crude. No one writes treatises
on Helium or Engineering without some sort of acquaint-
ance with the subject, but every one thinks that he or she
can write history and biography without any preliminary
training or any specific research; and the public will buy
any book if the author possesses a handle to his or her
name. A well-known man of letters and politician once
asked me how much a certain scholar received for a certain
book. I happened to know and told him. ' What,' he
exclaimed, ' do you mean to say that they insulted a man
like that with the offer of such a sum? ' I said that
scholars were often insulted that way. ' Well,' he said,
' let me give you a piece of advice; before you write a
book, get into Parliament, or still better get made a cabinet

minister; and I guarantee that the publishers will pay you ten times that amount for any book you may write on whatever subject you choose.'

Now I may be told that it is impossible to do the things which I have suggested without help and funds, which at present the university can scarcely hope to command. Nothing of course can be done by sitting still and sighing at the magnitude of the task. Perhaps not much will be done until London finds legs of it own and dispenses with borrowed crutches; but I do not think the question of funds is fatal, and I am sure there is no greater delusion than that the quality of work depends on the amount which is paid for it. Milton got £10 for *Paradise Lost* : it would have been no better a poem if he had received £10,000; and if some of our latter-day novelists received £10, instead of £10,000, their work could not possibly be any worse. There are scholars to-day doing historical research of a very high order for nothing more than the love of the thing; and some of them would be glad to give their services to the university for a price which in other professions might seem absurd. Their appointments need not be permanent, for fixity of tenure is often more pleasant than stimulating to the tenant; and you can get vastly more and vastly better work by paying a yearly succession of lecturers £100, than you can by giving one man £1000 a year for life. At any rate, nothing has done so much in recent years for historical teaching at Oxford as the establishment of the annual Ford Lectureship. For that lectureship the services have been secured of men like the late Dr. Gardiner, the late Sir Leslie Stephen, and the late Professor Maitland; and the result has been in each case to produce not merely a course of lectures, but a book of the highest historical value. Something similar might be done at London for even a smaller sum;[1] and two things at least we can do without any money at all.

[1] The Creighton Memorial Lecture was established in 1907, and the first was given by Dr. Thomas Hodgkin.

We can raise the standard of London degrees in history until they rank with or above the highest; and we can insist that no doctorate be granted except for work which shall be no mere juvenile essays, but solid contributions to historical knowledge based upon original research among published and unpublished sources.

One last idea I should like to mention; it is perhaps the most fantastic of all, for certainly it could not be carried into effect without financial support. I mean the idea that London should have its own University Press.[1] A scholarly but somewhat cynical friend of mine says that if he had a fortune, which he hasn't, and if, having this fortune, he felt disposed to part with it—which he certainly would not—he would not endow professorships, thinking that perhaps professors even now sometimes get too much and do too little; he would not endow libraries, although, or perhaps because, he is a librarian himself; but he would endow printing presses; for by that means alone could much of the research now fruitlessly done be made known to the world at large. It would possess a further enormous advantage for London University; we should not be hampered by the constant plea that such and such a subject must not be prescribed for examination or curricula because there are no good books or editions dealing with it, or else that those books are not within the means of the average student, for then we could always provide our own editions and text-books.

Now, it is often made a reproach to young men, that they dream dreams and see visions. But if it is commonly a reproach, it becomes once and again a privilege; for a vision may be one of the future and a dream does sometimes come true. And one of the dreams which I am sure will some day come true is this : that as we are citizens of no mean city, so shall we be graduates, undergraduates, fellow-workers in no mean university, a university every

1 The London University Press was instituted on a not very satisfactory basis in 1910; it has, however, published some good work.

school of which shall focus knowledge, radiate truth, and help to illumine the national mind.

(ii.) Twenty Years After

The vision outlined in the preceding paragraph was a dream of twenty-two years ago, recounted in a lecture which was delivered in October 1904, was based on a single year's experience as a teacher in the University of London, and was historical only on the assumption that historiography requires an imagination which can discern the possibilities as well as the facts of achievement, and can found its judgment on a comparison between the things men did and the things they could or might have done. Any final estimate of the change effected during these years must still be left to a later occasion and another hand; but it has become impossible to reprint as a veracious account of affairs in 1926 a farrago of facts and forecast compounded in 1904; and while judgment is out of the question, it is not impertinent in a witness or even a litigant to give evidence on facts and theories, of some which he may be the sole repository.

The essential facts, however, can be quoted from a lucid summary by a high authority. 'The change,' writes Professor Seton-Watson,[1] 'may be indicated very briefly under the triple heading of students, teachers, and research.'

(a) Between the years 1904 and 1911 the numbers of those taking a B.A. or M.A. in History rose twelvefold and sevenfold respectively (186 and 37); and since the war they have again risen to 368 and 39 (in 1919-24). In 1923-24 there were 250 internal students reading for history.

(b) In 1903-4 the history staff of the university consisted of two professors and one assistant at University College, one professor and one lecturer at King's College, and one lecturer each at Holloway, East London, Westfield, and Bedford Colleges. To-day there are twelve professors and ten readers whose subjects are definitely historical; and in addition there

[1] *Tudor Studies,* ed. R. W. Seton-Watson, 1924, p. vi.

are twenty-two 'recognised teachers' and fourteen 'other teachers' engaged in historical teaching. The mere list of historical lectures delivered in the university fills twenty-six pages of a special pamphlet.

(c) For the session of 1903-4 post-graduate courses of lectures were announced in fifteen subjects in the Faculty of Arts, but History was not among them. In 1923-4 the Institute of Historical Research was in its third year of existence, with 146 research workers, 17 seminars, a growing library, and its own *Bulletin*.

The product of twenty years' labour could not be more succinctly stated; but the historian is properly more interested in the methods and means of production than in the finished article, because, as it has been said, ' history never stops short '; and unless it goes on changing, the finished product in human affairs achieves sooner or later the *rigor mortis*. Change itself is a product of life which is not finished until it is dead, and the registered achievement of a School of History in London throws less light on its prospects than does a study of its growth. Sometimes, too, the bare record suggests more to the reader, at other times less, than is warranted by the facts. The meagre provision for teaching history in 1904 itself conveys an exaggerated notion, without a knowledge of the fact, that the three professors were paid for but a fraction of their time and mainly by fees from students sadly to seek. The professorial title was in fact used as an attraction, *honoris causa*, to atone for the lack of stipend, and such energy as the professors could devote to building up a School of History in the university had to be diverted from time spent in earning a living. Finance was the fundamental difficulty, and it was clear that what men could do would depend upon what they could do without. Twenty years later, on the other hand, the professors were receiving fixed salaries, less indeed than those paid for lighter duties and shorter terms in older universities, but a vast improvement on the earlier share of fees; and they were adequate in so vast and heterogeneous a community

as London where the profession of learning involves no
pretence to social position.

In another respect the position has improved. The three
professors in 1904 were only college professors; the twelve
professors and ten readers in 1924 held university appointments. But this nomenclature, owing to a peculiarity of
the University of London, implies a false analogy both
with the older Universities of Oxford, Cambridge, and
Scotland, and with the newer universities of England. In
all these the title of university professor or reader involves
a real university function; in London it does not necessarily involve any teaching outside the particular college
to which the professor belongs or any contact with other
pupils than his own; and in these cases the university
professor may be simply a college lecturer transfigured by
a university title. The so-called University professoriate
has in fact been created mainly by the 'conferment of
titles,' and it is one of the relics of the spiritual home out
of which the university came that it should shrink from
conferring *ad eundem* or honorary degrees (except or
members of the Royal Family),[1] but scatter with a
comparatively lavish hand the professorial titles which it
holds comparatively cheap. There is no need to wait for
the vacancy of a chair; for there is no limit to their
number, and titles can always be conferred, subject to
certain financial regulations which can be indefinitely
relaxed for the part-time recipients of more or less honorary
posts. The resultant ambition of every college is to seek
a 'university' title for every teacher it can afford to pay
at the university rate; and a Senate, in which centrifugal
forces have always been predominant, gladly connives in
the dilution of university teaching provided it can maintain
the standard of university examinations.

The dilution varies in different faculties and subjects
In History the attempt has been made to regard the

[1] The only honorary graduates of the University of London are the
King, the Queen, and the Prince of Wales.

University professoriate from a totally different point of view, that is to say, not as a means of gratifying College amour-propre, but as a means of creating out of the College staffs a University organisation for the co-ordination and furtherance of teaching and research. The view of the Board of Studies has been that the University—as distinct from the College—staff should consist solely of experts in the various branches of historical study, and that all historical students, irrespective of their College, should, as far as is practicable, have the benefit of their guidance and advice. The distinction between school and University standards depends upon this : in a school there can only be as a rule one historical expert, who has to teach all the history that is taught; in a University there should be at least half a dozen teachers of history, each more or less expert in the particular branch he teaches. For a University teacher should always be one who is adding not merely to the persons who know but to the things that are known; and it is impossible to add much to historical learning if one is trying to teach the whole field of history. A College which imposes on one historian the burden of teaching its students all their history is giving them not a University but a school education, and is precluding that historian from fitness to discharge a University function : the practice is itself a source not of strength but of weakness to a University, and is only tolerable when over and above these College teachers there is superimposed a higher grade of University professors and readers.

That is roughly the plan at Oxford and Cambridge. Its defects have been explained by professors at both Universities : students ignore professorial teaching, and College tutors are too busy preparing pupils for examination to give the time they would like to doing research or to interesting pupils in its prosecution. Other methods were imposed upon London by the original absence of endowment for research; only teaching was paid for, and there was no provision for a grade of professors who might write admirable history but could not provide their own emoluments in the form of students' fees. It was not till history had been made a popular subject with under-graduates, and had thus attracted the notice of educational authorities, that any organisation for research could be superimposed; and it was only by slow gradations that heads of departments could, through the appointment of assistants, be released for the higher work of their profession The release was never more than partial; the professor grew out of the college lecturer, but he had still to spend most of his time on work that was remunerative to the college; for even the university professor was paid by his college out of fees which were the main element in its finance, and the higher the education the more it costs and the less it earns in fees. The advantage in combining the work of a college tutor with that of a university professor was, apart from its economy, that no schism was made between teaching and research, and a far larger proportion of undergraduates than in the older universities go on to postgraduate work.

The first task, however, was to popularise history as a subject of undergraduate study in the university and in the schools which provided London with most of its students and drew from it most of their teachers. The attempt initiated in 1901, to create, as a memorial to Bishop Creighton, the superstructure of a School of Historical Research without the foundation of an undergraduate school had broken down. 'London,' said Mr. (now Lord Haldane on 3rd February 1905, 'has no school of historical research.'[1] In the autumn of that year I began, at the invitation of Mr. (now Sir) Robert Blair, the Education Officer of the London County Council, to give courses of evening lectures in history for teachers in schools. In January 1906, again at the invitation of Mr. Blair, I took the chair at a conference he had organised on the Teaching

[1] See above, pp. 243-4, and *Fourth Rep. of Comm. of Management Advanced Hist. Teaching Fund*, 1906, p. 4.

of History.[1] I might have hesitated had I realised that one
outcome would be the chairmanship of another conference
which sat for two years (1909-1911) and produced for the
County Council an elaborate Report on the subject.[2]
Another outcome was the Historical Association, the
formation of which was first publicly advocated by the
late Miss M. A. Howard at the above conference in January
1906. That Association comes of age next January, and
will doubtless ' to the listening earth, recall the story of
its birth.' Its early council and annual meetings were
held at University College until it grew too comprehensive
for a single local habitat.   It has now 4500 members
distributed among more than eighty branches, which extend
to New Zealand and Ceylon; its annual budget exceeds
£2000, and its official journal, *History,* which it acquired
in 1916, has a circulation larger than any other historical
periodical on this side of the Atlantic and a reputation
second to none. Its other publications include sixty-five
leaflets, many of which have gone out of print, an *Annual
Bulletin of Historical Literature,* a series of constitutional
documents, and an historical atlas. Without some knowledge of the leading part which University teachers in
London took in this remarkable development, the rapid
increase in the number of their pupils would not be
intelligible.

A third outcome of the connection between University
teachers and the London County Council was the Evening
School of History at University College. When two or
three courses of evening lectures had revealed the existence
of a latent demand[3] for further historical education, the
County Council was persuaded in 1909 that something
more than occasional courses was needed, and it adopted

1 See its *Report of Proceedings* (P. and S. King), 1906, pp. 35-47.
2 See its *Report* (P. and S. King), 1911.
3 One of the points on which I insisted most strongly in giving
evidence before the Haldane Commission in 1910 was that 'the
supply creates the demand' (*Haldane Commission,* 2nd Rep., App.,
p. 164).

a scheme for a three years' continuous general course in Ancient, Medieval, and Modern History, to be followed by a year's more intensive study of the sources for English History on the seminar method. The accommodation for this last year's course had just been provided at University College by the creation (in 1907-8) of seminar libraries to do for Arts subjects what is done for physical science by means of laboratories. Students who attended with sufficient regularity and passed an examination at the end of each year's course, and then a final examination over the whole, were given a diploma, which came in time to be sought even by some who had obtained degrees before starting their four years' course for the diploma, and was treated by Education Authorities as evidence of a ' special qualification' to teach history. Two hundred ' free " places in this evening school were ultimately reserved for teachers in London schools, but the scheme was designed as a general experiment in historical education for adults; it was intended to benefit other adults than teachers, and was not limited to a four years' course or to candidates for diplomas.   It was graded to lead up to continuous postgraduate study, and was based on the ideas (1) that education is a life-long process, not an episode of youth, (2) that as soon as one ceases to learn one becomes unfit to teach, and (3) that a university is not a harsh amalgam of crabbed age and youth, but a permanent association of men and women for the advancement of learning. Some of the original entrants are still, nearly twenty years later, members of seminars pursuing research which sometimes finds vent in books and learned periodicals, is always fertilising the soil of the minds of the successive generations they teach, and is ever repaying the University for the seed it has sown in a harvest of better taught candidates for matriculation.

With the establishment of this Evening School of History which involved at least four lectures or classes a week, the need for occasional courses at University College passed away, and they were succeeded by courses of free public lectures designed less for professional students than for intelligent adults who were interested, as journalists, publicists, politicians, or simply as citizens, in the past for its own sake or for the light it might throw on the problems of the present and the future. There had long been a tradition at University College that each professor should inaugurate each session's work with a lecture which should be open to the public. This tradition of a single lecture was expanded from 1910 onwards into short courses of six or ten public lectures, and extended—in the History Department—from professors to assistants; and during the war the short course was further expanded into a weekly lecture on its progress. Some restriction had, however, to be imposed upon admission owing to the impossibility of accommodating, in any hall at the disposal of the College, an audience of more than four or five hundred. It was clear that public lectures were one of the means by which universities, situated in the midst of vast populations, might 'help to illumine the national mind,' and the practice gradually spread throughout the University.

Upon this broad foundation of more or less popular education it became at length possible to begin the erection of an organisation for higher university teaching and research. The Haldane Commission on the University of London had been appointed in 1908, and it fell to me to draft the recommendations of the Board of Studies in History in 1909 and give evidence in their support before the Commission in October 1910.[1] Our demands were generally regarded in the University as ridiculously extravagant : we recommended fourteen chairs and five readerships. That is almost precisely the number now established In 1912 the County Council, owing mainly

---

[1] See *Haldane Commission*, 2nd Rep., App., pp. 158-65, 356; the evidence contains a fuller account of the initial stages than it has been possible to give here.

to the success of the Evening School of History at University College, provided the University with stipends for chairs of history and some other subjects, leaving their allocation to the Senate. There was the inevitable scramble in that representative body, and the chair of history went to King's College. It was the first chair in history that was independent of fees, and for that reason and because the teaching in the University was weak on its medieval side, the chair was definitely earmarked for Medieval History. Another chair, provided by the County Council, the professorship of French History and Institutions, was allocated partly to the School of Economics and partly to University College. In the same year Sir Sidney Low advocated before the British Academy and in *The Times* the establishment in London of a chair or department of Imperial Studies, not particularly associated with the University. Effective protests were made, though not by the Senate, against adding to the chaos of conflicting educational organisations; and the movement eventually took shape in the Imperial Studies Committee of the University, of which Lord Bryce was the first and Lord Milner the second chairman. Courses on Colonial history and law had for some years been regularly given at University College, and the development of these and other subjects by the Imperial Studies Committee led to the foundation in 1919 of the Rhodes Chair of Imperial History.

This Chair, owing largely to the energy of its late Principal, Dr. Ronald Burrows, was attached to King's College. But his historical interests lay mainly in the east of Europe, and he powerfully stimulated the development of historical studies in that direction during the war. Professor (now Sir Bernard) Pares was brought from Liverpool to become head of the School of Slavonic Studies. Dr. Seton-Watson was enlisted (bringing with him notable connections with Czecho-Slovakia, including its future President, Dr. Masaryk) and became the first occupant of the Masaryk Chair of Central European History. The Koraes Chair of Modern Greek and Byzantine History and Literature was the outcome of Burrows' friendship with M. Venizelos, and Professor Arnold Toynbee was appointed to it; he has since (1925) been appointed to the Stevenson Chair of International Affairs. Dutch patriotism, rather than internationalism, endowed a somewhat amorphous Chair of 'Dutch Studies,' which was attached to Bedford and University Colleges and was subsequently transformed into an effective Chair of Dutch History and Institutions, while the Oriental interests of the British Empire led to the establishment in 1916 of the School of Oriental Studies and the foundation of a professorship of the history and culture of British dominions in Asia with special reference to India. Internationalism inspired the endowment, in 1922, of a Chair of International Relations at the School of Economics, where Economic History was already repre- sented by one professor and two readers. A Readership in the History of the Roman Empire (University College), and another in General Ancient History (King's College), were added to the original Readership in Ancient History, and the County Council was persuaded to establish a novel but much-needed Readership in the History and Records of London (University College).[1] Chairs of History were also established at Holloway, Westfield, and Bedford Colleges, without any specific limitation of subject or reference to university co-ordination.

It is obvious from this enumeration that provision for historical education in the University of London has not been the outcome of any coherent plan or corporate consciousness. It has been the result of diverse sentiments, political as well as academic, sectional as well as scientific. The titles themselves are a study in anarchy, and inter- nationalism itself could hardly avert some friction between 'International Affairs' and 'International Relations.' Some of the moving spirits apparently regarded history as

[1] See above, p. 248.

a term without content and felt constrained to inject one of their own by appending to history ' and institutions' or ' and culture.' Generally the impulse has been less to strengthen historical science than to cultivate special affections, and less to fill up gaps in a University organisation than to complete competitive College armaments. The Board of Studies has at times made suggestions; but, although it is the statutory and social adviser of the Senate in all matters relating to provision for teaching and research in history,[1] it was rarely consulted thereon by a body which has never been able to think consecutively or collectively itself or to control the bias of others. Nothing but an examining body till 1900, it could neither expect nor desire endowments; twenty-five years later it still deprecates them from fear of ' the scramble for appropriation of University funds "[2] which would ensue in its academic arena, and prefers that public and private benefactors alike should earmark their benefactions for their own purposes in order to save the Senate the task of determining their destination and thinking out a university policy.

This administrative anarchy has necessarily involved the University in a great deal of waste and overlapping between one college, one faculty, one subject, and another. With the growth of equipment and of confusion produced by competitive action, it became ever more urgent to provide some sort of co-ordination and to limit so far as might be the needless expense of reduplication, at least in the field of training for research. The Board of Studies had attempted long before the war to co-ordinate undergraduate teaching by means of intercollegiate lectures and by combining in a single syllabus the whole of the historical

1 Statute 104.

2 Dr. Graham Little and others in *The Times*, 28th April, 1926: the object of this protest against the reform of the University was to preclude the furtherance 'of academic and scholastic interests rather than of the special interests of the graduates'—whatever they may be.

teaching provided by the various colleges; and it was hoped that this function of collecting would lead to co-ordination and to the elimination of superfluous competition. But the Board itself was constituted on the principle of representing rival colleges rather than the interests of historical study or of the University; and it was prohibited by statute from adding to its members more than a fourth from outside the University and the range of sectional feeling. It never proved equal to the task of prohibiting courses of lectures instituted merely to compete with existing provision elsewhere; and, indeed, it was not uncommon for the endowment of a new subject in one college to be immediately followed by its re-duplication elsewhere. The root cause of this was that, even when the endowment came from or through the University and took the form of a University chair, the College to which it was allocated was allowed to charge fees for the ' University ' instruction, and the rival provision was made to save one College from contributing to the finance of another. The Board was, however, able to agree in prescribing various ' Special Subjects ' to be taught by one or more of its members, and in providing—in order to meet the difficulties referred to above[1]—two series of historical documentary source-books, one which has run to nine volumes for Honours students, and another which has run to seven for Intermediate students. These were produced without cost to the University, and not only relieved teachers and students from reliance on less suitable books—and often finding them out of print—but produced a small revenue which has been used to publish results of research.

More far-reaching were the results of the regular but informal gatherings of university teachers and others which began in 1914 to be held at University College on every Thursday evening during term. The object was to provide common ground and occasion for the discussion of

[1] P. 253.

problems alike of historical research and historical organisation, and visitors were welcomed from other universities and other countries, especially the United States. The war, while it stimulated historical discussions, constrained academic activities; but its conclusion was soon followed by the movement which produced the Institute of Historical Research. It had become clear that the University could not do justice to itself and to London's unrivalled opportunities as a centre for that purpose so long as it acted not as a unit but on the centrifugal principle of individualistic and competitive enterprise. Room, equipment, and expert guidance over the many fields of historical investigation could not be reduplicated in all the various colleges concerned in historical teaching; governments, learned societies, and private donors could not be expected to lavish gifts on half a dozen or a dozen rival applicants; neither men nor matter could gravitate towards a centre until there was a centre of gravitation. No college would be suffered by others to monopolise the force of gravitation; it was equally irrational to isolate in a dozen different colleges the equipment for a dozen different branches of historical research. There must obviously be an organisation with a home which should be the common property of them all; in other words, the University must be made a reality at least so far as advanced historical studies were concerned.

The case seemed clear to those who knew. But those who know not what they do have a good deal to do with the government of universities; and wheels within wheels had to be set in harmonious though reluctant motion before the Institute could be constructed and opened in July 1921. The essential benefactor was fortunately forthcoming; the locality, which might otherwise have proved an insoluble problem, was determined by the coincidence of the advantages of proximity to the British Museum with the Government's offer of the Bloomsbury site to the University in 1920. The Treasury allowed the Institute to occupy land at a nominal rent,[1] private benefaction provided a rent-free building, and the Treasury made an annual grant which met the expense of rates, maintenance, and service. The cost of teaching prohibited an independent Institute staff; it had to consist of existing college teachers, who found in the Institute better accommodation and equipment than would otherwise have been available. The colleges were relieved of the necessity of providing for those growing needs, and also, since they supplied the teaching, received three-fourths of the fees paid for instruction at the Institute. The Institute, in fact, became the top storey of every college so far as historical education was concerned, and, apart from its other benefits, it provided a real university function for teachers whose services would otherwise have been restricted to their particular colleges. It was partly designed as a model of the way in which the Bloomsbury site might have been used to solve the general problem of higher university education in London. It is impossible to concentrate colleges or the teaching of undergraduates on that or any other site : it is equally impossible to multiply the equipment for research in dozens of subjects in dozens of colleges; it is fatal to divorce teaching from research and colleges from postgraduate institutes. The only solution is to construct, for college staffs engaged both in teaching and research, central *ad hoc* institutes where they can train their research students, while the rest of their time is devoted to more general teaching in colleges. The institutes should not be separate schools of the University, but the common property of the united colleges, *i.e.,* of the University. But this was, with rare exceptions, unfamiliar speech to governing bodies, whose conception of progress in university matters was the independent motion of colleges

---

[1] The formal agreement was eventually made between the University and H.M. Commissioners of Works, who were, however, unaware in March 1926, when the land was given back, of the existence of the Institute.

along their own strict lines tempered only by collision on the Senate; and most of the site was left derelict until, in 1926, the Government sold it back to the vendors.

Historical consolidation, however, soon produced its natural effect within its own particular orbit, and the Institute of Historical Research became at once a centre of attraction unrivalled in any other sphere of university research. Not only did the British Government present it with collections it had refused to colleges, but every Dominion in the Empire, the Government of the United States, and many in Europe followed suit. Learned societies and private donors were hardly less appreciative, and within five years 27,000 volumes, many of them rare and most of a documentary character, accumulated in their appropriate seminar libraries at the Institute. Other universities and university colleges, in the British Empire and in foreign countries, entered into arrangements by which their students might avail themselves of its facilities and guidance. The League of Nations sought its assistance for the higher purposes of intellectual co-operation. A standing Anglo-American Historical Committee was formed for the furtherance of the interests of English-speaking historical researchers; the weekly conference was moved to the Institute and supplemented by a more extended annual, and a still more elaborate quinquennial, conference. Visitors and students from all the chief countries of the world have come to study its organisation, methods, and equipment.[1]

Its methods are its most distinctive feature. Why there should be need for such an Institute in juxtaposition to the British Museum and not far from the Public Record Office sometimes puzzles the novice in historical research. But it is the mass of materials in London which creates the need for the Institute; it would have little justification for existence were there not archives in London to which

[1] See the annual *Reports* of the Institute and its *Bulletin* (Longmans, Green & Co.).

historical students must resort; no one wants a water-can where there is no water. The Institute exists to fertilise the use of London's archives, to train students how to find what they want and use it when found, and to save them from wasting their own time and that of archivists, paid at the public expense, in trying to make their way through historical jungles where they are lost until they can read the signs of the times and decipher ancient deeds. Some think that students should teach themselves, and that each child in learning should puzzle out the alphabet of research without instruction. That argument leads us back from civilisation to primeval forests and from university to elementary education. The real difficulty is that in the British Museum and the Record Office silence is the golden rule and seminars are barred. Hence the need for the Institute : it exists less as a place where students do their research than as one in which they learn how to do it and discuss its meaning and value when done. It is a laboratory rather than a factory, and in its seminars it is seeds that are sown and tested rather than fields that are ploughed or harvests reaped.

The word ' seminar ' has become acclimatised in the English language and is well described in general terms in the Oxford English Dictionary. But its methods are various, and since that in vogue at the Institute has been objected to elsewhere as ' the London method,' it merits perhaps some definition. It had been practised since 1908, when seminar libraries were first established in University College; and, while methods vary in the Institute itself, the general idea may be gathered from a statement I published in the first number of its *Bulletin*.

' One of the most interesting discussions at the Anglo-
' American Historical Conference in July 1921 was on the
' question " How to Conduct a Seminar "; and this *Bulletin*
' seems the appropriate place for a brief attempt to indicate
' the ideas to which seminars held at the Institute endeavour
' to give effect. It must, however, be remembered that

' there are a dozen or more of such seminars and that they
' deal with widely different periods and subjects to which
' widely different methods may be applicable. There is no
' simple avenue to historical truth, but many intricate and
' devious paths; and even were there but one broad or
' narrow way, there might be various methods of progression
' or propulsion along it. It is hoped that the following
' statement may lead to other suggestions.

' 1. Training in methods of research is based, so far as
' postgraduate historical education in the University of
' London is concerned, on the circumstances (i) that there
' is a limitless mass of ascertainable, but not yet ascertained,
' historical fact; (ii) that a great bulk of the material
' from which this knowledge is to be derived exists in
' London; (iii) that it consists of documents which are
' undecipherable and unintelligible to students who are
' familiar only with printed pages and narrative histories;
' and (iv) that it is contained in archives in which the
' student is lost until he has learnt how to find his way.

' 2. Some assistance is provided by calendars of state
' papers, of patent, close rolls, and the like, catalogues of
' MSS., lists and indexes, and similar guides; but these
' guides are themselves unknown to the untrained student,
' who may waste years of labour for lack of an introduction.
' He has first of all to be told what guides there are and
' taught how they should be used. He has, secondly, but
' simultaneously, to learn how to decipher the documents
' to which he has been guided. He must thirdly, before he
' deals with his documents, be given some idea of the
' meaning and value of original evidence; and fourthly,
' he must also know how to test their date and authenticity,
' and to discriminate between rough drafts and final
' versions, between letters that are written and those which
' are only signed by their authors, between originals and
' contemporary copies, and between contemporary and
' later copies. As an aid to this discrimination he should,
' fifthly have some idea of the methods of testing, not

' merely the date and handwriting of the document, but
' the date of the parchment or paper on which it is written.
' Sixthly, he must be able to distinguish by their form
' papal bulls from paper briefs, letters patent from letters
' close, privy seal from signs manual, parliamentary rolls
' from journals, treaties from drafts, and so forth. Seventhly
' he must learn how to weigh the conflicting evidence
' according to the source from which it comes, and how to
' get at the human or official mind behind the parchment
' and the paper on which it is imperfectly expressed.
' Finally, when he has collected, sifted and tested his
' materials, he must know how to construct and present
' his results. Historical research involves, in fact, a varied
' training in methods of discovering new facts, of inter-
' preting evidence, and of probing the work of human
' minds as recorded in what men have written and as
' influenced by material, moral, and other conditions.

' 3. Training in these methods of historical research is
' provided (i) by individual conference between teacher
' and student, and (ii) by co-operative research and
' discussion in a group commonly called a seminar. The
' individual supervision is by one or (preferably) more
' responsible teachers of the University, and is supplemented
' by the assistance voluntarily rendered to serious students
' by official archivists at the Public Record Office, British
' Museum, Guildhall, Lambeth Palace Library, and else-
' where. The highly technical help required for the
' decipherment of exceptionally difficult documents is
' naturally obtained from these expert archivists, while
' the responsible teacher's principal functions are to assist
' the student in ascertaining and interpreting the historical
' import of the materials and to advise him with regard to
' the construction and presentation of his results.

' 4. The value of seminar work, which should in no case
' take the form of a lecture or monologue by the teacher
' consists in the discussion of a common problem of historical
' research by a group of students who are individually

'dealing with different aspects of that problem or working
'at different categories of historical material. The subject
'of a thesis can never be more than a part of a larger
'whole, and the more intensive the research the smaller
'must be the part in relation to the whole. It is essential,
'therefore, that the intensive study by one student of one
'part should be brought into relation with the intensive
'study by other students of other parts. Otherwise the
'sense of proportion, of perspective, and even of meaning
'is lost. The fact of a number of students having a
'common teacher is not enough of itself : he may apportion
'their tasks with the utmost skill and give them invaluable
'assistance in private conferences. But if they are left
'without co-operation and discussion among themselves
'and he is made the sole link in the organisation, he
'inevitably becomes an autocrat and a taskmaster rather
'than a teacher, while they are reduced to the level of
'employés working out his designs and giving detailed
'expression to his mind rather than to their own.

'5. It is, moreover, a commonplace with those who
'have had experience that the most valuable finds are
'often made incidentally when in pursuit of something
'else. Historical investigators are constantly lighting on
'references, documents, facts which might take weeks and
'months to trace by direct pursuit; and these discoveries
'may have little bearing on the finder's particular thesis,
'but be of great importance to some one else. What
'may be a mere curiosity from one point of view becomes
'a vital link from another; and it is only by the production
'of such references, facts, and documents for discussion in
'seminars that their true importance and perspective is
'perceived. An incidental but invaluable ingredient in
'the organisation of the Institute of Historical Research
'is that not only are such points brought up at the various
'seminars of the Institute, but that they are carried to a
'sort of higher court of appeal in weekly meetings composed
'not only of the teachers who conduct the seminars, but

' of archivists from the principal archives in London, and of
' historians eminent in various fields of historical research.'

There are now at work in the Institute six preliminary
courses on historical sources and palæography and seventeen
seminars on different aspects of medieval and modern,
political and constitutional, social and economic, diplomatic, colonial, and American history.   Admission is
restricted to postgraduate students specially qualified for
historical research, and the number now approaches two
hundred. The Institute is not designed for the platform
method of lectures, but for the round table method of
consultation among researchers and the consultation of
authorities. No book may be taken out on any pretext;
for the books, maps, facsimiles, guides, catalogues, and
indexes are the equipment of a laboratory, and historical
study no more permits their removal than physical science
permits the borrowing of microscopes, telescopes, or other
apparatus essential to its work.   The Institute aims at
providing a comprehensive guide to historical knowledge,
means of testing its value, and a method of training
students to use them. Its *Bulletin* is devoted less to the
product than to the technique of historical research; and
' the very pulse of the machine' beats with the hope of
fostering a corporate spirit of research and a common
tradition of art beyond the compass of one man's achievement, and more lasting than such stuff as dreams are made
on or the little life that breaks into the circle of our sleep.

(iii) THE LATEST PHASE, 1926-31

The preceding section ended on a note that was tuned to
the somewhat depressing circumstances in which it was
written in the spring of 1926. His Majesty's Government
has just re-sold the Bloomsbury site on the ground that
after five years' deliberation the University had been unable
to make up its mind whether it wanted that or any other

site or how it would use one if acquired. The Senate was hopelessly divided and, outside its oligarchic circle, academic opinion was for the most part mute, save for a vigorous and enlightened but belated protest by the junior members of the university interested mainly in the fate of their University Union. A departmental committee of the Board of Education had, indeed, presented a scheme for reforming the government of the university; but a Convocation, which excluded the vast majority of university teachers from the university franchise on the ground that they were drawn from other universities, had returned as its representative in Parliament an independent member pledged to little beyond resistance both to that reform[1] and to the acquisition of the ' arid waste ' in 'the obscure and decaying suburb ' of Bloomsbury.[2] The Institute of Historical Research[3] itself seemed doomed in consequence to disappear unless it could perchance be reconstituted on a broader foundation less shifting than the University of London.

The danger, however, produced its antidote. A letter to *The Times,* signed by the principal historians in the United Kingdom not connected with the University of London, declared that it would be a disaster if the Institute were allowed to disappear. Similar expressions of opinion were forthcoming from the Dominions and the United States of America. The Chancellor of the Exchequer accordingly undertook to spare, out of the £415,000 he had recovered by the re-sale of the site, enough to enable the university to continue its activities already created on the Bloomsbury site; and in the autumn the confidential adviser of the Rockefeller Trustees with regard to their

---

[1] "In accordance with a very direct mandate from those whom I represent," wrote Dr. Graham Little to *The Times* on 27 July, 1926, "I have put down a motion to reject the present Bill at its second reading."

[2] F. J. C. Hearnshaw, *Centenary History of King's College,* 1929, p. 475.

[3] Along with the 'other encumbrances injudiciously and improperly erected thereon' (*ibid.,* p. 478).

European expenditure on the humanities reported that, of all humanistic organisations, the Institute of Historical Research most deserved and needed their support. The crisis in the question of the site suggested a wider scope of benevolence; and the Rockefeller Trustees resolved to offer the university a sum which would enable it to acquire the whole of the Bloomsbury site without the conditions attaching to the original offer by H.M. Government. The removal of those obstacles did not wholly eliminate opposition on the Senate and elsewhere, but it was reduced to slender dimensions and to argumentative incoherence; and its leader, who had objected mainly to dependence on American money, presently withdrew elsewhere to enjoy the well-earned emoluments of a foundation derived exclusively from American sources. The matter was settled in the spring of 1927, and for the first time after nearly a century's existence it became possible for the university to do something effective apart from conducting examinations, because at last it owned a place in which to do it.

The deferment of hope, distressing though it was to individuals whose time was short, proved a blessing in disguise to a university with an almost boundless future. The implicit, though not quite explicit, condition of the Government's offer of the Bloomsbury site in 1920 had been that half of it should be used to accommodate King's College, severely cramped in its narrow quarters between the Strand and the Embankment and condemned by Somerset House and the prohibitive cost of land to purely vertical expansion; and this condition was, apart from the lamented death of its Principal, Dr. Ronald Burrows, the chief cause of the rejection of the Government's offer. For, while the Government was prepared, over and above the six acres in Bloomsbury, to compensate King's College for its buildings between the Strand and the Embankment, valuers from outside, ignoring the fact that the college was prohibited from selling or using the premises for other than educational purposes, encouraged the belief that the compensation due was some five times that which the Government was prepared to pay; and the counter-suggestion was more or less seriously made that, instead of removing King's College, the Government should give it Somerset House. In the end the college remained without either, comforting itself with the reflection that size was not everything, and that quality, could it be won, was better than quantity out of reach. Was not ancient Athens also better than her barbarous, bulky rivals in the north and east? Moreover, as Dr. Flexner has remarked, 'at deliberately arranged co-operation the really gifted shy.'[1]

The University had no less ground for satisfaction : the whole instead of half the Bloomsbury site was now at its disposal for objects which it alone could achieve, and some causes of jealousy and misapprehension were removed. Previous attempts to solve the problem of a university site had been impeded by diverse conceptions of its scope and uses. The narrowest was that the only need was a permanent home for such functions as the University had hitherto discharged at Somerset House, Burlington Gardens, and the Imperial Institute, the successive premises it had been permitted to occupy as a tenant-at-will of the Government. These functions related mainly to administration, examination, and university extension; and this conception of university needs was fairly adequate so long as teaching for degrees and the provision for research were regarded as the exclusive function of the colleges and schools of the university; the idea indeed is still prevalent that, so far as its highest work is concerned, the university should act only in and through its colleges. The inherent difficulty in giving effect to such an idea is familiar to students of constitutional history, and may be indicated by the trite remark that, whereas the Crown once governed by means of ministers, ministers now govern by means of the Crown. The university did not, and does not, in fact act in and

---

[1] *Universities: American, English, German*, 1930, p. 120.

through the colleges: it is the colleges which act in and through the university; and the weakness of the ' Internal ' against the ' External ' case was mainly due to the fact that the ' Internal ' side was not so much a university, as a disunited college, party.

The inability of the university to act through its colleges became clearer as its theoretical means of action increased, notably through the ' incorporation ' of University College and King's College. The term ' incorporation ' illustrates the pervading ambiguity of language. Commonly it means that a group of persons are incorporated in a single legal personality, which can hold property, sue, and be sued in courts of law. The ' incorporation ' of University and King's Colleges meant, on the other hand, that—so far as the acts of incorporation extended—those colleges lost their legal personality, ceased to be capable of holding property, and of suing or being sued in courts of law; these rights and liabilities were merged in the University. The result was to increase the jealousy of those colleges felt elsewhere in the university; and the jealousy was based on the suspicion that instead of the university animating the colleges, the colleges would animate the university. The suspicion might have been well-grounded but for the mental and other reservations which underlay the acts of the incorporators. Shortly before the war I suggested to the Academic Council that it should put the Provost of University College on the governing body of King's, and the Principal of King's on that of University College, with the idea that the process should be extended until the two governing bodies became one, consisting of three equal parts representing each of the two colleges and the university. That would have meant a real instead of an academic incorporation. Needless to say, the idea was rejected and the incorporated colleges retained their practical independence; in 1914, as in 1827-36, two rival colleges were stronger than one university.

Incorporation nevertheless produced the second of the

general conceptions with regard to the use of the Bloomsbury site. Approximately half of it was to be devoted to
the agencies transferred from South Kensington, and half
to King's College removed from the Strand. University
College, with an area greater than either of these two
halves of the Bloomsbury site, was already in close
proximity, and something like a university quarter would
thus be created. Some hope was entertained that 'the site
of eleven and a half acres would be extended until most of
the colleges and schools of the university could be concentrated there; but this was a distant, if not impracticable
project, and meanwhile objections to the more immediate
prospect made themselves felt. The concentration of the
university with its two incorporated colleges in Bloomsbury
would undoubtedly give the combination a preponderance
over all other schools and colleges in London, and this was
naturally disliked. It would, however, probably have been
achieved but for internal doubts within the proposed
combination itself. The old maxim of Roman law that
husband and wife were one person and that person was the
husband, which dogged the steps of the statesmen who
sought through marriage the union of England and Scotland,
seems also to have haunted the unionists of the University
of London; and an exaggerated fear prevailed that
University College would dominate anything centred in
Bloomsbury, of which the local genii of South Kensington
and the Strand incidentally expressed an intellectual and
even a moral abhorrence. There were local loyalties of other
sorts in all quarters which were startled when pregnant
questions were asked whether a university and two incorporated colleges concentrated anywhere could afford, or
expect the public purse to pay for, two or three rival and
elaborate laboratories for each of the physical sciences.
Rationalisation had not then attained its later vogue, but it
cast its coming shadow over the prospects of the Bloomsbury site.

A third conception slowly and almost unconsciously

emerged from the confusion of ideas. The impossibility of crowding all the colleges and schools of the university on to one site was perceived before the incongruity was grasped of a university attempting to discharge its proper functions exclusively through the means of colleges. Even granted a governing body with a single university mind immune from college affections, it was impossible to distribute its activities and its endowments among colleges which had grown up as though each were a small university itself, covering most if not all of the wide field of humanistic and scientific education; and before the war a sound discrimination had been attempted on a very irrational basis. Conscious of the weakening appeal of examination for all as the exhaustive content of the idea of a university, the ' External ' side put before the Haldane Commission the suggestion that to it belonged in a special degree the sphere of research, inasmuch as the 'Internal' side enjoyed a monopoly of undergraduate teaching. The idea was sound so far as it rested on a recognition of the fact that the highest teaching in any university must be a matter of university rather than college organisation. The multiplicity of colleges and the multiplicity of the subjects taught prohibited any other solution, for the higher and more specialised the teaching, the more expensive and the less remunerative it becomes. No university could afford to equip all its colleges up to the highest level, and no college could maintain at that level more than a selected number of subjects. Conceivably it might have been possible for a powerful Senate, had such existed in 1921, to deal so drastically with the two incorporated colleges as to fuse them into one real university, distributing between them, for the equipment of research, such subjects as lay outside the spheres of the medical schools, the School of Economics, and the technological departments of the Imperial College. But the Senate was weak, the colleges recalcitrant, and the university site had not materialised.

Nor would that solution have been really satisfactory.

It would have meant that the two incorporated colleges would have become two groups of university departments rather than colleges, each group leaving to the other something like half of its previous content : the most plausible suggestion on these lines was that one should take Arts and the other Science, without prejudice to the ultimate fate of Theology, Law, Advanced Medical Studies, Economics, and Engineering. This would have had certain advantages : it would have avoided the paralysing schism of fixing a gulf between the teaching of undergraduates and the training of researchers; and it would have prompted efficiency, economy, and closer co-operation within each of the two selected faculties. But it would have severed those two colleges from the rest of the university. The two colleges would have become an inner ring with a vengeance, confronted with determined opposition from the majority thereby left outside and deprived of the possibility of competing on anything like equal terms with those within. Conflict between the two colleges would have been extinguished only at the price of conflict between them and the larger part of the university. For, great as the two incorporated colleges are, their combined numbers are less than half the registered Internal students of the university; and if the two colleges were restricted to Arts and Science, their students would be further reduced to less than a third.

The Institute of Historical Research was designed to avoid, within its limited sphere, these various evils. It was not itself to be a college or school of the university, nor a part of any one college more than another. It was to be part of all—the top storey of each—so far as they participated in historical research. No qualified student of the university, whether Internal or External, was to be excluded. It was to be the common possession of them all, that is to say, of the university. No gulf was fixed between teachers of undergraduates and professors of research. A line was indeed drawn between undergraduates and graduates, but that was a fundamental distinction already drawn by all universities; and having been universally so drawn, it inevitably determines the basis of discrimination between collegiate and university organisation.   It has become increasingly impossible to provide within the same walls adequate accommodation both for the numbers of undergraduate students and for the equipment required for post-graduate research. The British Museum itself has long had to exclude from its library those who merely wish to read; its comprehensive accumulation of books pre-cludes a like comprehension of students. Selection has similarly to be applied in the university and its colleges either to students or to equipment.   So far as history is concerned the selection in the colleges has to be mainly of books required by candidates for a first degree; the reduplication in each college of materials for research in the endless ramifications of history is impossible.   It is only accomplished in part by any university, and the condition of partial achievement is the selection of students in par-ticular need of the equipment.

The line between undergraduate and research students is inevitable, but a link remains in the teacher. The under-graduate benefits most by association with students of other subjects than his own. But with graduation he comes to the point at which he benefits most by association with fellow-workers in his own particular field; and, while it is a college function to associate both teachers and students of one subject with teachers and students of others, it is essen-tial for the university advancement of learning to bring together its researchers in the same subject scattered throughout its various schools and colleges. Commonly, historians had met before the War only at the Board of Studies in History, and that Board met for any purpose rather than the study of history. As for the students, they only met in the feeble and flickering light of a historical society or casually in the Record Office or the British Museum where, save for officials, the human voice is taboo. For almost all academic purposes the university had to depend upon the goodwill, the hospitality, and the convenience of its colleges. Was a distinguished foreign savant invited to address the university? He could find nowhere to do so except in some college or other, and then as a rule he found himself addressing a college rather than the university. Boards of Studies themselves had to meet at different colleges in turn, and carry their minute-books and other records from place to place, or else dispense with such aids to continuous policy. When the university had to perform a university function like the conferment of degrees, which could not in decency be discharged in any particular college, it had to hire the Albert Hall. It could not support itself because it had no *pied-à-terre*.

The colleges, on the other hand, had many, and were rather too self-supporting. Unlike the ancient seats of learning,[1] where the university existed before colleges began —and then were only hostels having little or nothing to do with university teaching or administration—the London colleges came into existence before the university, and assumed functions which the university, when it was created, disclaimed until the end of the nineteenth century. In 1900 it acquired, in a half-hearted sort of way, some of the academic functions of a university but with inadequate means to give them effect. Another quarter of a century showed that a university site would be wasted on university colleges. Even the concentration of the two incorporated colleges on the university site would compromise the essential needs of the university. The schools and colleges were needed where they were; what was needed on the university site was the university itself, something which others could see, like a sun and not a nebular constellation, and in which the university could act directly as a whole and not indirectly through its parts.

1 But even at Oxford and Cambridge to the foreign observer, 'it appeared that the colleges were all in all, and the University in both places merely a "geographical expression" as Metternich said of Italy' (Sir Charles Firth, *Modern History in Oxford*, p. 30). In London the expression was not even geographical.

The concentration of colleges thus faded into the background as the purpose of the university site, and its place has been taken by schemes of a purely university character. The central administration, at present housed in the Imperial Institute, will become more central in a more adequate home of its own, comprising a court- and senate-house, administrative offices, the university library, rooms for the numerous councils, committees, delegacies, faculties, boards of studies appointed by the Senate, and halls for university lectures. The Students' University Union, already on the site like the Institute of Historical Research and the School of Slavonic Studies, will acquire better and permanent accommodation. Other institutes, like that for the history of art, an institute of archæology, an institute of Education (limited by the capital E), are in contemplation, and claims are being staked out (on paper) which would occupy all and more than all the available space. Fortunately the original eleven and half acres were already extended, not in theory but for all intents and purposes, before the site was actually acquired; and on the west side of Malet Street contiguous to, but not actually on, the University site, the School of Hygiene and Tropical Medicine has realised, in a spacious and dignified home, the first fulfilment of the proper ideas for the university site. To the north of it cognate conceptions are taking shape in a residential hall for women students; and east of the site, but in close proximity, a larger scheme for a residence for students from the British Empire overseas has received generous financial support. Libraries as well as homes for students are growing in the neighbourhood; and the need, the advantages, and the uses of a university site in Bloomsbury, so obscure to obscurantists a few years ago, have become obvious to the least enlightened minds.

Meanwhile the twin-project of a reform in the government of the university had been achieved, at any rate on paper; and the university had received the fourth of its parliamentary constitutions.   But the object of American legislators has been crudely described as to put their moral aspirations on record; and, while British Acts of Parliament commonly have a more practical end in view, they are mostly matters of machinery which depend on other than parliamentary agencies for their working and driving force.   The Act of 1926 modified, re-arranged, and re-inforced certain parts of the university engine.   But an engine is not driven by the mere fact of being repaired; it may move forward at various speeds, it may be reversed, it may even break down.   The case for reform by Act of Parliament was that previous Acts of Parliament prevented the engine from working smoothly and efficiently; and Parliament was asked by a departmental committee of the Board of Education to amend its own parliamentary handi-work.   There was not much scope for idealism : the departmental committee had to tread delicately and consider what was likely to commend itself to politicians.   There was, however, no political capital in the question : not a seat would be lost or won by any party, whatever attitude it adopted.   The independence of the university's M.P. was perhaps an advantage; being independent, he could depend on no party but himself.   But the complexity and unfamiliarity of the problem might easily enable one or two skilful critics to delay, if not to frustrate, the bill.   Its passage without a division in either house was due to the absence of effective criticism, the moderation of the departmental committee's report, and the firm support of a Government with a great majority.

The principal changes effected in the government of th⸍ university were the creation of (1) a Court with suprem⸍ control of the finances of the university, and (2) a Collegiate Council giving the principal schools and colleges of the university direct representation on the Senate and enabling those representatives to act as an advisory body independently of the Academic Council, which represented the

Faculties, and of the External Council which represented Convocation. The need for some such body as the Court had been urged both outside and within the university Outside, grant-giving bodies such as the Treasury and the London County Council had indicated in no uncertain terms their misgivings about entrusting the administration of public money to a body constituted like the Senate. The university's representative in Parliament had himself deplored the ' scramble for appropriation of funds '[1] in the academic arena, though he alleged that circumstance not as an argument for the court but as an argument against the endowment of the university. The Court was to consist of the Chancellor, the Vice-Chancellor, the Chairman of Convocation, four persons nominated by the Crown, two by the London County Council, and six by the Senate, with one member to be co-opted. Its efficacy would depend upon its personnel. The Crown could be trusted to nominate able, experienced, and impartial administrators : and the London County Council would do the same, subject to restricting its choice to its own members. The critical selection would be that made by the Senate.

The allocation of seats in the Court had been more discussed by the Departmental Committee than any other single point. There was no difficulty about the size of the court; sixteen was readily accepted as the limit of members. It was also agreed at once that, considering the extent to which the university would depend upon the Treasury for its finance, the Crown should nominate to the Court not fewer than the four members it had since 1900 appointed to the Senate. A similar argument was used in favour of an equal representation of the London County Council. But its representatives on the senate had only been two,[2] and its grants fell far short of those which came from the

1 See above, p. 264 *n.*
2 And these two had commonly cancelled the L.C.C.'s representation by voting on opposite sides of most important questions on the Senate.

Treasury. The real question was whether the Senate should, considering the purely financial functions of the Court and the past financial record of the Senate, have as large a representation on the Court as the Crown and the County Council put together, and thus with the help of the three *ex-officio* members enjoy the preponderance of power. The Treasury and the London County Council, moreover, represented the taxpayers and the ratepayers who were taxed to support the University; and it seemed an odd principle of taxation and representation to give as large a representation to those who received, as to those who paid, the rates and taxes. On the face of it the suggestion of equality appeared absurd; it was accepted in fact as a matter of faith. The Senate was *ex hypothesi* to be reformed mainly by the introduction of the new collegiate third element : when called upon to act *en bloc* in the selection of its representatives on the Court, it might surely be trusted to choose its best qualified members; and, in any case, the departmental committee would be stultifying its own report if it implied that a Senate, re-constituted on the lines of that report, was not to be trusted in so simple a matter as the choice of its representatives on the Court.

Faith, however, is often misled by reason, because reason itself is fallacious. No process of ratiocination could have anticipated that the reformed Senate, when actually called upon to choose members of a Court created to enlist financial support for the university, would choose persons who had publicly protested against its endowment and were, after their appointment as members of the Court, to oppose its acceptance of munificent foundations on the ground that the maintenance of those foundations would involve the university in expense. The mind of an accountant had been the Senate's old ideal of financial statesmanship; and 'nip expenditure in the bud' of endowment was the maxim conveyed by some of the elected of the Senate into the precincts of the Court. Human nature in fact is stronger than reason : the roll of French Presidents shows as clearly as senatorial elections how seldom the elect are elected, and how often the secrecy of the ballot serves ends not meet for public avowal. The new Senate, like the old, contained men of the highest distinction in many walks of life including public administration, and not one was unwilling to serve the university on its Court; but only one or two survived the test of a secret ballot. Habits more ingrained than reason determined the result. Consisting so long for the most part of two equal opposing parties, the Senate's idea of executive impartiality had been to refer any contested proposal to a committee composed impartially of its advocates and its opponents. Similar reasoning would produce similar results on national policy, if the Cabinet, the executive committee of the House of Commons, were composed equally of the government and the opposition. So the Senate's personal contribution to the Court was to consist of the foes as well as the friends of financial reform, with a strong infusion of those who were happy and skilful enough to be able to take both sides of a question at once or at least at alternative crises. The strongest recommendation was seniority in service, an ever-present help when discrimination fails.

The event to outsiders seemed a curious effect to come from a reform which changed the Senate from a body consisting roughly of two equal parties, Internal and External, into a body consisting of three parts, two of them Internal and one alone External. But that introduction of collegiate representation had been accepted with an acquiesence which was itself a surprise to the uninitiated. The truth was that the distinction between Internal and External was itself fallacious: the Internal side had always suffered more from its own internal weakness than from External opposition. Heads of colleges and professors were not infrequently chosen as External representatives on the Senate, and the elected of Convocation have found seats on the new Collegiate Council Across the nominal lines of difference ran a serious cross division, based on the natural interest of the smaller and more isolated schools of the university in two important objects common both to them and to the isolated external student. Both appertained to the idea of equalising, so far as might be, the opportunities of all students of the university—external students, students of small colleges more or less remote, and students of large colleges in the inner ring of London enjoying ready access to all the facilities it might provide. Equality, benevolence, and impartiality here joined hands to combat the claims and pretensions of any particular excellence and contend that a democratic university must at least (1) attempt to level up the endowments of the smaller and poorer to that of the greater and richer colleges; and (2) accommodate university teaching and examination to standards to which the poorer as well as the richer colleges could attain.

Theoretically and superficially attractive as these aims may appear, they are fundamentally fatal to university organisation. It is impossible to place these various categories of students on the same level of opportunity with respect to library and laboratory equipment, university teaching or intellectual intercourse, except by bringing the student to where these advantages are provided. The real difference between the Internal and External ideals is that between bringing the student to the university and bringing the university to the student. The latter is possible up to a point, but the point is reached in a university when extension means dilution; there is a limit to the extent to which a university can get outside itself. Water and horses are common and mobile enough for either the horse to be brought to the water or the water to the horse. But students must be brought to the university rather than universities to the student. In London, with its vast number of county council scholarships, the difficulty of access to the sources would not be so great were it not impeded by lack of collegiate co-operation. As between poorer and richer colleges, it need only exist where distance intervenes. It does not exist at Oxford or Cambridge : the present writer was at one of the smaller and poorer colleges of Oxford; yet during the whole of his course for his honours degree in history he attended without extra cost lectures at Balliol, New College, Magdalen, University, Oriel, and other colleges, but not one in his own. The intercollegiate system established at Oxford in 1876 was the very foundation of its magnificent undergraduate history school.[1]

In London the intercollegiate system halts on lagging feet; an hour or so a week is the utmost a student is encouraged or allowed to spend outside his (generally her) own college, and college endowments have not seldom been used simply to keep students inside, irrespective of the intellectual attractions elsewhere. In one case a recently appointed and endowed ' university ' professor complained that he had to 'mug up' Stubbs' *Select Charters,* which he had not looked at for twenty years, in order to teach students of a college who had previously got all they wanted from a life-long specialist in the subject in a college a few minutes' distance away. The idea that the atmosphere and equipment of a university can be repeated in each of the schools is but a half-way house from, or to, the delusion that they can be brought to the doorstep of every student by post. Its prevalence however, explains the frequent obscurity in the lines of demarcation between the Internal and External sides and the perpetuation of much the same personnel and policies after the apparent change of constitution.

Next to the personnel of the Court the most surprising sign of conservatism was the immediate reappointment of a finance committee by the Senate after its financial powers

[1] Its chief defect was indicated at the time by the Oxford Board of Modern History itself: 'There is in the inter-collegiate arrangement no security for the encouragement of research—the special province of a university' (Sir Charles Firth, *op. cit.,* p. 20). 'This view about the functions of a university' Sir Charles describes as 'since abandoned'; cf., *ib.,* p. 28.

and responsibilities had all been transferred by authority of Parliament to the Court. The possibility had not escaped the notice of the Departmental Committee, but no express prhoibition had been recommended, partly because of the suspicion it would imply and partly because the danger was thought remote : it was assumed that the old finance committee of the Senate was *functus officio* : and, indeed, its resuscitation is not easy to reconcile with the new statutes. It arose out of domestic arrangements ostensibly made to give those statutes effect. Each of the schools or colleges of the university (incorporated in it or not) was authorised and required to present its finance direct to the Court without the intervention of the Senate. This left over what are called the 'central activities' of the university, concerned mainly with administration but including such diverse elements as matriculation examinations, extension lectures, and the Institute of Historical Research; and this incoherent complex, in its relations with the Court, was treated as a financial unit, a collegiate miscellany, governed by the Senate on the advice of its finance committee just as a college or school is governed by its delegacy or college committee. From the point of view of finance the effect may be expressed by saying either that the Senate was reduced to the status of one of its schools, or that the schools were raised to the status of the Senate. Senate and schools alike framed each its own estimates, presented them to the Court, asked for a block grant to meet its expenses, and retained a free hand to spend it, subject, of course, to its estimates and to review by the Court when the block grant came up for renewal.

The detailed consequences of a general plan can seldom be foreseen with any precision, and some results of this scheme were disturbing. The University Institute of Historical Research found itself in no closer touch with the source of financial supply than the smallest department of history in a school of the university. It had only been maintained for the first five years of its existence by the

direct action of H.M. Treasury's University Grants Committee. Three additional bodies were now interposed, the
Court, the Senate, and the Senate's finance committee; and
to all intents and purposes the finance committee, before
which it claims had to be measured with those of matriculation and school-leaving examinations and extension lectures,
was the final authority. The Court could no more be
expected, however admirably it might have been constituted, to allocate to a department under the jurisdiction of
the Senate's finance committee more than the Senate on
the advice of that committee asked, than to allocate more
to a college department than the college desired : every
such grant would be not only a work of supererogation but
a reflection upon the finance committee's discrimination or
impartiality. Nor was the Court supplied with the grounds
of action. The Senate always had an admirable rule that
whenever a superior body, such as the Academic Council,
reported its disagreement with an inferior body like a
Board of Studies, it must submit to the Senate not only its
own recommendations but those from which it was differing.
But the Senate has not applied its own principles to its
own practice; when disagreeing with the estimates of its
subordinate organisations, it does not communicate those
estimates to the Court from which it is seeking grants.
University organisations like the Institute of Historical
Research can therefore only obtain, not what the Court
can afford or thinks fit to grant, but only that for which
the finance committee thinks fit to ask.

That perhaps is a detail interesting to few and not worth
discussing were it not for two general considerations. The
first is that, owing to the loose-jointedness of the university, there is no forum therein for the discussion of general
university problems and nothing that can be called a
university public opinion; and the second is the danger
in which these financial anomalies involve the whole
future development of the university on its new site. For
the institutions located there will not be schools or colleges

with their independent access to the Court, but university organisations or departments in the constitutional position of the Institute of Historical Research and dependent upon what influence they can bring to bear upon the finance committee of the Senate; and the more specialised and advanced their ideas and methods, the less influence they will have on the normal organs of university administration and finance.   To belong wholly to the university, without such qualifications and limitations of their dependence as are enjoyed by schools, is at present a serious handicap; for it means control by a committee which represents neither the learning of the Senate nor the financial eminence of the Court.   The first experience the Institute had of the new arrangement was, after generous increases in the Treasury and County Council grants to the university for current expenditure during the next quinquennium, to find its own estimates cut down twenty-five per cent. by the finance committee of the Senate;[1] and the new pro-jected institutions on the university site would all be liable to the same haphazard risks of a policy, if such it can be called, which thinks only in terms of pounds, shillings, and pence, with little comprehension of the intellectual values of the various objects of academic expenditure.

These are the defects in the new organisation which most invite criticism and require re-consideration, because they impair the university's capacity for framing any policy at all.   Some welcome signs have been recently given of a new capacity for corporate action and discrimination. The new chairs—such as those of American,[2] Military,

---

[1] In significant contrast, the Treasury's University Grants Com-mittee, reverting to its earlier practice, earmarked a grant of £1,500 to the Institute to fill the gaps in its chief collections of printed historical materials.

[2] Most of these chairs were advocated in a memorandum (see Appendix) I submitted to University College on 26th November, 1918, and the American chair publicly in a letter to *The Times*, 6th December, 1919; the chair in that subject at Oxford was established in 1922. More important for this country than the

Economic, and Byzantine History, and the History of Art—
are real university chairs, at least in idea, with definite
limits enabling the professor to represent the university as
an expert in the subject, and are not simply disguised college
lectureships with a scope indistinguishable from that allotted
to historical ' experts ' in secondary and even elementary
Schools.[1] More care has lately been shown in filling vacancies
on the Court and Senate, and the honorary degrees of the
university are no longer restricted to members of the royal
family.[2]   A vacancy in its chancellorship provided an
opportunity for introducing the thin end of the wedge, and
soon after Earl Beauchamp's election to succeed Lord
Rosebery he received an honorary doctorate. A more
distinctive step was taken in conferring the same distinction
on Lord Macmillan in recognition of his eminent services
to the university as the first chairman of its Court. The
centenary meeting of the British Association in London in
September, 1931, was happily seized as an opportunity for
conferring honorary degrees on its President, General
Smuts, and on the President and three ex-Presidents of the
Royal Society, while President Masaryk, who lectured at
King's College during the war, received the Hon.LL.D. At
the next Foundation Day the Bishop of Gloucester (formerly
Principal of King's College) received the Hon. D.D.;
Lord Passfield (famous as Mr. Sidney Webb, for no less
eminent services to the London School of Economics) the
Hon. D.Sc. (Econ.); Lord Tomlin (Chairman of the
Statutory Commissioners) the Hon. LL.D.; Mr. Samuel
Courtauld (part-donor of the endowment of the History of
Art) and the Rector of the University of Paris the Hon.
D.Lit.; and Sir Edward Elgar, the Hon. D.Mus. Thus

chair of military history was a chair of naval history. Efforts to
found it failed in London, though one was subsequently founded
at Cambridge; and even the lectureship which was started has
now lapsed.

1 The objection is not to allotting chairs to colleges, but to giving
their holders titles in no way indicating the university functions
they should fulfil.

2 See above, p. 256.

London has broken some of the ice which froze its
approach to the comity of universities and chilled the
advances to it of possible benefactors.

A spirit had stirred in the valley of dry bones. They
were coming together with sinews and flesh, and the
whisper perhaps of a breath which might make them live
and stand up on their feet. An academic memorandum
early in 1931 referred to the ' absence of an academic
policy' which ' is liable to result, as suggested above,[1] in
a more or less haphazard development in the University.
This has been so in the past when new departures were due
to various and sometimes conflicting interests rather than
to any conviction of the University as to the most desirable
lines of development.' It proceeded to urge that the time
had come when the Senate must devise a plan in order to
ensure a well-balance development of the various subjects
of university study and convince the Court of the
desirability of the requisite expenditure. This is new and
admirable doctrine coming from the head, or at least the
headquarters of the University. Hitherto initiative had
been left to its schools, to casual groups, or to outside
bodies. If any body proposed a new university chair and
provided the appropriate salary and equipment, the Senate
would appoint or confer the title on the selected professor.
There might be half a dozen colleges wanting university
titles for half a dozen teachers of an identical subject, and
the Senate's practice was to let them all come, provided
they came with the requisite funds and plausible qualifications. The notions that the university should attempt
to discriminate between subjects that should and those
that should not be taught in the university; that it should
plan a professoriate and co-ordinate the teaching of its
nominal professors (some with identical titles) scattered
throughout its colleges; or even require them to lecture to
the university as a whole, were dismissed as irrelevant or
impracticable. In 1912 a motion that the conferment of

1 Pp. 263—5.

professorial status should entail the delivery of at least three public lectures in the university was rejected by the Senate; and about the same time the late Lord Moulton protested against the idea that the Senate could possibly exercise any real academic discretion.

The university, in short, existed, so far as its internal side was concerned, solely to serve its colleges. At Oxford or Cambridge a college—even when it provides the whole of a professor's remuneration—has no voice in the work he does for the university; in London, strange as it may appear, he is responsible to the college for his duties to the university—even when the university provides the whole of his stipend. If he is the head of a department at all, it is of a college and not a university department; but, as often as not, the university professor is not even the head of a college department. Abdication could no farther go : the university throne was vacant; and, there being in fact no real university, there could be no university departments. Their place was taken by an indefinite number of incoherent college departments quite incapable, owing to rival ambitions and diverse standards and ideas, of devising co-ordinate university plans or policies. There existed a sort of academic feudalism; and just as in a feudal society there can be no real State, in London there could be no real university : the ' overmighty subject' in collegiate form reduced the sovereign university to a *roi fainéant*. The chronological order is, strictly speaking, somewhat different : the university had been condemned to academic incompetence by its initial restriction to examining functions, and the colleges had no option but to cultivate the vacant academic space on their own and thereby increase their independence, resources, and strength.

The renaissance of the University is exemplified in the new-found desire of the Senate to make plans and exert a will of its own. But the initiative was not entirely due to a growth of self-determination; it is imposed by the new constitution and the creation of the Court. Its functions

are indeed financial, but its name implies that it exists to
hear cases; and the Senate has to produce a case before it
can go to the Court for supplies : hence the demand for a
plan.   Under the old dispensation, the Senate had no need
to plan because there was no one to whom to present a
case, and it disclaimed the functions of a court mainly
because it had as little to dispense as discretion in dispensation.   Nor, indeed, can it now do much of the planning
itself : it has to rely for the most part on its advisory
Board of Studies, to whom the academic memorandum
was addressed.   The response is the thing that matters,
and that depends upon qualities of comprehensive outlook
in which highly specialised Boards of Studies, often composed of localised minds, are not apt to excel.   Collegiate
predominance therein has, it is true, been reduced by the
multiplication of university professors which increased
endowments have produced.   But, for reasons stated above,
the university professor's mind moves in a collegiate atmosphere[1] : one eminent member of the species recently
proposed to eliminate the ambiguity by erecting his
particular college into a university; and the plea is often
heard that the great London colleges are really universities
in themselves.   That is the principal difficulty in making a
university out of them; not the least of the advantages of
Oxford and Cambridge is that not one of their colleges has
ever pretended to be a university.

Nor do increased endowments always produce the
expected improvement in *personnel*.   Historians are familiar
with the tendency of second generations to fall into second
classes.   It is happily a generalisation to which there are

[1] The reason is, of course, that in London university professors
lecture mostly to undergraduates of a single college.   Why, asked
a witness before the Oxford Commission of 1877, should a professor 'lecture to undergraduates?'   Another witness said : 'What
I should like is, to have professors to teach us, the teachers'; and
T. H. Green suggested that the proper function of professors was
to teach post-graduate students (Firth, *op. cit.*, p. 25).   Freeman
repudiated the idea that it was any part of a professor's duty to
prepare pupils for examinations (*ib.*, p. 32).

many exceptions, but the exceptions are seldom produced by a rate of remuneration. Nor, whatever its intellectual product, will remuneration redound mainly to the advantage of the university so long as it proceeds mainly from a diversity of schools and colleges. It is rare that streams from different sources run in the same direction or reach a common issue. A nation confronted with an urgent need for economy will sooner or later turn its attention to the waste accruing from the competition of all its universities to provide, mainly at the public expense, for every stage of education in every subject and branch of a subject from matriculation to the highest research; and guardians of the public purse, when they escape from the miasma of war expenditure and competitive armaments, may even insist that the elaborate existing equipment of one university for a special purpose is an argument not for but against its repetition in every other.[1]

The case of the State against university rivalry for redundant equipment is still more strongly the case for a university against its component schools and colleges. The moral is stated in words which may fitly conclude this argument, because they sum up the position of those who have striven during a generation to realise a vision of twenty-seven years ago.[2] The words were addressed in 1917 by Mr. Herbert Fisher, then President of the Board of Education, to the oldest college out of which the university grew[3]: they might have been addressed with no less point to the youngest.

[1] See below, Appendix, pp. 313-14, and my 'plea for a national policy' in *The Times*, 6th and 17th December, 1919. The argument was taken up by a number of distinguished men interested in medical studies in London (*ibid.*, 13th December, 1919) on the ground that the principles I 'enunciated for history apply with even greater force to medical science'; and, on the report of the Athlone Committee, to School of Hygiene and Tropical Medicine was founded in Malet Street on somewhat the same lines as the Institute of Historical Research, though with much ampler accommodation, equipment, and endowment.

[2] See above, pp. 253-4.

[3] *University College Calendar*, 1917-18, p. lxxxviii.

'What the University of London may eventually become depends upon the degree of allegiance which the idea of a great London University may be able to command among its members, and upon the extent to which the various interests and collegiate bodies at present composing the University are prepared to make concessions to a common purpose. . . .

Universities . . . do find a great difficulty in working together, and the colleges within the universities have their little rivalries and contradictions of policy. . . . Another obstacle to academic union is erected by virtue herself. Members of colleges readily acquire a sentimental affection for any system which has helped them in youth, and in particular for the foundation to which they owe their first taste of the generous wines of sociability and liberal learning. . . . The College becomes part of himself, a parcel of his virtue, and a darling point of prejudice and contentious defence. To challenge its utility, to suggest an alteration in its frame wears the air of treason to a long succession of treasured memories. Yet a time may come when it becomes an act of virtue to extricate oneself from the mesh even of the most meritorious tradition.'

NOTES

CHAPTER I

Page 2, ll. 16-23. Utopias begin with the Paradise of Genesis
and the golden age of Hesiod, and the first, at any rate,
has inspired many revolutionists, *e.g.* John Ball with his

> When Adam dalf and Evé span
> Who was thanne the gentilman?

More elaborate were the utopias of the revolutionary
leaders of the Peasants' Revolt in Germany in 1524-5 and
the Anabaptists in 1534; see my chapters in the *Cambridge
Modern History,* ii. 183-6, 222-6. Utopias in England
were more academic and platonic save for the Fifth
Monarchy men, the Levellers, and the Diggers in the time
of the Commonwealth; and the first French Revolution
was too bourgeois a movement, and succumbed too soon
to militarism, to give much serious attention to dreams
of an earthly paradise.

Pages 3-4. English History, as Maitland said, can never be
an elementary subject (*Collected Papers,* iii. 310-11). It
consists, in fact, of an infinite series of intricate, if not
insoluble, problems. But so, too, does Nature; and if
history is less easy and less popular than Nature-study,
it is because man is so much the most complex and variegated animal in existence.

Page 5, l. 19. Sir Francis Palgrave.

,, ,, l. 26. The 'myth of Magna Carta' is a phrase of
Professor Edward Jenks who attacked the traditional
view in the *Independent Review* for November, 1904. A
more elaborate criticism is the late Professor W. S.
McKechnie's *Magna Carta* (1905; 2nd ed. 1914); and
various points of view are expressed in the Royal
Historical Society's *Magna Carta Commemoration Essays*
(1917).

Page 6, ll. 5-7. The witticism that there are 'lies, damned
lies, and statistics' may be exaggerated; but in one
university, at any rate, there has been a long feud between rival schools of opinion on the very foundations of
statistical science.

Page 7. The most familiar of these false antitheses in history
is, perhaps, the question whether Mary Queen of Scots
was guilty or not, the very form of which precludes
any truthful answer. The real question is one of degree,
and there are endless degrees of guilt in connection with
murder. Crime attaches not merely to the actual
murderer and those who participate in the deed, but to
the accessories either before or after; and there are many
ways, passive as well as active, of being 'accessory,' such
as connivance before, and condonation or even concealment, after. No one supposes that Mary actually
murdered Darnley; it is improbable that she took an
active part in planning it. But it is equally improbable
that she had no idea of what was in the wind or took any
active measures to save her husband; and whether she
did so before the murder or not, she certainly afterwards
showed conclusively that she viewed the murderer with
no disfavour.

Page 8, ll. 24-36. These lines were written in 1911 the
'three main reasons' then urged have all become
increasingly urgent during the twenty years which have
since intervened. The historical education which has
spread so widely in universities and secondary schools has
hardly affected 1 per cent .of the present electorate. The
primitive mind, says Prof. Elliot Smith, has no ' craving
for historical knowledge ' (*Early Man*, 1931, p. 13).

CHAPTER II

Page 14, ll. 19-20. The allusion is to a speech of Joseph
Chamberlain's in 1905 on his tariff-reform proposals, in
which he said he had only used facts (which were disputed)
as illustrations of his argument.

Page 17, l. 32. See M. Jacques Flach, *Les Origines de l'ancienne
France* (Paris, 1904, iii. 88 *n*), ' l'organisation féodale s'est
trouvée dans la société Anglo-Saxonne en avance sur celle
de la France.'

Page 21, l. 25. Christopher Ocland; see *D.N.B.*, xli. 365,
which should now be corrected and supplemented by
reference to J. R. Dasent's *Acts of the Privy Council*,
1581-2, pp. 389-90. That patriotism did not exist till the
18th century was a view expressed by Joseph Chamberlain; he was probably thinking of Chatham and subcon-
sciously indentifying patriotism with imperialism.

Page 23, ll. 24-27. In January, 1897, Mr. Louis Schlesinger was adopted as Conservative candidate at a by-election for Romford, was nominated on the 26th as Mr. Louis Sinclair, and elected on 1st February (*Annual Reg.* 1897, p. [54]; *The Times,* 22nd January to 2nd February, 1897).

Page 24, ll. 10-14. The first of these Irishmen was Richard Wall (1694-1778 : see *D.N.B.* lix. 96). The second was John Acton, 'né à Besançon de parents irlandais' (Lavisse and Rambaud, *Hist. Générale,* vii. 976); but this is a mistake, for John Acton was ancestor of Lord Acton and therefore came from a Shropshire and not from an Irish family (see *D.N.B.* i. 67-8 and Second Suppl. i. 8). The third allusion is to Marshal Maurice Francis Lacy (1725-1801 : see *D.N.B.* xxxi 387-8, and Carlyle's *Frederick the Great, passim*). The fourth allusion is to Comte Thomas Arthur Lally, baron de Tollendal, Sir Eyre Coote's opponent at the battle of Wandewash (see *Encycl. Brit.,* 11th ed. xvi. 95). Frederick the Great's 'right-hand man' was Marshal Keith (Carlyle's *Frederick, passim,* and *D.N.B.,* xxx. 324-5). Peter the Great's grandmother was a Hamilton (Lavisse and Rambaud, *Hist. Générale,* vi. 673-4). Napoleon's marshal who became King of Sweden was, of course, Bernadotte.

Page 27, ll. 21-23. The revolution in Germany, which followed the Great War, promoted its unification by abolishing these territorial sovereignties.

Page 29, ll. 36-37. The incident of the Oxfordshire election is related by Sir Francis Palgrave in his *Merchant and Friar,* 1837, pp. 81-3. The fact that he gave his M.P.'s fictitious names in his text has misled some readers into thinking that the incident itself was fictitious; but in his 'Dedication' (pp. xv.-xvii.) Palgrave gives their real names with a reference to his *Parliamentary Writs* (II ii. p. 273, No. 47) whence the official information was derived; they also appear in the *Official Return of M.P.'s,* i. 67.

The opinion that membership of Parliament was in the 14th century regarded as a burden rather than a privilege was vigorously stated by Prynne, as a result of his monumental labour on parliamentary writs, and has been adopted by most constitutional historians since. It has recently been challenged in the *English Historical Review* (July 1931, pp. 372-388) on the ground that the attempted exclusion of sheriffs, lawyers, esquires, 'valetti' and other inferior persons from election as knights of the shire implies that knights themselves were, or would have been, willing to take their place. But surely this is a fallacious argument : I may wish to prevent the election or appointment of unfit town-councillors, jurymen, or municipal scavengers, without in the least wishing to be a town-councillor, a juryman, or a scavenger myself. It is admitted, moreover (*ib.* p. 384) that ' the return of these " valetti " seems to have met with no opposition.' But why not, if knights were anxious or even willing to serve themselves? The invariable practice of ' mainperning ' M.P.'s and the use of the Chiltern Hundreds as ' a sanctuary in which the knight of the shire took refuge in order to avoid being dragged into Parliament against his will ' (Palgrave, *op. cit.,* p. 82) leave little ground on which to base the attractiveness of knight service in Parliament. Palgrave's chapter on 'The County Election' in his *Merchant and Friar* is still worth reading by those who wish to know what a mediæval county election was like without labouring through his *Parliamentary Writs* or Prynne's *Briefe Register* of 2,200 pages.

CHAPTER III

Page 33, ll. 15-19, and pp. 34-35. Cf. Hilaire Belloc's *Wolsey* (pub. October 1930) pref., ' history, whose function it is not only to chronicle a series of events but to say *how* and *why* such things happened.'

Page 34, ll. 3-7. The ' profound scholar ' was the late W. H. Stevenson, and his article on Alfred the Great's death is in *Engl. Hist. Rev.,* xiii. 71-7 : it had in fact been published in 1898, but the projectors of the celebration had not kept up with the ' Notes and Documents ' in the *E.H.R.*

Page 46, l. 30. On the ' myth of the three estates in England,' see my *Evolution of Parliament* (2nd ed. 1926,, cap. iv.).

CHAPTER IV

Page 63, l. 18. The now almost-forgotten ' Fashoda incident ' nearly precipitated war between England and France in 1898. Fashoda was a post on the Upper Nile occupied by the French commandant Marchand, while Kitchener was completing the conquest of the Sudan; and French occupation threatened Rhodes' popular Cape-to-Cairo policy.

Page 69, l. 15. The reference is to Sir H. Beerbohm Tree's production of *King John* at the Haymarket Theatre in September 1899.

Chapter V

Page 74, ll. 3-5. By the late Martin A. S. Hume in his *Wives of Henry VIII.* (1905).

Page 74, ll. 34-37. The four English cardinals were Bainbridge, Wolsey, Fisher, and Pole; and the four dukes were the two dukes of Norfolk and the dukes of Buckingham and Suffolk. The cardinal who was executed was Fisher and the duke was Buckingham. Cardinals and dukes represented the two forces with which Tudor monarchy was at grips.

Page 85, l. 7. 'Both the husbands,' *i.e.* Louis XII. of France and Charles Brandon, Duke of Suffolk.

Page 85, l. 9. Margaret was divorced from her husband, the Earl of Angus, by papal sentence on 11th March, 1527, in order to marry Henry Stewart, Lord Methven, who had also been divorced from a former wife for the same purpose.

Page 85, ll. 10-2. This king of Castile was Henry IV. and the terms of the papal licence to him are given in the *Calendar of Spanish State Papers*, ii. 379.

Page 91, ll. 14-15. Cranmer's Lutheran phase has been denied on the ground that after his initial conversion from the Roman doctrine he 'embraced, consistently maintained, and never abandoned the Suvermerian theory of the Eucharist' (C. H. Smyth, *Cranmer and the Reformation*, 1926, p. 25). But this 'Suvermerianism' appears to have been a work of imagination deduced from a misreading of 'svvermeriasmus,' a latinised form of the German 'schwärmerei' (see *The Times Lit. Suppl.*, 1927, pp. 456, 488).

Chapter VI

Page 95, ll. 21-24. The 'aspiring politician' was Sir Henry Bagnal (see *D.N.B.*, First Suppl., i. 95-6); and his letter to the Earl of Rutland is in *Rutland MSS*. (Hist. MSS. Comm.) i. 207.

Page 95, ll. 25-26. Norfolk's list is in *Letters and Papers of Henry VIII.*, x. 816, but he includes Gatton, which is in Surrey; the other boroughs were Horsham, Shoreham, Steyning, and Lewes; it is odd that he does not include

Arundel or Bramber. The reference to the Bishop of Winchester should be deleted : he probably meant clerical proctors, not burgesses (Foxe, vi. 54).

Page 105, ll. 25-26. Cf. *Official Return of M.P.'s,* i. 376 *n*; in 1547 the two M.P.'s were returned by ' Sir Roger Copley, knyght, burgese, and only inhabytante of the borowghe and Towne of Gatton.' In 1554 the return was made by his widow Dame Elizabeth Copley (*ib.,* i. 391 *n.*).

Page 105, l. 36. The constituency is printed ' Oxford ' in *Letters and Papers,* iv. App. no. 238; but the fact that Sir Thomas Rush was to be consulted whether Cromwell should represent it or not shows that Orford is meant. Rush had considerable influence in Suffolk and was himself returned for Ipswich, while he had no connection with Oxford.

Page 109, ll. 4-7. The member whose name is given (Hall, *Chron.,* p. 788) was Thomas Temys, M.P. for Westbury. So far from suffering any ill consequences, he received various grants of monastic lands, chiefly from Lacock Abbey, of which his sister, Joan Temys, had been abbess.

Chapter VII

Page 125, ll. 20-24. The bishop was John Scory; see *D.N.B.* and my *England under Protector Somerset,* pp. 210-211. These remarks about unemployment date, of course, from 1905, long before ' rationalisation "—the modern counterpart of the enclosure movement—had produced a similar result.

Page 133, l. 19. ' A sympathetic divine ' was Francis Trigge (1547 ?-1606); see *D.N.B.,* lvii. 230.

Chapter VIII

Page 135, ll. 1-2. Professor E. A. Freeman.

Pages 137-138. On Luther's political thought see the acute criticism of current misconceptions by J. W. Allen in *Tudor Studies,* ed. Seton-Watson, pp. 90-108; Mr. Allen's *History of Political Thought in the 16th Century* (1928) is the best general work on the subject.

Page 150, ll. 9-11 . I have here given ' State ' a capital letter to make Hobbes' meaning clearer; his point is that the ' state of Nature ' is no ' State ' at all.

CHAPTER IX

Page 156, ll. 16-17. 'One writer': see *Social England,* ed. H. D. Traill (1895), iii. 171.

Page 160, ll. 25-28. An allusion to the dissolution of the first and second Russian Dumas on 8 July, 1906, and 16 June, 1907, respectively; the former occasion provoked from Sir H. Campbell-Bannerman, then Prime Minister, the ejaculation 'Le Douma est mort; vive le Douma.' The Third Duma, which met on 15 November, 1907, was satisfactorily Conservative and subsided into an insignificance which preluded the Great War of 1914 and the Russian revolution of 1917.

Page 160, ll. 30-37. The quotation is from Hume Brown's *Hist. of Scotland* (1902), ii. 117.

Page 161, ll. 32-35. This sentence was editorially eliminated from the *D.N.B.* art. on Sir Thomas White.

P. 162, ll. 28-37. On 25 February, 1629, the Speaker, Sir John Finch, who wished to adjourn the House at Charles I.'s command, was held in the chair by Holles, Valentine, and others while Sir John Eliot read a remonstrance on tonnage and poundage. The name of the woman who hurled a stool at the head of David Lindsay, bishop of Edinburgh, when he attemped to read Laud's service-book in St. Giles', Edinburgh, on 23 July, 1637, is supposed to have been Jenny Geddes (*D.N.B.*, xxi. 102).

Page 169, ll. 35-36. James Sharp, archbishop of St. Andrews (who must not be confused with John Sharp, archbishop of York, 1645-1714), was shot in High Street, Edinburgh, on 8 July, 1668, by James Mitchell, who escaped capture and execution till 1678.

CHAPTER X

Page 179, ll. 26-29. The Parliament Act was not, of course, passed till 1911.

Page 180, l. 33 *et seq.* On the other hand, Alexander Hamilton contended in the *Federalist* that such 'abridgements of prerogative' as Magna Carta, the Petition of Right, and the Bill of Rights, had no application to constitutions 'founded upon the power of the people' like that of the United States; and Hobbes' *Leviathan* has recently come to have an ominous vogue across the Atlantic: 'the shade of Hobbes began to haunt the sanctuary of John Locke' (see my *Factors in American History,* 1925, pp.

216-17, 249; and Charles A. and William Beard, *The American Leviathan,* 1931).

Pages 183-195. These Cromwellian attempts to limit and define the powers of Parliament no doubt suggested the American idea of a government with ' enumerated powers ' (*Factors in American Hist.,* p. 218). Bacon, however, had written of fundamental laws in his *New Atlantis,* published in 1627.

Page 187, l. 23. The Channel Islands are specified in clauses ix-x of the *Instrument,* but apparently made no return to Cromwell's Parliaments.

CHAPTER XI

Page 201, ll. 26-29. Lord Rosebery gave the signal for this in his lecture on Oliver Cromwell, published in 1900 but delivered a year or so earlier; and this, Lord Morley told the present writer, provoked his own more elaborate volume on the same subject in 1900.

CHAPTER XII

Page 217, l. 17. ' Teleological conception ': *cf.* Flexner, *Universities* : *American, English, German,* p. 15. ' In the social as in the physical sciences, the university is, in so far as scientific effort to understand phenomena is concerned, indifferent to the effect and use of truth '; and pp. 30-1, ' Have I lost sight of the importance of " training"—training college teachers or educational administrators or candidates for governmental posts? I think not. . . . Society requires of its leaders not so much specially trained competency at the moment as the mastery of experience, an interest in problems, dexterity in finding one's way, disciplined capacity to put forth effort.' I have therefore preferred the shorter title of Sir C. Grant Robertson's Creighton Lecture (1928) on *History and Citizenship,* in which he treats the subject from a more philosophical and academic point of view. Dr. Flexner has a great deal to say on what he calls (p. 72) ' the confusion in our colleges of education with training.'

Page 222, l. 29. *Cf.* F. W. Maitland, *Collected Papers,* iii. 289 : ' The language of any and every science must be in the eyes of the etymologist a mass of metaphors and of very mixed metaphors.'

Page 224, l. 19. *Cf.* Graham Wallas, *Physical and Social Science,* 1930, p. 1.

Page 225, ll. 6-10. Bacon, in his *New Atlantis,* attempts to
provide an escape from this dilemma : he makes the
' father ' of his ' Solomon's House ' say, ' we have consul-
tations which of the inventions and experiences which we
have discovered shall be published, and which not; and
take all an oath of secrecy for the concealing of those
which we think meet to keep secret, though some of those
we do reveal sometimes to the State, and some not.' Here
the scientist is made responsible for choosing between
three courses, (*a*) keeping inventions secret, (*b*) revealing
them to ' the State,' and (*c*) making them public property.

Page 225, ll. 12-15. *Cf.* Flexner, p. 15. ' The modern university must neither fear the world nor make itself responsible for its conduct.' Dr. Flexner is dealing with the savant
or scientist as such, not with him as a citizen, nor with
any possible conflict between a civic Dr. Jekyll and a
scientific Mr. Hyde. Nor, apparently, would he defend
the special representation of universities in Parliament;
for surely that special representation gives the British
university of to-day a special responsibility for the conduct of its country if not of the world. ' Taste and
reason,' he remarks later on (p. 21), ' do not intervene to
stop the scientist prosecuting his search for truth; they
do sit in judgment on the uses to which society puts the
forces which the scientist has set free.' Taste and reason
are here regarded as the qualities of the citizen but not
of the scientist; and the difficulty, which lawyers sometimes acutely experience, of drawing a line between
professional and political practice remains unsolved.

Page 225, ll. 24-27. See my *Commonwealth at War,* 1917,
pp. 102-125.

Page 225, ll. 34-37. See *The Times,* 2 December, 1929. Presumably, like General Smuts, Dr. Flexner regards
' universal science ' as an expert adviser to ' universal
suffrage '; and he cites (p. 15 *n*) the recently-established
Economic Advisory Council as an example; ' The Council
does not decide policies : that is left to the Government.'

Page 226, l. 9. ' Like the scientist, the humanist creates as
well as solves problems. . . . He has, I repeat, no
practical responsibility for the trouble he makes; it is
his business and duty to preserve his independence and
irresponsibility ' (Flexner, pp. 21-22).

Page 226, ll. 12-14. See below, p. 308. Bury's answer would
probably have been that Thiers and Treitschke proved
his point : they did *not* study, or at any rate, did not

write, history ' as if it had no bearing on anything beyond itself,' but with specific reference to political ambitions.

Page 226, line 7. This famous maxim of Bacon's has been derided on the ground that knowledge how things are done is quite different from the ability to do them. Yet, when we say a man knows how to write, we mean that he can write; and teaching children to write is practical work producing power and not theoretical knowledge. The criticism is a mere quibble based on the ambiguity of ' knowledge ': no one has the power to write without ' knowledge ' of how to write.

Page 227, ll. 19-20. That the worship of youth has characterised earlier periods of disturbance may be seen from the following passage from the Hist. MSS. Comm. *Report on Various Collections,* iv. 268; ' 1652—Thomas Hastlyn, a youth described as of twenty years of age " or thereabout," is elected mayor [of Orford]. And in the next year William Marsh, of the same age. These became by virtue of their office justices of the peace. It may be inferred that older and more responsible persons were withdrawing themselves from taking part in any public business, at any rate for a time. 1654, Thomas Hastlyn is elected coroner at the age of 22.'

Page 232, ll. 4-6. *Cf.* Joseph de Maistre's protest against the humanitarianism of the eighteenth century, ' I have seen Frenchmen, Italians, Russians; but as for Man, I declare I never met him in my life ' (my *Factors in American History,* 1925, pp. 231-2). Professor Ernest Barker complains that history panders to the nationalisms of mankind (*History,* vii. 82); and the Historical Association itself has at times been almost persuaded to lend itself to Imperialist propaganda on one hand and League of Nations propaganda on the other. Since there is not the same reason for secreting historical facts as there is for poison gas or high explosive, the only sound rule for the historian is Bury's that ' History must be studied *as if* it had no bearing on anything beyond itself ' (*The Ancient Greek Historians,* 1909, pp. 244-5). Mr. Norman Baynes in his *Bibliography and Memoir of J. B. Bury,* 1929, pp. 109-10, emphasises the words in italics, and shows that Bury did not mean that history *has* no bearing on any thing beyond itself. It must not be used to inculcate even citizenship, but it is not history at all unless it exhibits the feelings and enlightens the passions of men; and out of that enlightenment alone can any true citizenship come.

Page 232, ll. 9-11. *Cf.* my paper on 'The Dominions and Foreign Affairs' (*Proc. of the British Institute of International Affairs,* 24th May, 1921, p. 12) : 'The less we talk about independence or dependence, the better. For neither the one nor the other is the vital fact in the situation, but the interdependence of all the parts.'

Page 232, ll. 35-36. W. J. Cory, 'Mimnermus in Church' (Palgrave's *Golden Treasury,* p. 440).

CHAPTER XIII

(i) IN 1904

The first section of this chapter was published in 1904; the footnotes were added in 1907 except two appended in 1911.

Page 236, *n.* I. To some extent this guidance has now been provided by the establishment of an Advisory Service for External Students.

Page 238, ll. 6-7. S. R. Gardiner told me this himself. He received nothing for the first six volumes of his monumental *History of England,* 1603-1642 (*D.N.B.,* 2nd Suppl., ii. 76). On the other hand, he was offered but wisely declined £1,000 in lieu of royalties on his schoolbook entitled *The Student's History of England,* which covered nineteen centuries in three volumes (1890).

Page 238, ll. 28-33. The allusion is to the late William Duncombe Pink. His MSS., still unpublished, are now among the valued possessions of the John Rylands Library at Manchester, and, besides being used by various research students of Manchester University, have been of great assistance to Colonel Wedgwood's Committee on the Records of the House of Commons, appointed by Mr. Baldwin in 1929.

Page 240, ll. 15-16. Dr. Abraham Flexner would definitely exclude from the university all 'secondary, technical, vocational, and popular education' (*Universities,* 1930, pp. 27-8).

Page 245, *n.* I. For the difficulties still prevailing at Oxford and Cambridge, see Flexner, pp. 270-2 : (1) 'The University is really the creature of the colleges' which 'are on the whole well-to-do,' while 'the University has little'; (2) 'the colleges are mainly undergraduate; a graduate development would be a University matter, but the University lacks the requisite funds and a governing body interested in graduate work and capable of in-augurating and pursuing a far-sighted and continuous policy.'

Page 247, ll. 26-27. Admiral Mahan.

Page 248, ll. 5-10. This was, of course, a reference to the 'Great' Boer War of 1899-1902 : the remark is still truer of the Great War of 1914-18.

Page 248, ll. 11-12. Moltke.

Page 248, ll. 14-27. See p. 263.

Page 250, ll. 1-2. The late Sir William Ramsay, F.R.S., K.C.B.

Page 250, l. 32. Dr. G. P. Gooch.

Page 251, ll. 30-34. The 'well-known man of letters and politician' was Lord Morley, the scholar was Sir Charles Firth, and the 'certain book' was Sir Charles' *Oliver Cromwell*.

Page 253, ll. 1-18. Dr. Alfred William Pollard, F.B.A., C.B.

(ii) TWENTY YEARS AFTER

Page 256, *n.* But see p. 293.

Page 257, ll. 30-31. *E.g.*, by Stubbs in his *Seventeen Lectures* (1887), lectures ii.—v. and pp. 382, 435-7; by Freeman (Flexner, *op. cit.*, p. 277, *n.*) ; and by Sir Charles Firth in his inaugural lecture, *A Plea for the historical teaching of History* (1904) and *Modern History in Oxford,* 1841-1918 (1920).

Page 259, l. 12. The number is still given as 'about 4,500 members' (*History,* July, 1931, p. xvia).

Page 259, l. 28. The Evening School began work in October, 1910, and some 2,000 teachers in London schools have since attended its courses.

Page 266, ll. 31. This benefaction to history and the university has been described in terms of comprehensive censure by one of the professors of history in the university itself : 'With extreme rashness and with the very improper connivance of the government, it [the Senate] had placed on a large plot of the site in question an Institute of Historical Research costing over £20,000' (*Centenary History of King's College*, p. 476). The cost, of course, was not to the Senate but to the benefactor, now Sir John Power, Bart., M.P., who presented the Institute to the University; and his benefaction was not available for any other purpose in any other place.

Page 267, ll. 23-30. On the general problem of University 'institutes' as distinct from 'colleges' and 'schools,'

see Flexner, *op. cit., pp.* 31-5; but his reference (p. 240)
to the Institute of Historical Research implies a somewhat idealised conception of the conditions prevailing
therein. The staff of the Institute is administrative
rather than academic; its endowment for research
consists almost exclusively in its libraries; and research
there, as elsewhere, has for the most part to be pursued
and directed ' in fragments of time snatched from routine
duties ' (*ib.,* p. 10).

Page 268, ll. 8-15. Perhaps the most notable and gratifying
of these gifts was one of 226 volumes from the Government of the United States of America, including 84
volumes of its rare *Diplomatic Correspondence and
Foreign Relations* : for to complete the Institute's set
the United States Government not only gave what it
possessed but purchased volumes difficult to obtain, and
accompanied the gift with the remark that it was given
because the United States Government ' believe that the
Institute of Historical Research of the University of London is so situated that its library will be able to put this
series of volumes to the best possible use ' (*I.H.R. Fifth
Annual Report,* p. 7). Another notable gift was that of
1,281 volumes from the library of George Louis Beer
' given for the furtherance of a better understanding
among the English-speaking peoples through the study
of a common past ' (*ib., Second Annual Rep.,* p. 14).

Page 268, ll. 18-19. More than half the universities in the
United Kingdom have now entered into this arrangement.

Page 269, l. 22. The seminar was originated by Ranke in
1830. In France, provision for post-graduate training
began earlier with the establishment of the Ecole des
Chartes in 1821, but took a somewhat different form
laying more stress on the preparatory training of researchers than on the production of original work. There
followed in 1846 the foundation of the Ecole d'Athènes,
in 1868 the Ecole Pratique des hautes Etudes, and in
1877 the Ecole de Rome. In America, Yale organised
a department for post-graduate studies in 1847 and
Harvard in 1872. In 1876, Johns Hopkins was founded
as an exclusively post-graduate university, but soon
found itself hampered by the ambition of most other
American universities to develop post-graduate schools
of their own. Generally speaking, it is on its post-graduate
school that an American university prides itself most
(*cf.* Flexner, *op. cit.,* p. 73), while in English universities

the history and other schools commonly mean under-graduate schools (*cf.* Firth, *op. cit.*, pp. 41-51). The difference in point of view with regard to the meaning of research is quaintly illustrated in Freeman's ' Impressions of the United States ' (1883, pp. 184-5; *cf.* my *Factors in American History,* 1925, p. 293).

In England, Stubbs talked about the seminar some-what vaguely in 1884 (*Seventeen Lectures,* 1887, p. 429), and twenty-five years later Sir Paul Vinogradoff and Sir Charles Firth were actually holding serious seminars at Oxford, being joined afer the War by the professor of American History (Mr. S. E. Morison). But two of these professors came from abroad, and none of the seminars survived their founders. Mr. Fisher, at Oxford, has spoken of the seminar as not being ' accordant with Oxford tradition ' (*Paul Vinogradoff* : *A Memoir,* 1927, p. 32), and Professor Trevelyan, at Cambridge, of its being ' alien to the genius ' of that university (*Inaugural Lecture,* 1927, p. 24), while Dr. Flexner, who admirably describes what he calls ' the unique value of the seminar,' says it ' is in England almost an accident ' (*op. cit.,* p. 254). It is not, however, an accident but the property of the Insitute of Historical Research which has endeav-oured to learn from a century of experience in Germany, France, and America without slavishly following any precedent. Its essential purpose is to create a corporate tradition of historical technique which shall not be dissi-pated—like the biographical technique accumulated during twenty years in the office of the *D.N.B.* (see *Bulletin I. H. R.,* iv. 13)—by the conclusion of any par-ticular task, the disappearance of individuals, or the dispersal of equipment; but shall have, like ' Solomon's House ' in the *New Atlantis,* fellows, novices, and appren-tices, ' that the succession do not fail.' Only in a univer-sity with post-graduate as well as undergraduate students is there any guarantee of such conditions, or any hope of redemption from the reproach that ' the climate of the English University is not favourable to the production of finished historical technique ' (Fisher, *F. W. Maitland,* p. 171).

APPENDIX

The Needs of Historical Studies in the University of London.

26th *November, 1918.*

(1) The approaching end of the War provides an opportunity and emphasises the necessity, for a comprehensive reconsideration of the position of Historical Studies in the University of London. The Board of Studies in History has already reported to the Senate on the radical changes in the curricula which the situation requires; and the Imperial Studies Committee has long been engaged in preparing recommendations on the problem of historical education so far as it relates to the development and administration of the British Empire. But neither of these advisory bodies possesses the means of providing for the execution of its own recommendations, and the task of giving effect to them falls in practice upon various College authorities. One of the incidental disadvantages of leaving University policy to be determined by the different, competitive, and sometimes discordant, parts of a University is that the problem can only be attacked piecemeal, and often from points of view that are irrelevant to its proper consideration and injurious to its satisfactory solution. It is a defect in College as well as in University organisation. An educational policy can only be framed after a comprehensive survey from a general point of view; yet there is no general Department of History, not only in the University but even in the College itself,[1] and the head of any one of the Departments can only present an adequate report on the question at the cost of transgressing the limits of his own jurisdiction.

(2) The ultimate position of a School of History in the University of London depends on considerations which transcend the limits of College and even University policy, and intrude on the domain of a national policy of education which has hardly yet been broached. It is fundamentally a question

---

[1] The University College department consisted in a number of professors, readers, etc., arranged in order of seniority, and my name never, during the twenty-eight years of my professoriate, stood at the head of it.

313

whether each University is to pursue an independent policy of its own, generally seeking to cover the whole field of knowledge and frequently making provision for studies for no better reason than that adequate provision has already been made elsewhere, or whether the various universities are to be brought within the scope of a national organisation and a national policy which would insist upon co-ordination rather than competition, and upon specialisation rather than reduplication. For the purposes of undergraduate education reduplication is inevitable, though even here reflection will show in time that undergraduate education should not be of the same type in every university; and the fundamental divergence of type will be between universities like Oxford and Cambridge, consisting mainly of undergraduates who by private means or liberal scholarships are enabled to spend three or four years exclusively on their studies away from their homes and unhampered by having to earn the means of subsistence, and on the other hand universities like London and Manchester, situated in the midst of vast populations and making provision (a) for those who cannot afford to live away from home, and (b) for those who must spend part of their time at least in earning a living.

(3) The former of these two categories of students (a) and (b) has hitherto been the main preoccupation of the newer universities, but the latter will become more and more important in the future. For it is certain that, if democracy is to have a university education, democracy will for the most part have to receive that education where and while it works for a living. The restriction of university education to the few, whether selected by the haphazard incidence of private means or by the more rational method of scholarship examination, will not long satisfy democratic sentiment or democratic needs; and the disadvantages of diluting university studies with bread-and-butter distractions is more than compensated by the circumstance that a university education, provided while and where the student works for a living, need not be compressed into three or four years, but can be prolonged throughout life. University College has made some not unsuccessful experiments, with inadequate means, in the direction of this adult and democratic education; its future, and the future of all universities similarly situated, will depend largely on its success in fulfilling this function rather than on its success in imitating and competing with other universities in the semi-monastic conception of university education handed down to modern democracy from the Middle Ages.

(4) The solution of this problem obviously affects the relative emphasis to be placed on undergraduate and postgraduate studies, and this in turn bears on the relation of universities to one another and the respective importance of various studies within the university. It is clear that where the normal student is one whose university career is limited to three or four years, the type of education must be undergraduate; but where the education may be spread over an indefinite number of years postgraduate study may become more normal, and the provision for it the determining factor in university organisation and equipment.   There are also some subjects which by their character are more proper to undergraduate education. Sufficient mathematics can, for instance, be acquired in three or four years to enable the student to deal with the mathematical aspect of most problems he will encounter in later life; and within the same period sufficient mastery of a foreign language can be obtained to enable the student to speak and write it. There are other subjects whose complexity and infinity makes them less adaptable to undergraduate education than to life-long study; and it is among these subjects of postgraduate research that universities have to choose for purpose of specialising their functions.

(5) Hitherto no university in the British Empire has made adequate progress in specialisation for the postgraduate study of historical, political, and legal science. The greatest of legal historians, the late F. W. Maitland, complained of the difficulty of establishing such a school at Cambridge, and other historians have made similar laments in regard to Oxford, while one of the effects of the War has been to emphasise the national importance of some such development. It has been a matter of public comment that it was not found possible in this country, as it was in the United States of America, to improvise a Board of National Historical Service for the purpose of bringing to bear upon present problems the light of historical knowledge and experience.   Something like a rudimentary national laboratory of History was eventually improvised under the somewhat incongruous auspices of the War Office, the Admiralty, and the Foreign Office; but it was an organisation with which Universities, as such, had nothing to do, and was hampered throughout by its empirical character. The principal reason for this defect in national organisation was that there are not in British Universities properly organised Departments of History which could be converted to purposes of government investigation; and all that could be done was to make more or less haphazard

application to individual historians and rely upon the results of their single-handed and unco-ordinated efforts. A remedy for this national defect will undoubtedly be sought as an item in national reconstruction, and whether it will be found depends largely upon the action or inaction of the University of London.

(6) For in this respect the University of London stands in a position of peculiar, not to say unique, importance. From the point of view of national equipment, which is the supreme consideration, it is a matter of comparative indifference in what university the highest specialisation is developed in such subjects as classics, mathematics, or chemistry; for these studies are not dependent for their material upon any particular locality. Any university, given the funds, can build the finest chemical laboratory in the world and supply it with all its requirements. But the wealth of Crœsus will not enable any university other than London to develop the highest specialisation in historical, political, and legal science. The original materials for such research are to a very large extent all concentrated in the government and other archives of the capital of the Empire; they are unique, they cannot be reproduced, and they cannot be transported. If there is to be a national school of research in those branches of study, it cannot be established in any other university.

(7) This unique advantage is accompanied by another not less important from the point of view of university finance. The material for chemical research, the laboratories in which to treat it, and their equipment have all to be provided at no inconsiderable cost. The unique materials for historical, political, and legal research are all already provided, housed and cared for at the public expense, and postgraduate students in these branches can pursue their researches in libraries and archives and with expert assistance maintained from public funds. The university can, if it wishes, develop the greatest school of postgraduate research in the world in these subjects for a fraction of the sum required to establish a mediocre laboratory and equipment for some of the physical sciences. What is needed is merely sufficient room and equipment to train students for their work in these national muniments and archives. They cannot be taught or trained in the British Museum, the Public Record Office, or the libraries of government departments, the use of which is restricted to those who are presumably already acquainted with what they want to find and how to find it.

(8) But, while circumstances which cannot be altered have

placed within the reach of London and its university opportunities which might constitute almost a monopoly of advantages with regard to the development of a national post-
graduate school of historical, legal, and political science, these
advantages are not, and cannot be, under the existing arrangement of the University, the monopoly of any particular
college; and herein the treatment of the problem must be on
different lines from those which have apparently been followed
in other departments. Whenever and wherever a great engineering, chemical, or physiological department has been
established, its design has seemingly been to cover the whole
field of that particular study, irrespective of what has been
done elsewhere within the University. The result has been a
number of college departments and schools, but an absence
of university departments and schools. The School of Economics, the new School of Oriental Studies, the proposed
Institute of Modern Languages, and presumably the Imperial
College of Science and Technology, represent piecemeal
attempts at university reconstruction on diametrically opposite
lines to those upon which the older university institutions
were founded, and no effort, so far as I know, has been made
to reconcile these mutually destructive principles. But no
report on the development and reconstruction of historical
studies in the University—even for college purposes—can be
satisfactory which takes no account of the problem so far as
these studies are concerned.

(9) The objections to the University organisation on the
plan of specialised schools or institutes are obvious enough to
college authorities. But the objections to the alternative plan
are hardly less serious. The history of the numerous Hospital
Medical Schools, which prevented the University of London
from developing a School of Medicine comparable with its
opportunities, is perhaps the most striking illustration. But
others have been, or are being, rapidly provided. Every year
one or other of the colleges sees distinguished professors
leaving this University for more attractive Chairs elsewhere
because, while nominally they might be university professors
here, they were really the heads of one among several college
departments in the same subject, and not one of them stood
on a proper university footing. This personal wastage is perhaps less important than the endemic loss of efficiency caused
by perennial reduplication, conflict, and competition. Nor from
the national point of view does the transference of those professors of science to other spheres matter so much, because
presumably they will be able elsewhere to pursue their re-

searches with equal or greater effect than they could in the
University of London. But that is not the case with researchers in the political sciences. Their materials are in
London, and the researcher's removal elsewhere means a loss
not only to this University but to the cause of national learning. Moreover, it is not by a collection of college departments
that the University can respond to the growing demand for
advanced instruction in the political sciences on the part of
postgraduate students from the Dominions and the United
States of America. In spite of the unrivalled advantages
possessed by London these students will go elsewhere, as they
have done in the past, unless we can appeal to them, not as
a number of disjointed colleges, catering mainly for undergraduate needs, but as a university organised and co-ordinated
for the highest instruction and research.

(10) There is yet another factor in the situation, which
should not be ignored, and has a special bearing upon these
particular subjects. It was said by one of the most eminent
men ever connected with this college that he did not regard
it as his main function to turn out chemists but to make
chemistry; and to a considerable extent equipment and
endowment have enabled professors of natural science to fulfil
both these objects. Their laboratories were fitted for their
own especial investigations; research was considered a part
of the duties for which their stipends were paid (some Chairs
being even research Chairs in the main), and it was further
assumed to be the duty of the Library Committee to provide
them with the books and the periodicals they required.

No such conditions have ever obtained in the History
departments; it is impossible for teachers of History to pursue
their own researches in college; their emoluments are based
upon fees or grants earned by more or less elementary teaching without reference to the research they might or might
not be doing; and the utmost that the Library Committee
has aimed at doing has been to provide, not them, but their
students, with the books they require. To some extent this
discrepancy is inevitable. It will never be possible for the
historian to combine the teaching of History in London with
the equipment and time for continuous research and reflexion
required for making any serious contribution to the writing
of history. It is possible for the holders of Chairs under the
totally different conditions of Oxford and Cambridge; but for
the rest the writing of the history that counts and survives
has to be left to historians with ampler time than a professorship permits. The dilemma cannot be evaded; but in making

his choice the historian will naturally be influenced by the respective attractions of the alternatives. He may prefer a position as head of a department or school and the service which the direction of the researches of pupils enables him to render to the advancement of learning; or he may prefer the individual reputation, and possibly wider influence, in the world at large which accrue to the scholar who can by concentration on the task produce a great historical work. In many cases, no doubt, private circumstances and the inadequate remuneration for the writing of history leave him no option. But, when the opportunity of selection does arise, it is a material consideration whether the teaching post is one of adequate university standing and equipment. The inducement to surrender his individual chances of writing history will depend upon the circumstances of his Chair and the opportunities it affords of developing a real University School of Research; and that in its turn depends upon whether the school is a university school or merely one of a number of college schools.

INDEX

A

Abraham, 151
Absolutism, 54, 56, 65, 71, 101-2, 147-8, 150-1
Achilles, 35, 224
Act, the Parliament (1911), 305
Actium, battle of, 36
Acton, Lord, 37, 136-7, 301
Acton, John, 24, 301
Adam, 151, 299
Adult education, viii., 259-60, 262, 310, 314
Africa, South, 31, 40, 62, 203
Agriculture v. pasture, 25-6, 48-9, 115, 120-6
Albany, 213
Albuquerque, 41
Alexander the Great, 15, 36, 199
Alexander vi., Pope, 204
Alexander, Sir W., Earl of Stirling, 208
Alfred the Great, 27, 34, 302
Algiers, 62-3
Alice in Wonderland, 15
Aliens, 18, 23-4, 142, 301
Allen, Cardinal, 100
Allen, J. W., 304
America, 23, 25-6, 35, 38-42, 189, 197-216
See also United States of.
Spanish, 116
American history, chair of, 292*n.*
Factors in, 305-6, 312
Anabaptists, 299
Andalusia, 58, 61-2
Andros, Sir Edmund, 215
Angevins, 24, 29, 63
Anglicanism, 20-1, 86-92, 141, 151, 166-7, 170-1, 174

Anglo-American historical committee and conferences, 265, 268-9, 272-3
Anglo-Saxons, 21, 24, 27-8, 34, 55, 122, 156, 300
Angus, Archibald Douglas, sixth Earl of, 85, 303
Anjou, 24, 58, 63
Annapolis, 207
Anne of Brittany, 84
Anne of Cleves, 13, 91
Anthems, national, 21
Anthropology, 25
Antony, Mark, 156
Antwerp, 116
Apostolic succession, 138
Aquitaine, 62-3
Arable land v. pasture, 121-2
Aragon, 58-9, 61, 63-4, 84
Arc, Joan of. *See* D'Arc, Jeanne
Archery, 29, 124
Archives, British, 246-7, 268-73, 316
Argyle, Earl of, 169
Aristocracy, 6, 114-15, 175
Aristotle's *Politics,* 15, 114, 175, 217, 230
Arithmetic, 35-6
Armada, Spanish, 112, 135, 144
Armagnacs and Burgundians, 58
Army, Cromwell's, 181-95
Arnold of Rugby, Thomas, 249
Arrest, freedom from, 109-110
Art, history of, 293
Arthur, King, 138
Articles, Lords of the, 160
Arundel, 95, 303
Assembly, General (Scots), 161-2
Westminster, 167-8
Athens, 52, 79, 111, 235
Athlone, Earl of, 297*n.*